D1558606

OUT OF A WILDERNESS

In memory of John Robison

A symbolic relief on Lansing City
Hall. The state capitol represents
Lansing's role as capital city, the
log cabin suggests Lansing's earliest origins, the geared wheel
represents industry, and the book
represents education. Courtesy
of The Warren Holmes-Kenneth
Black Company.

OUT OF A WILDERNESS

An Illustrated History of Greater Lansing

By Justin L. Kestenbaum

ISBN 0-89781-024-4
Library of Congress Card Number 80-51650
Windsor Publications, Woodland Hills, California 91365

Printed in the United States of America

First Edition

TABLE OF CONTENTS

PREFACE

Since the historian is deeply affected by the times in which he lives, the writing of history cannot be an exact science. *Out of a Wilderness* appears at a time of uncertainty in the life of the capital region. Inflation, the high cost of energy, and foreign competition have cut deeply into automobile sales; dwindling tax receipts have forced two of the mainstays of the area's economy—Michigan State University and the State of Michigan—to examine priorities and reduce expenditures. *Out of a Wilderness* has been written in the light of these uncertainties; it seeks, by integrating the economic history of the area with other aspects of its growth, to provide fresh perspectives on the concerns of the moment.

But *Out of a Wilderness* attempts more than this. It has sought to integrate the thousands of facts and diverse streams of development which are the raw material of the history of the capital region into a coherent and readable narrative. The book is based on a wide range of sources, including the older histories, published and manuscript primary sources, official records, a wide range of secondary sources, and the local newspaper press. The book, however, cannot be exhaustive; a "complete" history of the capital region would require a much longer work. The serious student of the history of the area should supplement this book with those by Durant, Cowles, Darling, Ceasar, and others. A good starting point is *Ingham County Histories: An Annotated Bibliography for Students, Buffs and Collectors* (1977), compiled by Eugene G. Wanger. The earliest full-scale history of the Greater Lansing area—Samuel I. Durant's *History of Ingham and Eaton Counties, Michigan*—was written in the wave of euphoria which greeted the centennial of American independence. It reflected pride in accomplishment, boundless optimism for the future, and nostalgia for a rapidly disappearing past.

And so it was with the later capital region historical and biographical works; they appeared during waves of interest in local history and sought to keep alive the record of illustrious citizens and notable events. A *Pictorial and Biographical Album of Ingham and Livingston Counties, Michigan* (1891), is almost entirely biographical; it celebrated the remarkable growth and prosperity of the area. Albert E. Cowles' *Past and Present in the City of Lansing and Ingham County, Michigan* (1905) appeared at a time of great optimism as the automobile industry began Lansing's modern industrial history. In 1924 the indefatigable Mrs. Franc L. Adams of Mason published the *Pioneer History of Ingham County,* an exhaustive compendium of raw material and recollections on many aspects of the pioneer period. This work, like its predecessors, appeared during a time of heightened social and technological change and sought to preserve historical experience which might otherwise have been lost.

The first interpretive history of the City of Lansing—Birt Darling's *City in the Forest: The Story of Lansing* (1950)—appeared when the centennial of Lansing's selection as state capital sparked a new wave of interest in local history. Darling's book, which appeared as the city stood on the brink of a new spurt of growth, was for years the standard history of the area. Ford Stevens Ceasar's *Bicentennial History of Ingham County* (1976), a compendium of information, was published during the celebration of the bicentennial of American independence.

Research for this volume was carried on in local libraries, historical archives, and private collections. The Local History Room of the Lansing Public Library is the leading local repository of materials bearing directly on Lansing; it contains thousands of newspaper clippings, pamphlets, other publications, manuscripts, and artifacts on the history of the city and surrounding area. The Michigan State Library's clipping file and newspaper microfilms—including almost all of those published in Lansing—is an indispensable source. The State Library also holds the Orien A. Jenison Collection, a large series of scrapbooks containing documents and mementos on the building of the state capitol in the 1870s. A social history of Lansing in that decade might easily be constructed from that collection.

The Michigan State Archives' holdings include much material bearing directly on Lansing and the capital region, including such records as the "Correspondence of the Mayors of Lansing, 1929-37," and many records of the Lansing Chamber of Commerce (now the Lansing Regional Chamber of Commerce). At the Michigan State University Archives and Historical Collections the author examined the Papers of Orlando M. Barnes, Ransom E. Olds, Charles Hutchinson Thompson, Courtland Bliss Stebbins, and the Records of the Reo Motor Car Company and the Novo Engine Company.

Much of the material for this volume was gleaned from Lansing newspapers; the dates for quotations are in almost all cases cited in the text. To avoid confusing the reader, the *Lansing Republican*—variously entitled the *State Republican, Lansing State Republican, Weekly Republican,* and *Tri-Weekly Republican,* and others, has been cited as the *Republican.* This newspaper generally upheld the Republican party point of view; for much of the period from 1855 to 1911 its principal rival was the *Journal,* a Democratic party newspaper, whose title also varied (*Lansing Journal, Lansing State Journal,* and others). In 1911 the *Journal* faltered and was absorbed by the *Republican;* the title of the new, merged newspaper was then changed to the *State Journal.* Other newspapers have appeared from time to time; the author examined issues of the *Lansing Press* (also *Lansing Evening Press* (1912-16), and the *Capital News* (1921-32).

Justin L. Kestenbaum
East Lansing
May, 1981

Local history is the record of a community's interaction with its past and environment. It is a history that can be known firsthand—history that means a personal involvement with the past in a far more intimate way than from reading accounts of elections, booms, busts, and natural catastrophes. Histories of a neighborhood, town, city, or state are pieces, of course, of a larger design. But the history of local people, events, customs, institutions, and even buildings can illustrate, enliven, and expand our understanding of the past in ways that the usual generalized histories cannot.

To know why Meridian Road is so called, or how Lansing got its name, tells us something of the American westward movement and of the settlement of the Northwest Territory. One cannot explain the name of Ingham County without knowing about Jackson and his cabinet, or without feeling a bit more certain of one's own identity as a link in a human chain stretching back into the past. Historian Clifford Lord has explained this well. "The study of history at a local level," he wrote, "reveals how things really happen, how things act and react, how the wheels of history mesh and cog with one another. It shows people living together, working together, getting along together (or not getting along together), at work, at play, in politics, business, government, social and cultural pursuits."

This book is the outgrowth of a recognized need for a fresh background to an understanding of the potential of a city, and of the problems—as well as the triumphs—created by its development. There is a need for breadth and depth of vision to give significance to facts, and to make facts basic to understanding.

The bibliography of traditional printed sources about Lansing is notably lean for a region so rich in primary sources for historical research. Few have been written by historians; none have been widely distributed and made available in popular style. In the 20th century, when the image has become so important, history must be visual as well as verbal. The marriage of words and pictures, represented by this volume, adds a new dimension to Lansing's history. During the months that this volume has been under preparation we have observed the orderly progress of research; the wide-ranging search for photographs of historical value; the careful analysis of sources not exploited by earlier works; and the constant critical attention paid to the structure of words, which creates literature. Here are personalities located in their place and time; here is the pattern of events that molded a community and made it meaningful and viable. Since no historian can ever tell it all, these chapters of Lansing's history give us only a portion of the story. To some it will be exciting and sufficiently informative; to others it will serve as a challenge to know more.

Justin Kestenbaum's book, then, is a way of getting our local history back to the people of Lansing who made it. Reading it may give, we hope, the reader a clearer and better sense of his or her place within a heritage, of one's position within the stream of time.

Although this volume is concerned primarily with the greater Lansing community, the narrative of its development is essentially a reflection of the histories of other cities throughout the nation. All of those concerned with its publication hope that it will alert a new audience of readers and stimulate the continued study needed to illuminate future alternatives, as history illuminates those past, to the fundamental problems affecting people's lives.

Geneva K. Wiskemann
Past President, Historical Society of Greater Lansing
President, R.E. Olds Museum Association, Inc.
Chairperson, Clinton County Historical Society

For centuries after the European discovery of America, little was known of the interior of Michigan's lower peninsula. The region was heavily forested, remote from the main centers of settlement, and inhabited only by Indians. In the 17th and 18th centuries, French explorers, missionaries, and fur traders penetrated its rivers and built strong points on its fringes, but left few descriptions of the interior. However, an early French map correctly locating and describing the Grand, Huron, and Shiawassee rivers suggests that French voyageurs traversed these streams no later than 1703.

After their decisive defeat by the British on the Plains of Abraham, the French lost their North American empire, and in 1763, sovereignty over what is now Michigan passed to the British. In the treaty of 1783 that ended the American Revolution, the territory was formally surrendered to the United States. Practically speaking, the British continued to control Michigan until 1796, when they withdrew at last from their western military posts.

Having acquired the former French possessions, as well as British territory south of the Ohio River, the United States suddenly found itself with an enormous preserve of land—half a million square miles—beyond the borders of the original states. Hardly had the American Revolution ended when land-hungry speculators and settlers began demanding entry into this region, and Congress set about creating the public-land policies that would open the area to settlement.

Under the Ordinance of 1785, all western lands were to be divided into townships of 36 square miles; these, in turn, would be divided into "sections" of one square mile, or 640 acres. Section 16 of every township was to be set aside for the support of schools—a provision that was to prove of special importance for Michigan and the Lansing area.

Michigan became a territory in 1805, but not until after the War of 1812—after Illinois, Ohio, and Indiana had become states—did settlers turn their attention to the territory farther north. In 1810, the population of Detroit was still only about 800, and many of these left during the War of 1812. Of the interior of Michigan's peninsula, the inhabitants of Detroit knew little or nothing.

Michigan's potential for settlement first came to public notice during the War of 1812, when soldiers stationed in the area liked what they saw. In 1812, Congress authorized land bounties of about 6 million acres of western land for war veterans. Each soldier was to receive a land warrant authorizing him to select 160 acres, or a quarter section, of land in Michigan or other areas.

Lewis Cass, who became governor of the Michigan Territory in 1813, pressured federal authorities to begin the survey of Michigan lands as soon as possible. "It would be desirable that the exterior [i.e., township] lines be run if possible this fall," he told Edward Tiffin, superintendent of the general land office, in August 1815. "By bringing the public lands of the United States [in Michigan] into the market, the current of immigration would be turned towards us." Cass was careful to point out the strategic considerations, sure to carry weight in light of recent military disasters: "Our population would be such, as would be adequate to the defense of the Country, and a barrier interposed between the British and the Indians."

The first important treaty by which Indians ceded their claims to Michigan lands was the Treaty of Detroit, 1807, in which the Indians gave up a huge land area in southeastern Michigan. The western boundary of this territory later became the principal meridian, or north-south line, for land surveys; Meridian Road, which divides Ingham County in half, is named for this line. By the Treaty of Saginaw, 1819, the Indians ceded their claims to other parts of the lower peninsula; all of the Lansing area west of the meridian was ceded in this treaty. By 1842, additional treaties had extinguished all Indian claims throughout both peninsulas of Michigan.

Surveying of the Lansing area began late in 1824 and was completed in the spring of 1827. The men who conducted these surveys contributed more to the development of the area than is generally appreciated. Though their names are all but forgotten today, theirs was a profession that carried a great deal of prestige. At a practical level, their firsthand knowledge of good lands enabled them to serve as "land lookers" for buyers interested in good investments, and thus to exert a substantial influence on the actual course of settlement.

The best-known surveyor in the greater Lansing area was Lucius Lyon, for whom the town of Lyons, in Ionia County, was named. During the territorial period Lyon served as a delegate to Congress, and after statehood he became one of Michigan's first United States Senators. Lyon, one of the most prominent Michigan citizens of his time, surveyed land in Wisconsin and Illinois in addition to laying out 27 townships all over Michigan. In the greater Lansing area, he surveyed several townships in the northern tier of Jackson County.

Hervey Parke, who surveyed extensive areas in Iowa and Wisconsin as well as Michigan, had a remarkable career. He was born in Connecticut and actually walked

Lewis Cass became governor of Michigan Territory in 1813. During his term as governor the federal government undertook the great task of surveying Michigan lands; a project designed to bring settlers to the area. Courtesy of Saginaw Historical Museum.

9

the entire distance to and from Michigan on his first visit in 1821. In the greater Lansing area, he surveyed townships in Ingham (Leslie, Onondaga, Aurelius, and Vevay), Clinton (Bath, De Witt, Waterford, and Eagle), and Eaton (Hamlin and Eaton Rapids) counties from 1825 to 1827. In the winter of 1826-27, he and his party subdivided six townships on the Looking Glass River in Clinton County, a survey that extended, as he later recalled, "to the north line of the township [Lansing] in which the State capital is located." Park Lake and Park Lake Road in Bath Township are named for him.

Musgrove Evans, who in 1826 and 1827 surveyed Meridian, Lansing, Alaeidon, and Delhi townships in Ingham, as well as Delta and Windsor in Eaton, was remembered by a contemporary as a Quaker and "a worthy, well-educated surveyor and Gentleman." Evans was the first settler in Lenawee County and served as its first probate judge. But since "a year elapsed between the first and second petitions in his court," Judge Evans had ample time in which to survey land.

Joseph Wampler, of whom little is known, surveyed the township and section lines east of Meridian Road in Ingham County. Wampler, who lived in Tuscarawas County, Ohio, was said by some early settlers to be a Methodist preacher. His surveying duties included the townships of Woodhull and Perry in Shiawassee County; Lake, Wheatfield, Leroy, Ingham, White Oak, Bunker Hill, and Stockbridge in Ingham; and several others in Jackson County.

John Mullett, who settled in Meridian Township in 1852, was the only surveyor who eventually took up residence in the area. Mullett was born in 1786 in Vermont and emigrated to Detroit in 1818. Because of his interest in science and mathematics, he served as surveyor for Michigan Territory and laid out a number of new streets and avenues in Detroit. In 1825, while he was surveying townships in Eaton and Calhoun counties, there occurred an incident that has made the name of John Mullett unforgettable to several generations of schoolchildren. A group of Indians objected to the surveyors' presence, and a fracas ensued; two of the Indians died, and Mullett's party hastily left the woods. A stream near the site of the incident has been known ever since as Battle Creek.

Since the land surveys of the townships in the greater Lansing area were made about a decade before settlement, the surveyors' field notes are the earliest reasonably accurate descriptions of the region. These notes, once closely scrutinized by land buyers, are now a valuable source for the local historian. Musgrove Evans' field notes for the February 1827 survey of "Township 4 North Range 2 West" are of particular interest; the area was organized in 1842 as Lansing Township and is now the core of the capital region.

The survey began at the southeast corner of Lansing Township at what is now the intersection of Jolly and College roads, where the men presumably set up their base camp. From here, they laid out the southern boundary of the township, running a line six miles west along what is now Jolly Road to its intersection with Waverly Road. Running this line must have required at least a full day's

work, since it involved walking a round trip of 12 miles and preparing and setting 12 markers—section and quarter-section posts—situated at half-mile intervals. Thirty-one trees that stood athwart the sighted line had to be "blazed," and their species and distance from the last marker entered in the notes. In addition to blazing the "line" or "station" trees, other trees in the vicinity of the marked posts were also blazed and entered in the notes.

The surveyors then drew the eastern boundary of the township by running a line north from the place of beginning. This line runs along College Road, across the campus of Michigan State University, and along Abbott Road past downtown East Lansing to the county line, two miles north of Burcham Drive. From the northeast corner of the township, they drew the northern boundary by running a line six miles west to Waverly Road; then they walked back to the southwest corner (Jolly and Waverly roads) and surveyed the western boundary.

With the survey of the township's perimeter complete, the next step was to survey the section lines. Once again, the survey began in the southeast corner and proceeded to the north and west. This process involved considerable backtracking, and Evans' field notes show that the party walked a minimum of 116 miles, placed 156 markers, and blazed hundreds of trees. They also measured distances to topographical features and—of particular importance to land buyers—observed the quality of the land at intervals of one mile. In addition, the surveyors had to make 450 separate measurements of the "meanderings" of the Grand and Red Cedar rivers and lesser streams.

The work of surveying land would have been arduous under ideal conditions—and conditions were often far from ideal. If the area to be surveyed was several days' journey from a supply of food, the party would have to transport its own provisions. When food spoiled, or if a party was in the woods longer than planned, rations would be short. On occasion, Parke recalled, "we were ... reduced to a short allowance of only buggy peas," and more than once surveying parties experienced starvation for days at a time.

Since the sightings required clear visibility, much of the work was done in winter—thus adding exposure to the catalog of hazards. Various parties encountered blinding snowstorms, severe spells of cold weather, or, as Parke recalled of an area near Lansing, "the most terrific gale of wind I have ever witnessed in Michigan." Toward the end of his life, Parke—who died in 1879 at the age of 89—vividly remembered that "we suffered much from frozen feet, the effects of which I am hourly reminded, even after a lapse of forty years."

Since the surveyors recorded completion dates for most of the townships, it is possible to reconstruct the order in which the work progressed; the length of time required to complete each one depended on the terrain and weather.

Joseph Wampler completed his survey of Stockbridge Township on November 22, 1825; the survey of White Oak Township, directly north, was completed six days later on November 28. Apparently Wampler interrupted his work for a time; he completed Bunker Hill, just west of Stockbridge, on February 7, 1826, and Ingham Township, just north, on February 18. Continuing north, Wampler completed Wheatfield on March 3, Williamstown on March 13, and Woodhull Township in Shiawassee County on March 20.

The surveys of the western portion of Ingham County— across the meridian from those already surveyed—began later in 1826 and continued until they were completed early in 1827. Judge Musgrove Evans completed the survey of Alaeidon Township on December 23, 1826, and on January 8, 1827, completed Delhi, in Eaton County, the adjoining township to the west. The survey of Meridian Township was completed on February 8, 1827, and that of Lansing, the last township to be surveyed in Ingham County, on February 21, 1827.

The completion of the surveyors' work did not immediately bring a rush of settlers to the area. Time-consuming tasks remained, including the preparation of plats for the district and general land offices and for the Surveyor General of the United States. At last, in June of 1829, the eastern portion of Ingham County was declared open for sale; the western portion, including Lansing and Meridian, was not offered for sale until October 1830— more than three and a half years after Evans had completed his survey.

The public-lands policies of the United States determined not merely the pattern of land sales, but also the kind of society that would emerge in Michigan and its neighboring states—a society of small, independent farmers. The system of surveying land in advance of settlement assured an orderly pattern of land distribution. The townships marked off by surveyors, known as "congressional townships," became, with only minor changes, the basic units of local government in Michigan. And since Michigan was settled fairly late in the history of the Great Lakes region, its settlers benefited not only from progressively liberalized land policies but also from the experience of settlers on earlier frontiers.

As the surveys progressed, Governor Cass and the legislative council of Michigan Territory took further steps to assure a flow of settlers. By a series of measures, they created the basis for a system of strong local government and home rule that would affect powerfully the course of Michigan's subsequent development.

When Congress, in 1825, authorized Michigan Territory to create local units of government and to provide for the selection of their officers, Michigan went so far as to provide for the popular election of all local officials except judges. This was an extraordinary measure at a time when property qualifications for voting and officeholding had only recently been abolished and entrenched conservatives remained extremely suspicious of popular rule.

A series of acts approved by Governor Cass on October 29, 1829, officially "set off" the 12 so-called "cabinet counties," named for President Andrew Jackson, Vice-President John C. Calhoun, and the members of Jackson's cabinet. Ingham County was named for Samuel D. Ingham, secretary of the treasury; Eaton County was named for the secretary of war, John H. Eaton. So far as is known, neither of these men ever set foot in the county named in his honor.

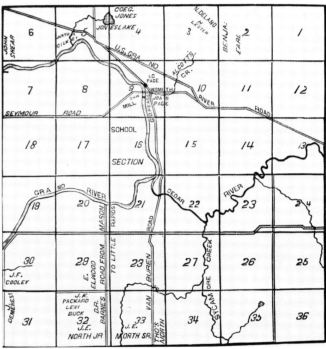

TOP: **This 1725 map shows how many geographical details of Michigan's lower peninsula were still unknown. From *Indiana and the Old Northwest*, 1980.**

BOTTOM: **This map shows Lansing Township, "Town Four North Range Two West," divided into sections. The names of the earliest settlers are included. The town of Michigan, later named Lansing, occupied all of section 16, the north half of section 21, and the south half of section 9. From Durant, *History of Ingham and Eaton Counties*, 1880.**

Chapter 2

In 1835, recalled Edward W. Barber of Vermontville, his father and neighbors in Vermont began talking about the Great Lakes, "about magnificent forests ... [and] the wonderful richness of the soil which only needed to be tickled with the hoe to yield a bounteous harvest." His father, Edward H. Barber, made several "land looking" expeditions to Michigan, and in September 1839, the Barber family "bade adieu to the old Vermont home," never to see loved ones again.

Having succumbed to "Michigan fever," the Barbers joined one of the great population movements of American history. In 1820, the population of Michigan Territory was 8,896, mostly around Detroit; in the following decade, it grew to 31,639, an astonishing increase of three and a half times. Yet the Michigan fever had hardly begun. By 1835, the population reached 87,000, an increase of tenfold since 1820. Over the next three years—from 1835 to 1838—population doubled again; more land was bought and sold in the single year of 1836 than in the entire previous history of Michigan. The federal census of 1840 showed a total of 212,267 persons; the state census of 1845 counted 302,521; and on the eve of the Civil War, Michigan's population stood at 749,113—an increase of 84 times since 1820.

At first, settlers took up land in areas most accessible to Detroit—Wayne, Oakland, and Washtenaw counties. Then they turned to the south and west, to Jackson, Kalamazoo, and Calhoun counties. Eaton County, to the west of Ingham, and Clinton, to the north, both had settlers before Ingham. Not until the middle and late 1830s, when the Michigan fever was subsiding, did an appreciable number of settlers come to the capital region.

Reaching the Ingham County area required a journey of several stages. From Vermont or other areas of New England, the pioneer hauled his possessions to Whitehall, New York, the head of the Champlain Canal, which led into the Hudson River and then to the Erie Canal. So great was the traffic on the Erie Canal at the height of the Michigan fever that one New York newspaper reported, "every boat ... is literally overloaded with passengers, chattels, wares, and merchandise. ... [And] in some instances passengers have been literally *pushed ashore* to prevent the boat from being overladen." Steamboat traffic from Buffalo to Detroit increased correspondingly, and by the mid-1830s, some 45 steamboats offered almost daily service.

The facade of an abandoned farmhouse on Lovejoy Road, Woodhull Township, Shiawassee. This photograph shows the "board and batten" type of rural architecture which often succeeded the log cabin. Photograph by author.

William A. Dryer, an early Lansing settler, remembered his passage across Lake Erie on the old steamboat *Michigan*. The vessel "was a sort of Chinese junk—nearly as long as she was broad ... crowded with five hundred passengers, at least a third more than her comfortable carrying capacity." Shortly after departure, gale winds churned the lake into enormous waves and submerged the decks. The *Michigan* finally reached Detroit "after a hazardous and seasick journey of five days"—twice the usual sailing time.

But nature has another face; sometimes the journey was an idyllic cruise—the scenery majestic, the sunsets spectacular, the waters silvery smooth. The most eloquent account of a passage across Lake Erie at the height of the Michigan fever was that of Alexis de Tocqueville, who took passage in July 1831 aboard the *Ohio* from Buffalo to Detroit. The *Ohio* plied within hailing distance of the south shore of the lake, often in the shade of a magnificent forest, the like of which de Tocqueville had never seen, even in America. "The wilderness was before us," he wrote, "just as, six thousand years ago, it showed itself to the Fathers of Mankind." Here and there in the "vast ocean of leaves" would appear signs of civilization—a church steeple or a farmer's rude habitation. Occasionally huge flocks of birds would darken the sky, swoop down to the surface of the lake, and just as suddenly fly off again in great sheets.

Detroit was an exciting place in the 1830s. As the entry point not only to Michigan but to Illinois and Indiana by way of the Territorial Road, it was crowded with settlers, land speculators, "timber cruisers," and "land lookers," who sought out choice acreage for wealthy investors. In one six-week period in the spring of 1830, 2,400 settlers arrived at Detroit; on one day—October 7, 1834—more than 900 passengers arrived.

In Detroit, the pioneers began the arduous part of their journey, the overland foray to Ingham County, a distance of about 80 miles. Later in the decade, part of this distance could be traversed by rail to Ann Arbor, Ypsilanti, or Jackson. From Ann Arbor, the Dexter Trail led to the southeast corner of Ingham County. Some traveled on the Territorial Road, or later by rail, to Jackson, and from there through the woods to Ingham. But most of Lansing's pioneers appear to have traveled by ox team along the Grand River Trail, a "brushed out" or improved road that ended at Howell in Livingston County. From there, an Indian trail led to the Ingham County area.

Driving a wagon and ox team through the Michigan forest meant cutting dense vegetation, fording streams, and suffering exposure to all kinds of weather. "Many times the blazed trail was so thick with mud," recalled Mrs. Robert Wright of Leslie Township, "that the goods had to be taken from the wagon, carried to higher ground, then after the wagon had been pulled out of the slough, it was reloaded and started again." Mrs. Eliza Haltz, who came to Leslie in 1836 with her father, John K. Leach, remembered an eight-day trek from Detroit to Jackson. Streams had to be forded, as "there was scarcely a bridge between Detroit and Jackson."

William A. Dryer and his wife, after their rough crossing

of Lake Erie aboard the *Michigan,* continued their journey from Detroit to Lansing by way of the Dexter Trail. Dryer had brought "the gearing of a wagon" from New York; in Detroit he purchased rough boards, built a wagon box, and bought a yoke of oxen.

The journey to Dexter took five days; mud and water in the wagon impeded their progress. They pressed on until they reached the southeastern corner of Ingham County, where the trail ended. "Having no compass, and the sun being obscured by a hazy mist, we were obliged to travel by intuition." Traversing the forest without landmarks, they got lost, and "a dismal rain set in." Having neither food nor camping equipment, they had to keep moving until, at midnight, they saw a light. It proved to be an unfurnished log house, occupied only by a woman whose husband was away. The woman had heard rumors of a cholera epidemic and was at first reluctant to take them in. The next morning, however, she directed them on to their destination of Unadilla, just west of the Ingham County line, and even offered an extra team of oxen to help pull them through a "bad slough" about a mile beyond the house.

A tradition of frontier hospitality developed. Taverns dotted the trails, and isolated settlers delighted in the company even of strangers. Nancy Meach of Leroy Township recalled that when settlers began to fill in the area after 1837, "I hailed them with joy, for I had not seen a woman for months . . . and I had had no communication with the outside world."

The Rolfe family of Vevay Township was famous for its hospitality to scores of stranded settlers. Augusta Chapin, who grew up in Eden, about four miles south of Mason, remembered that her family entered Ingham County in midwinter after several weeks' journey from New York. "The snow was deep, and only a half-trodden road wound in and out among the great trees of the primeval wilderness." They had been directed by travelers to "the famous Rolfe settlement"; but believing themselves lost in the woods, and suffering from exposure, the Chapins thought they were at their last extremity.

Suddenly a man appeared from behind a large tree. "He looked as though he himself were part of this wild scene," the Reverend Chapin later recalled. "An ample cap of raccoon skin almost hid his face, and he wore a great tunic shaped coat of the same material." He carried a gun and a deer he had just shot. Asked if he knew where the Rolfe settlement was, "His keen eyes at once took in the whole situation. . . . He saw that we were newcomers, with no idea of what life in the backwoods must be, and before we could speak he broke out into a loud ringing laugh that echoed and re-echoed through the woods as though twenty men were laughing, and then he said, 'The Rolfe settlement? Why, this is it.' Sure enough, within a few rods we found shelter in the hospitable home of Ira Rolfe."

Having arrived on their land, the pioneers set about the urgent tasks of survival. Shelter was the first imperative. Sometimes a family camped out, or used its covered wagon, until a crude shanty could be built; an ingenious Stockbridge pioneer, John Davis, actually hitched his ox team to a sled bearing a small house and dragged it to his land. The pioneer family's first, temporary shanty was usually about eight by ten feet and just high enough for a standing adult; a settler with an ax and a few other tools could easily build such a house in a day or two. It was made of small logs, "chinked" on the inside with small pieces of wood and "mudded" on the outside to keep out rain and snow. The shed roof was usually covered with bark or easily constructed wooden troughs.

Eventually a substantial log house was built, and this, in the fullness of time, gave way to a frame or brick house. Some log houses were elaborate, two-story structures; most appear to have been small, with 12 by 16 feet a popular size. Early houses were made of round logs; a pioneer who hewed or squared his logs was thought to be "putting on the style." The logs were notched near the ends; the gaps were filled with "chinkers" or split pieces of wood held in place with clay mortar. When the necessary number of logs had been assembled, neighbors from miles around were invited to a "raising," always a festive occasion.

A crosscut saw was used to make openings for windows, doors, and fireplaces. Doors were made of rough boards, if available, and hung from wooden hinges. There was no doorknob; the door was fastened by a wooden latch on the inside and opened from the outside by means of a leather string passed through a hole—the origin of the hospitable phrase, "You'll always find the latchstring out." To permit the family cat to go in and out, a small notch was cut near one of the lower corners of the door; a piece of board, hung over the opening, swung freely in either direction. This was known as the cat hole.

The log cabin has a special place in American folklore; in 1850 it was estimated that half the American population lived in such houses. No political candidate who was born in a log house would neglect to dwell on the simple, honest, Lincolnesque virtues thereby acquired. As time passed and the log cabin became a memory, a wave of nostalgia set in. "Those were days of hallowed contentment," recalled Silas Bement of Leroy Township. Bement remembered the simplicity of life, the cherished evenings by the firelight, and when company came, the joy with which even strangers were received and the pride in sharing even the simplest fare. "If the meal," said Bement, "consisted only of roast potatoes and salt, with what relish it was received."

And life was indeed simple. For heating and cooking, there was only the chimney, built of sticks and plastered with clay on both sides. A fire back consisted of stones, against which a great log was placed. This was the back log: a smaller log, the fore log, was placed in front of it. The fire was carefully kept, especially in the early days before the invention of "lucifer" matches, so that one would not have to go some distance to a neighbor to "get fire." Pots hung on hooks, and cuisine, by all accounts, was often excellent.

Sometimes there was a trapdoor in the middle of the split-wood floor; a ladder gave access to a cellar, most often just a hole in the ground. There the family kept vegetables, butter, fruit, and the inevitable pork barrel, "from whose briny depths," recalled one early settler, "came the crisp and savory accompaniment of every morning meal of baked beans or boiled vegetables." To this aged pioneer, it seemed that "there was never a more delicious dish served" than buckwheat griddle cakes "garnished with pork gravy, having the rich savory taste of the hickory nut, beech nut, [and] sweet acorn."

Most cabins were one-room structures. They were typically furnished with a bed, cradle, and fireplace, and not always with curtains for privacy. John Price of Lansing recalled that "when the women went to bed, the men went outdoors to give them a chance to undress." The bed was often built into a corner of the house, with its sidewalls notched into the walls in such a manner that only one leg was needed to support it.

Rain made a tremendous clatter on the shakes of the roof, and since rain and snow drifted in through the roof, the only safe place for clothing was under the bed. It was common in winter to wake up and find two inches of snow covering the entire interior of the cabin. More than one pioneer remembered the "delight of making one's toilet" when the inside temperature was below zero, and having to put on clothes full of drifted snow.

With shelter arranged, the settlers chopped down a few trees, planted seed between the stumps, and defoliated other trees by the Indian method of "girdling," or removing a strip of bark around the trunk. The forest provided wild game in spectacular profusion—flocks of wild turkeys, ducks and geese enough to darken the surface of a lake, millions of passenger pigeons, as well as black bears, wolves, foxes, deer, raccoons, minks, otters, muskrats, rabbits, skunks, chipmunks, black and gray squirrels, gophers, opossums, and even an occasional wildcat. No pioneer gathering was complete without at least one bear or wolf story.

Seasoned pioneers regarded the wolves as "cowardly whelps [who] seldom attacked a person," but new settlers were often frightened. John A. Barnes of Mason recalled his fright at the nocturnal howlings of wolves "which broke out with such hilarious strains that the very hairs on our heads seemed to stand up." Dr. L. Anna Ballard, daughter of Mrs. Epiphene Ballard of Lansing, remembered a summer spent south of Okemos in the late 1840s. "Another horror ... was the wolves. I have heard [my mother] tell of their howling around the house at night, even scratching at doors. Then the men of the neighborhood would have wolf hunts, and for a time there would be peace at night."

Bears were a major annoyance, and their audacity astonished the pioneers. The settlers quickly learned to keep their pigs in pens, for bears found them irresistible and would take great risks to obtain them. A particularly audacious bear was the central figure in what Barber remembered as the most exciting event in the early history of Vermontville. The swine pens had been raided repeatedly by this "brazen bear ... whose depredations were so frequent and numerous ... that a hunt was organized for his capture." Rev. Sylvester Cochrane, the first Congregationalist minister to settle in Vermontville, led the expedition, "and all the men, boys, and guns of the colony were mustered into service." The party surrounded

a section of land where the bear was suspected to be and at a signal marched toward the center. The bear somehow broke through, with men, boys, and dogs giving chase. Eventually the bear was killed, loaded on poles, "a procession was formed, and the hunters marched to the public square." There the meat was dressed and distributed to families; the skin was sold and the proceeds used "to purchase the first installment of Sunday school books that were brought into our village."

Wild animals were only one of the hazards faced by the pioneers. Disease was rampant, and medicine primitive.

The most prevalent disease was malaria, generally known as "ague." It began after the spring rains and continued until October, and there were few families in which at least one member did not come down with the disease. "Sometimes," recalled Dr. Charles H. Sackrider of Mason, "one would no sooner leave his bed, than his place would be taken by another ... until all had suffered from the disease."

"We could always tell when an attack of the ague was coming on," wrote Anson de Perry Van Buren, a Battle Creek pioneer, "by the preliminary symptoms—the yawnings and stretchings—these were soon followed by cold sensations that crept over your system in streaks." The victim might shake in the "frigid zone" for an hour or so; "then commenced hot flashes," in which the sufferer shook even more violently and sweated copiously. A victim would invariably feel "relieved and happy" when the attack ended. Since attacks occurred at predictable intervals, people learned to organize their daily schedules around them.

Malaria, however, was only one of the medical problems of pioneer Michigan. Cholera was epidemic in Detroit in 1832, 1849, 1850, and 1854, and sporadic at other times. Before the epidemic of 1832 had run its course, it decimated the Indian population; in 1849, half of Detroit's panic-stricken population fled the city; the 1854 epidemic claimed 1,000 lives. Closer to the capital region, cholera epidemics struck Marshall in 1832 and 1834, and an 1848 epidemic in Shiawassee County claimed scores of lives before it ran its course.

Other serious diseases were smallpox, typhoid, meningitis, and dysentery. The recollections of T.W. Huntoon of Leslie Township include a description of "a scourge of dysentery" that visited the area about 1850. "A young lady by the name of Schoolmaker died, and Lyman Case and I were the only ones able enough to carry the casket to the grave. One family of mother, father, and four children died."

In the winter of 1835-36, the wife of Samuel Searles, one of the first settlers near Charlotte, died; a coffin was needed, and the closest sawmill was at Bellevue, 15 miles away. There was neither a road nor even a marked trail from Searles' home to his destination. The aggrieved settler, said Barber, "yoked his oxen, hitched them to a sled, and laying his dead wife thereon, started alone one winter morning on his journey to Bellevue." Searles had to stop repeatedly to brush out a trail and fell trees. "All day long," said Barber, "the melancholy funeral procession, a touching incident of pioneer life and death, journeyed

15

through the moaning wilderness.''

Even where there were roads, they were frequently impassable. Heavily laden wagons made deep ruts, and rain made quagmires that immobilized ox teams. A journey of 10 miles by ox team was a major expedition; a foray of 20 miles could take several days. Yet the pioneers needed access to gristmills and sawmills and a few store-bought provisions. The closest mill to early Williamston settlers was at Dexter, 35 miles away, while the nearest doctors were in Ann Arbor or Howell.

Clearing the forest was the work of a generation. Today the virgin forest is largely gone, and the present generation wonders whether its forebears were overzealous. But the pioneers were hemmed in by the forest, and to them its removal was a noble undertaking, the first vital step away from savagery and toward civilization. As Barber put it, ''it required steady and continuous blows for years to change the wilderness into pleasant homes and fruitful fields.'' He even made his case poetically.

Cheerily, on the axe of labor
Let the sunbeams dance
Better than the flash of saber
Or the gleam of lance!
Strike! With every blow is given
Freer sun and sky
And the long-hid earth to heaven
Looks, with wondering eye!

The pioneers, awesome woodsmen, spared few trees. The ''foremost chopper'' in Vermontville was William F. Hawkins; he could ''slash down an acre of average timber in a day.'' Moreover, he could fell a tree with incredible accuracy. ''Bore a hole in the center of a tree, stick a pin in the hole, and . . . [Hawkins] would fell another tree, thirty or forty feet away, and hit the pin almost every time.'' Axes, according to Barber, were much discussed—''the best weight for efficient use, the proper length of helve''; in Vermontville, axes made by Isaiah Blood of Hoosac Falls, New York, were especially esteemed.

Skilled woodsmen learned to reduce the labor required to clear the land of trees. ''Windrowing'' began with partially chopping parallel rows of trees, about 40 feet apart, in such a manner that ''the tops of the trees, felled from either side inward, would cross each other and lodge there.'' Sometimes the rows of trees were half a mile long, or the entire length of a quarter section of land. Then, one large tree was felled with pinpoint accuracy, in such a way that it would bring down all the others like falling dominoes. The result, recalled one pioneer, was ''a sight, a noise of paralyzing grandeur that none will ever see again.'' The fallen trees were left to dry and, when the wind was right, ''set on fire . . . [which] swept through the great mass of dry timber like a volcano.'' After the fire, ''nothing remained but huge blackened logs and the upraised burial mounds of upturned roots.'' A logging bee would follow, in which eight or 10 ox teams made short work of removing stumps and tree roots.

Local government came early in the history of the area. The boundaries of Ingham County were ''set off'' in 1829, after the area had been surveyed but before the land was placed on the market. Until Ingham's government was organized, the county was informally attached to Washtenaw County as part of Dexter Township; for a brief period, Ingham's western half was attached to Jackson County for judicial purposes. But when the state census of 1837 showed a population of 822 in Ingham, the legislature, in an act signed by Governor Mason on April 5, 1838, authorized Ingham County to ''organize,'' or elect officers to discharge the functions of county government.

Under territorial law, the governor appointed three commissioners to locate county seats; these had visited the county in March 1836, examined several sites, and established the county seat ''at the quarter posts between sections 1 and 12 of Vevay.'' As there was no house on that site at the time—or for several years thereafter—the first polling place was the house of Hiram Parker, the habitation nearest the designated county seat. Here, on June 7, 1838, Ingham's citizens—those who were male and over 21—cast a total of 260 votes. The officers elected included a sheriff, clerk, register of deeds, associate judges, probate judge, and three county commissioners; by the time of Ingham's organization, even judges were subject to popular election.

The originally designated county seat, known as the village of Ingham, retained its status only until 1840, when the state legislature designated Mason as the county seat. There is no clear evidence as to where county business was transacted between 1838 and 1840. The village of Ingham soon languished and was eventually plowed under.

In the first contest for sheriff, Richard R. Lowe, who ran as a Democrat, narrowly defeated his brother Peter, a Whig. The Lowes were an early Stockbridge family for whom Lowe Lake is named. Since the early election records have been destroyed, the names of the other unsuccessful candidates are unknown.

Minos McRoberts of Mason, the second physician to settle in Ingham County, was elected register of deeds. He combined politics and medicine for a time, but gave up his medical practice after 1850. Dr. McRoberts held many township and county offices, was the first president of the Ingham County Pioneer Society, and is the best known of all the first county officeholders.

Peter Linderman, Ingham's first probate judge, operated a general store in Mason and also held many county, township, and school-district offices. County Clerk Valorous Meeker is remembered mainly because he was the first physician to settle in Ingham; the village of Leslie was known as Meekersville in the early days. Meeker, however, did not remain in the area.

The functions of county government were limited at first to maintaining courts and records; township government had a far more immediate effect on the lives of early settlers. Michigan's system of local government was modeled on that of New England, in which the town (or, in Michigan, the township) had a unique vitality. The township provided a legal framework in which settlers could act to meet some of their most pressing needs—notably, schools and roads.

Townships, unlike counties, appear to have been organized by the direct initiative of the settlers. When a

LEFT: This log cabin was the birthplace of Lansing architect Darius B. Moon. The cabin, which was built around 1860 and later modernized, stood in Delta Township. It was moved to the Woldumar Nature Center in 1980 and is now in the process of being restored. Moon was one of Lansing's leading architects during the late 19th and early 20th centuries. Photograph by author.

ABOVE: This black walnut mitten facer was made in 1845 by Leslie W. Winne of Ingham County. Most probably, it was used as a form when darning mittens. Courtesy of the Michigan State University Museum.

RIGHT: In the 1870s, Sylas C. Overpack invented huge 10-foot-tall wheels to facilitate the hauling of timber over obstructions such as tree stumps. Courtesy of Michigan State Archives.

surveyed township had a dozen or so families, little time was lost in submitting a petition for organization to the legislature; the legislative enabling act defined its boundaries, designated a place and date for the first meeting, and almost always approved the name proposed in the petition. In Ingham, the creation of townships began with Stockbridge in 1836, and continued until the organization of Lansing Township in 1842 completed the process. The "civil" or "charter" townships organized by the legislature had the same boundaries as the "congressional" townships originally marked off by the surveyors.

Organizing townships put names on the map, and many of these show the New York origins of the early settlers. Joseph E. North, Jr., suggested the name for Lansing Township, in honor of the Tompkins County, New York, community in which he had lived. Locke, Delhi, Wheatfield, Leroy, Aurelius, Stockbridge, and Onondaga were also named after communities in New York. Other townships derived their names from a variety of sources: Ingham was named for the county, Meridian for the survey line on its western border, White Oak for a tree that predominates in the area, and Vevay, apparently, for a town in Indiana. Phelpstown Township, later subdivided into Locke and Williamstown townships, was named for David Phelps, the settler in whose home the organizational meeting was held. Williamstown was named for the two brothers who filed the original village plat, and Leslie was named after a family of that name in western New York.

It does not appear that there was much conflict over names. The name originally proposed for Bunker Hill Township was Emma, to which some objected; the Bunker family objected to having the town named for them. The name Bunker Hill was a compromise proposed by Jonathan Shearer, a member of the legislature, in honor of his father, who had fought at that battle in the American Revolution.

William A. Dryer was present at the first meeting of Ingham Township, held at the home of Caleb Carr in the spring of 1838. The township then comprised an area more than four times its present size, including the present townships of Leroy, White Oak, and Wheatfield in addition to Ingham. "We felt the need for some proper authority to lay out roads and organize school districts," recalled Dryer. The 25 eligible voters at the meeting had "no records, no laws, nothing to guide us." They had come from several different states, each with its own traditions of local government. After an animated discussion, it was agreed to elect the same officers as in Stockbridge Township, which had been organized earlier.

"Now commenced an interesting scene," reported Dryer. The men did not know each other, and "they knew still less of each other's abilities or qualifications." The voters, with some embarrassment, described their respective qualifications, and a slate of candidates was agreed upon. Then arose the question of "who should receive the votes," and someone nominated their host, Caleb Carr, as chairman. Carr "doffed his hat into which the votes were cast," and when the votes were counted "we swore each other into office, adjourned, shook hands all around, a happy and independent people with full-fledged government fairly inaugurated."

In the newly organized townships, there were often as many offices to fill as there were voters. Vevay's 24 voters filled 23 places; there was one case of 13 voters filling 21 offices. The officers elected generally included a supervisor, a town clerk, justices of the peace, constables, "directors of the poor," school inspectors, road commissioners, "fence viewers," and a "poundmaster." "Fence viewers" determined that "lawful fences," at least four and a half feet high, were built; "poundmasters" cared for stray livestock.

To many settlers, the school inspectors were the most important local officials. Their duties, under Michigan law, included dividing the township into school districts, seeing that schools were built and organized, hiring teachers, and overseeing the operations of the township's schools much in the manner of a modern board of education. Michigan law required that "every township containing fifty inhabitants or householders shall employ a schoolmaster of good morals to teach children to read and write ... as well as arithmetic, orthography, and decent behavior."

The settlers hardly needed prodding by the authorities; pioneer accounts reveal that after meeting the physical needs of their families, their "greatest solicitude" was for "a suitable educational training" for their children, who had been suddenly withdrawn from schools and other sources of culture. "The pioneers," said Flavius J. Littlejohn of Lansing, "became a prey to the keenest anxiety lest the mental powers of their children might be clouded by ignorance or dwarfed by neglect."

The residents of School District No. 3, Alaeidon Township, assembled for their initial meeting on November 11, 1841, and agreed to build a log school 22 feet square, "with a shingle roof and a good box stove." A similar meeting two years later in Aurelius Township voted to erect a log school 20 feet square and to raise $100 for its construction. It was agreed that residents could contribute their share in labor at the rate of 50 cents a day, the labor of ox teams not included. "When the house was up and enclosed," recalled William M. Webb, for whom the Webb school was named, "134 days of labor had been performed, amounting to $67, leaving $33 with which to finish the inside." The modest sum of $100—the typical sum spent—paid only the cost of school construction; the teacher's salary was paid by means of a "rate bill," with each family paying according to the number of children enrolled and the length of time they spent in school. The teacher, hired by the township school authorities, was paid a minimal salary and "boarded round."

The log schoolhouse, immortalized in the paintings of Winslow Homer and in the poetry of John Greenleaf Whittier, has a secure place in American folklore. As a source of virtue and dispenser of the pristine values of American civilization, it was believed to have no peer, unless it was the log cabin itself. In creating log schools, the pioneers of the area were, despite primitive conditions and cultural isolation, participants in the common-school movement, one of the great humanitarian crusades of the time. And the schoolmaster or schoolmistress, more often

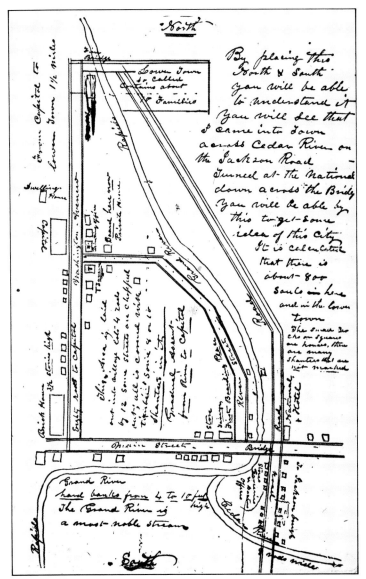

By placing this North & South you will be able to understand it. You will see that I came into town across Cedar River on the Jackson Road. Turned at the National down across the Bridy you will be able by this to get some idea of this city. It is calculated that there is about 800 souls in here and in the lower town.

This Area of Cde cut into alley lot 4 rod by 12 Some Streets are chopped out; all is covered with timber. Shanties Some 8 or 10

The small Sqre cho on Squres are houses, there are many Shanties that are not marked

Grand River hand banks from 4 To 10 feet high The Grand River is a most noble stream

LEFT: This 1848 Map of Lansing was drawn by Senator Luke Hazen of Hillsdale County and sent to his wife. Senator Hazen wrote on his map: "By placing this north and south you will be able to understand it. You will see that I came across Cedar River on the Jackson road, turned at the National down across the bridge. You will be able by this to get some idea of this city. It is calculated that there are about 800 souls here and in lower town." In the center of the map, he writes: "This area is laid out in village lots, 4 rods by 12. Some streets are chopped out; all is covered with timber. Some eight or ten shanties in it." Courtesy of Lansing Public Library.

BELOW: The First Congregational Church of Vermontville, Michigan, was built in 1864. It is the oldest church in the area still in continuous use. Although the interior has been modernized, the original pews are still in use. Photograph by author.

BOTTOM: A typical logging crew in the pine forests. Courtesy of the Saginaw News.

19

than not, appears to have been a person at least of diligence.

The interior of a log school was as Spartan as the houses in which the pupils lived. There was usually one door and one window; the door swung on wooden hinges and was kept closed by the inevitable wooden latch and opened by the leather latchstring. A fireplace took up one whole side of the room, usually opposite the door. Against the log walls were desks or planks supported by pegs. The school year was short—three months in summer and three in winter—and the building was "chinked and mudded up" for winter use. Few boys attended school after the age of 12 or 13; girls, however, usually attended school somewhat longer.

In the early days, books were scarce; in Onondaga Township, 40 acres of land were once exchanged for a quantity of spelling books. Blackboards were uncommon, and even the school bell was unknown; school was "called" by rapping a book on the window sash. The books most widely used—Noah Webster's *Elementary Spelling Book,* Lindley Murray's *English Reader,* Jesse Olney's *Geography,* and Nathan Draboll's *Arithmetic*—give a sense of the schools' intellectual diet.

The speller, one of the most popular American schoolbooks until well into the 19th century, contained ingeniously organized lists of words for spelling exercises ("words of three syllables accented on the third syllable") and "copybook maxims"—all manner of aphorisms, good advice, proverbs, and fables. The "copybook maxims" reflected the prevailing view that education without character training was incomplete; it was believed that morality would somehow rub off as the child used them for penmanship exercises.

The language arts—or, in those times, spelling, writing, parsing, penmanship, and reading—were stressed, especially spelling. Competition was encouraged; a pupil "went down" for improperly spelling a word. In spelling bees, all syllables were spelled and pronounced; for example, a speller would render *infantry* as *i-n, in; f-a-n, infan; t-r-y, try, infantry.* "This," said Van Buren, who taught in log schools for a decade, "we called spelling. Merely rattling off the letters is not spelling."

For reading, declamation, and parsing, Lindley Murray's *English Reader* was widely used. "There is not a line in the book," said Van Buren, "that the most scrupulous moralist would wish to erase, not a sentiment to unsettle any man's faith, or mislead by a false principle." The book contained heroic poetry and inspiring selections from the classic English writers, and was seen in later years as having helped the pupils form a "correct taste" in intellectual and literary matters.

Arithmetic seems to have received less emphasis than the language arts, but a whole generation of Michigan pupils learned to "cipher" from the "formidable old volume" of Nathan Draboll. "Authors of arithmetic books then," according to Van Buren, "were concerned lest the pupil learn the material too easily "and not get the benefit of drill and study."

The pioneers, adults as well as children, had a thirst for intellectual stimulation. Books were scarce, treasured, and read threadbare. The age of cheap printing, when books of all kinds poured from the press in profusion, had hardly begun. To meet the need for entertainment, culture, and what would now be termed "continuing education," the log schoolhouses became community centers. In the evening and during the long winters, the entire community would attend cultural activities at the log schoolhouse; many communities had singing, debating, spelling, and other cultural meetings, quaintly called "schools."

Sometimes an itinerant teacher taught one of these schools; Margaret Lindsey of Alaeidon Township remembered that the man who sold the school district a set of outline maps taught an evening "geography school." His method of teaching, said Miss Lindsey, was very effective. He would point to the features of the earth's surface and "the class followed the pointer and sang the facts to the tune of 'Old Dan Tucker.'"

"For entertainment and information," said Webb, the evening schools "were second only to the information we received in the day school." For more than a decade, Webb attended a debating school which met once a week; it had a constitution and bylaws and "aimed to conduct ... its meetings with as much propriety and dignity as in any legislative body." Among the propositions debated were: "Resolved, that the mental faculties of the sexes are equal"; "that a lie is sometimes justifiable"; "that it requires more skill and ability to be a successful agriculturist than any other calling." It seems probable that the topics came from a widely used manual, since pioneers all over lower Michigan seem to have debated the same topics. Some of the issues appear quaint to the modern reader. Mrs. Carolyn Kirkland, who lived in Pinckney in neighboring Livingston County during the late 1830s, reported an avid debate on the proposition, "Resolved, that the ass is superior to the ox as an agricultural animal." In addition to the topics mentioned, all the other "live" topics of the day were vigorously contended; there were plenty of these, as the controversies over slavery and other issues heightened during the 1840s and 1850s.

As time passed, the old log schoolhouse gave way to a frame or brick building; specially trained teachers supplanted the old schoolmaster or schoolmistress; graded classes and a lengthened school year altered the role of the teacher. As early as the 1850s, new educational ideas began to change the rote teaching style of many log schools; by the 1880s, the entire curriculum had been transformed. But to Van Buren and other pioneers, the modern schools lacked the vitality and effectiveness of the early log schools; the new schools, he said, made children indifferent to reading. "The young people of today," he declared, "are dying of *ennui* in a well-stocked library." And the teacher who "boarded round" knew his pupils far more intimately than those who taught after that practice had become only a memory.

During the late 1830s and 1840s, the forest retreated, civilization advanced, and population increased. Sawmills and gristmills multiplied; "corduroy" or log roads improved access and eased travel; schools proliferated. The panic of 1837 was followed by an economic recession; by 1840, however, a slow recovery had set in.

book, dŏve, full, use, can, chaise, gem, thin, thou.

No. 69.—LXIX.

Bāy	jay	slay	dray	tray	sway
day	lay	may	fray	stray	prey
fay	clay	nay	gray	say	trey
gay	flay	pay	pray	stay	dey
hay	play	ray	spray	way	bey

No. 70.—LXX.

boy	joy	toy	haw	claw	raw	saw
coy	cloy	caw	jaw	flaw	craw	law
hoy	troy	daw	draw	maw	straw	paw

No. 71.—LXXI.

swamp	smalt	swart	pōrt	live	glŏve
wasp	spalt	quart	mōst	cŏme	wŏrk
was	salt	pōrk	doll	sŏme	wŏrst
halt	want	fōrt	loll	dŏve	shŏve
malt	wart	spōrt	give	lŏve	mŏnk

No. 72—LXXII.

bow	mow	sow	wŏrm	dĭrt	squĭrt
cow	now	vow	frŏnt	flĭrt	fĭrst
how	brow	kēy	wŏnt	shĭrt	ward
plow	prow	buoy	wŏrt	skĭrt	warm

The farmer cuts his grass to make hay.
Bricks are made of clay baked in a kiln.
You may play on the mow of hay.
A dray is a kind of low cart.
When we eat we move the under jaw; but the upper jaw of most animals is fixed.
Little boys are fond of toys.
The sting of a wasp is very painful.
A swamp is wet spungy land.

Webster's Speller, a popular American schoolbook used well into the 19th century, had organized lists of words for spelling exercises. Courtesy of Michigan State Archives.

The Branch School in Williamstown Township, Ingham County. The school was originally known as the "Africa" school and the road it stood on was called Africa Road. This name derived from the fact that there were many abolitionists in the vicinity of the school. The school was later named the Branch School for a family in the area, and the name of the road was changed to Sherwood Road. Photograph by author.

By the late 1830s, Michigan fever had subsided, but the population of Ingham County continued to increase; the federal census of 1840 showed a population of 2,498, up considerably from the 822 of 1837. By 1845, the first census for which township population figures are available, the population of Ingham County had more than doubled, to 5,267. "This county, for a new county," said John W. Longyear, who settled in Mason in 1840, "was considerably advanced. ... One could even then get to a railroad in four or five days. ... [A] real pioneer couldn't accomplish that feat in as many weeks."

In 1845, the county's population averaged nine persons per square mile, but these were by no means evenly distributed. Lansing Township, the last to be organized, had a population of only 88, or 2.4 for each of its 36 square miles; Vevay, the most populous, had 16.7. The only village of any size was Mason, known originally as Mason Center and named for Governor Stevens T. Mason, which became the county seat in 1840.

The *Michigan Gazeteer* of 1838 described Mason as "a village of recent origin, situated on Sycamore Creek," near the center of the county. The land on which the village stood had been entered in 1836 by a firm of land speculators, the Charles Noble Company of Monroe, Michigan. In 1836, the company, hoping to attract settlers, sent one Lewis Lacey to build a dam and sawmill on the site. A member of the firm, Ephraim P. Danforth, who became one of Ingham's first county judges in 1838, came to look after the company's interests. In 1838, a gristmill was added, and early settlers found about 20 acres of cleared land. A county courthouse was built in 1843.

If Mason thrived partly because of its fortuitous selection as county seat, other settlements did not. By the mid-1840s, the area had three "ghost towns": Ingham, the first designated county seat, about three and a half miles east of Mason; Columbia, seven and a half miles west of Mason; and Jefferson, three miles north and one mile west, which for a time vied with Mason to become the county seat.

Silas Beebe visited both Jefferson and Mason in February 1838. At Jefferson, he found 10 or 12 acres "cut down ready to clear, five or six log houses peopled, [and] a schoolhouse"; Mason, with its dam frozen over was not much more advanced. But with the selection of Mason, Jefferson languished, as did Columbia, and there is no record of settlement at Ingham. Soon all three sites were plowed over.

In these early days of land speculation, there were also "paper cities," entirely fictional communities in which land of questionable value was sold at high prices to the unwary. One such scam, known as Biddle City, actually led to the first permanent settlement in Lansing Township.

Little is known about the two brothers, William and Jerry Ford, who promoted Biddle City, which covered the southern half of Section 21 in what is now the city of Lansing. Evidently they did have clear title to the land, which they entered with the government land office. In addition, they recorded a plat of Biddle City, which may be examined in the office of the Ingham County Register of Deeds.

The fancy (or fanciful) plat divided the 320-acre, half-section site into lots, and boasted an "academy square," "church square," and "public square." The plat was shown to prospects in Lansing Township, Tompkins County, New York, and it is known that at least 16 persons, including Daniel Buck and Joseph E. North, Jr., purchased lots.

Jacob Cooley, a German immigrant who lived in New York, and his wife, the former Lucy Barnes of Hartford, settled in Leslie Township in May 1836, became discouraged, and returned to New York. In November 1837, Cooley, having heard of Biddle City and apparently attracted by the prospect of living in a settled area, returned and visited the site with one of the Ford brothers. Instead of buying land there, however, he entered a deed for land in Section 30, two miles east, near the present intersection of Jolly and Waverly roads.

Meanwhile, the 16 purchasers of Biddle City lots traveled from Lansing Township, New York, to Detroit, where no one had heard of Biddle City. Most of the party remained in Oakland County and settled there, but two of its members—Joseph E. North, Jr., and Daniel Buck—pressed on to De Witt. There, David Scott referred them to one Justus Gilkey, who lived 10 miles south. Gilkey, who knew the area, led the settlers to the flooded peninsula between the Grand and Red Cedar rivers and said, as tradition has it, "There, gentlemen, is Biddle City." North and Buck realized they had been swindled, but Gilkey reassured them that "the land can be had for ten shillings an acre and the timber is of the finest quality in the world." North settled in Section 33, about a mile from Cooley.

Cooley remained alone on his land from November 1837 until the following spring, when his wife arrived with their two children, Jacob F. and Lansing J. Cooley. "In fixing for winter," according to Cooley's grandson Frederick, "he got buckskins from the Indians and made himself a suit of clothes." For shelter, he felled a large tree, left the butt on the stump, then piled on leaves, dirt, and brush. He followed the Grand River to Jackson for winter provisions, but while he was floating the provisions back, his raft broke at the Dimondale rapids. Cooley managed to get ashore but had no fire and had to run to keep warm. He was almost frozen to death and would probably have died, but a kindly Indian couple "rubbed him until he was warm, and then gave him some hedgehog and muskrat to eat." The Indians helped carry what was left of his provisions to his land, then camped nearby; Cooley "had Indian neighbors ever after that."

In the spring of 1838, Cooley built a log shanty and invited his wife to join him. After arriving in Detroit, Mrs. Cooley hired a teamster to take her and the children to Jackson; a short distance from the city, the sheriff pursued the teamster, who absconded into the woods, leaving Mrs. Cooley to drive the team herself. In Jackson, the authorities confiscated the wagon and team, and the Cooleys "started walking through the woods to Eaton Rapids." They got lost, and in a scene that has become famous in Lansing history, Mrs. Cooley "set the children on a log and went to find a way out." She found the clear-

Stevens T. Mason, the first governor of the state of Michigan. Mason, Michigan, known originally as Mason Center, was named for him. Courtesy of Michigan State Archives.

ing of a Mr. Blakeslee, who then helped her find the children after a long search. Informed by an Indian of his wife's arrival, Cooley went to Eaton Rapids, built a boat, and the entire family arrived in Lansing Township on June 15, 1838.

But the Cooleys' troubles were far from over. Without a team or other animal power, they had to clear land and plant a crop; the work must have been excruciating. Since they had no calendar, they "kept time" by marking a board with a piece of coal. They celebrated the first Fourth of July in Lansing Township on a rock near the Grand River, singing patriotic songs while their children played nearby. In mid-July, 1838, the Cooleys got sick "and lost the day of the month." They ran out of provisions, and only the Indians kept them alive. At one point, Cooley was not expected to live; he instructed his wife "to lay him in a bark trough, cover him with dirt and get the children out of the woods." Fortunately, however, he recovered.

Late in 1839, Cooley went to Jackson to pursue his trade of tailoring; for 14 months, his wife and the children were alone in the woods, except for the fortunate presence of Indians. On January 6, 1840, the Cooleys' third son was born—Nathan F. Cooley, the first white child born in Lansing Township. About that time, they heard that another family had moved into the woods. The new family was that of Joseph E. North, Jr.

The Cooleys' situation improved, but the area remained for some time the least populated in Ingham County. Much of the land north of Biddle City had been bought by investors. William Townshend of Rochester, New York, had purchased 1,280 acres, or two square miles, in the heart of what would become the city of Lansing, including parts of Sections 8, 9, 20, and 21. Other investors, including James Seymour and Frederick Bushnell, also of Rochester, purchased parts of Sections 9, 15, and 17. Bushnell, not a well man, went to Baton Rouge, Louisiana, in the winter of 1836-37 and died; in 1839, Seymour bought out his interests in the Lansing area.

Seymour understood the potential of his centrally located holdings, including the waterpower possibilities of Section 9. He sold its southeast quarter to John W. Burchard of Mason, the first lawyer to settle in Ingham County, apparently with the understanding that Burchard would build a dam and sawmill on the site. Burchard was slow getting started. Not until August 1843, about four years after he bought the land, did he move with his wife and children to what is now the heart of downtown Lansing. Probably he built his log cabin—the first permanent residence in Lansing—sometime before that. In any case, there is no doubt that John Burchard, his wife, the former Frances Haynes, and their two children were the first permanent settlers within the original boundaries of the city of Lansing.

Burchard completed the dam and returned to his native New York to obtain some of the equipment needed for the sawmill. A flood in the spring of 1844 damaged part of the dam. When Burchard and three other men ventured out in a canoe to examine the break, the vessel capsized, and Burchard was drowned. "By the above decease," said an obituary notice preserved by Burchard's widow, "a wife is bereft of a kind and affectionate friend and bosom companion . . . in one sad and unexpected moment."

On learning of Burchard's death, Seymour, residing in New York, sent a letter to Joab Page, a Vevay Township settler who had built the first sawmill in Jackson County. Seymour offered Page, his sons and sons-in-law, and any men they could hire 50 cents a day for a five-day week to build the mill. Page accepted and made the move to Lansing with his son Chauncey and sons-in-law Whitney Smith, George D. Pease, and Alvin Rolfe. There, they repaired the dam and built and operated the mill. At the first Fourth of July celebration held in what would become North Lansing, in 1844, Indians assisted in the raising of the liberty pole.

At the time of settlement, there appears to have been about 500 Indians in Ingham County, with perhaps a comparable number in Eaton. According to Dr. Frank N. Turner, nephew of pioneer James Turner and a leading local historian, the Indians were seminomadic. In the spring, when the sugar maples flowed with sap, they camped in the woods; in summer, they cultivated corn and pumpkins and gathered wild berries. There were two stable villages in Ingham—one at the site of the present village of Okemos in Meridian Township, which appears to have been "the Indian metropolis" of the area, and another near Lowe Lake in northern Stockbridge Township. The city of Charlotte in Eaton County stands on the site of an old Indian cornfield. Indian burial grounds dotted the entire region, and Indian trails, "well-beaten and apparently quite old," traversed all the counties in the area.

Important remains of the "mound builders," an early group of Indians of whom little is known, have been found in Ingham County. Orlando Mack Barnes, a Lansing pioneer and early local historian, reported one such discovery in Southwest Aurelius Township in the vicinity of Barnes and College roads. When Barnes saw the mounds in 1839 or 1840, "the largest was five or six feet high, and on it large forest trees were standing." When opened in 1874, the mound contained human bones, beads, and other Indian relics, and the remains of a wooden container. Barnes described another find nearby, four miles south and two miles east, "an earthwork, manifestly the work of man . . . oblong in shape, one-hundred-thirty feet by one-hundred and eight feet." This site, in the vicinity of Newett and Tomlinson roads in Leslie Township, included the remains of moats, ditches, and an embankment.

The Indians who remained after settlement lived a precarious life until they died off or were sent to western reservations. It seems likely that those in the Lansing area were Ottawas, but it is possible that they were of mixed Pottawatamie, Chippewa, and Ottawa descent. Their most important leader was Chief Okemos, a nephew of Pontiac (himself of mixed Chippewa and Ottawa origin) and a leading figure in the early history of the area. Okemos became a chief not by hereditary right but by military prowess. The village of Okemos in Meridian Township is named for him.

LEFT: **This carved spoon, made by a Chippewa Indian, is representative of spoons used by Indians in the Lansing area. Courtesy of the Michigan State University Museum.**

TOP: **Prehistoric projectile points typically used by Indians in central Michigan. Many of these have** been found in the Lansing area. Courtesy of Michigan State University Museum.

ABOVE: Chief Okemos, an Ottawa leader in the early 1800s, achieved leadership through military prowess rather than hereditary right. Courtesy of Michigan State Archives.

When his fighting days ended, Okemos, who ranged widely over lower Michigan, hunted, fished, and traded with the white settlers. About 1837 or 1838, smallpox decimated his tribe, while increasing white settlement destroyed the hunting grounds. The three or four families of Indians who regularly visited the Lansing area were members of Okemos' tribe; they usually stayed only briefly, trading baskets, venison, or wild berries for flour and other goods.

The Indians were of inestimable value in aiding the white settlers in their adjustment to life in the woods. Excellent hunters, they taught the settlers some of the finer points of this essential survival skill. The Indians also taught the pioneers a superior method of tanning hides. Buckskins prepared in this manner were permanently soft and could be made into almost any article of clothing, including coats, trousers, mittens, gloves, and moccasins.

Indian trails, extending through the forest in all areas, were essential to the settlers. These trails avoided some of the worst obstacles, crossed streams at the points where they could be forded most easily, and led to the better hunting and fishing areas. Pioneer accounts often told of Indians rescuing settlers stranded in the woods, serving as midwives, and performing many other humane acts.

In 1840, the United States authorities removed the Pottawatamie Indians from Michigan, including most of the Indians of Eaton County. David Lucas, a Bellevue pioneer and friend of the Indians, saw them just after they received the news that a detachment of federal troops was after them. "Mounted on the backs of their ponies as close as they could stand, they were in deep, anxious consultation around their wisest heads. Soon they scattered like a flock of blackbirds." They were captured after a two- or three-day siege in a swamp and were brought to Marshall, the collecting point for Indians rounded up in this part of the state. "I am informed," said Lucas, "that during the last night of their stay the moans and lamentations were heart-rending. ... They were going to a strange land where corn grew only knee-high, and pumpkins no larger than potatoes." No Pottawatamie Indians remained in the area after the removal.

"The woods seemed lonely after the banishment," said Edward Foote of Eaton County. "They had not been gone for six months when we wanted them back." The Indians had served the settlers as guides, had helped in hunting and in keeping track of cattle. In pioneer days, cattle were permitted to range the woods. "If we lost any animal and described it to an Indian," said Foote, "he was sure to bring back information as to where it could be found."

There were other poignant scenes, indelibly impressed on the memories of all who saw them. Mason D. Chatterton remembered that in the summer of 1852 some Indians were camped "about eighty rods east of where the college buildings [the present MSU] now stood." Okemos' daughter had died, and 300 to 400 Indians had gathered for a funeral service. They made a drum by stretching a deerskin over a hollow log, "upon which the Indians kept up a constant thumping night and day." All night long, they danced around a fire and "gave vent to the most horrid groans, screeches, and gesticulations imaginable; echoes of their wild, hideous cries and lamentations reverberated through the dense forest." Okemos' daughter was buried at Shim-ni-con, next to where Okemos himself would finally be laid to rest in 1858.

An artist's conception of a Chippewa Indian Village. The Indians of Michigan lived in wigwams constructed of an arched framework of poles overlaid with bark, rush mats, or hides. Courtesy of Michigan Historical Collections, Bentley Historical Library, University of Michigan.

BELOW: **A barn scene photographed on Park Lake Road in Bath Township just north of East Lansing, 1968. The equipment shown would suffice for a one-horse conveyance. Photograph by author.**

ABOVE: **This basketry rattle was made by Ottawa Chief Okemos and given to Mary L. Sherman sometime in the early 1850s. The basket contains kernels of corn which produce the rattle. Courtesy of the Michigan State University Museum.**

RIGHT: **An archaeological map of Ingham County and its surrounding region showing Indian trails. Courtesy of Michigan State Archives.**

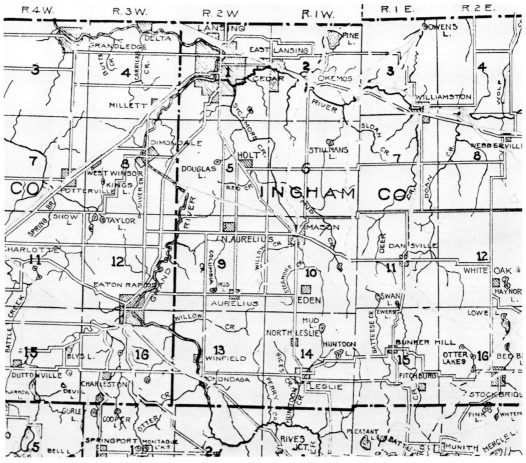

27

Chapter 3

"When the Legislature of '47 was first organized," said Enos Goodrich, a representative from Genesee County, "the man who could have supposed it possible to wrest the capitol from Detroit and set it down in the midst of a dense forest on the banks of the Grand River would have been considered a fit subject for an insane asylum." Yet by the end of that same legislative session, the incredible had come to pass: Lansing had been designated as the new state capital.

Since territorial days, the capital of Michigan had been at Detroit. The constitution of 1835, however, required that a permanent site be selected by 1847, and communities all over the lower peninsula—seeking the enormous economic growth certain for the capital site and its hinterland—had flooded the legislature with petitions and memorials. As 1847 approached, newspapers in Detroit, Ann Arbor, Jackson, and Marshall, strongly pressed the advantages of their own communities as capital sites while disparaging the claims of rivals.

Detroit had much to commend it, and it was within the discretion of the legislature to retain the capital there. Of all the communities in the state, many of which had a strong backwoods flavor, Detroit "looked" most like a capital city, with its many fine residences, churches, hotels, and public buildings. Not moving the capital would have saved the considerable cost of relocation, an important consideration to the economy-minded legislators of 1847. And Detroit, despite the marvelous growth of the interior, was a major lake port and terminal for rail and stage lines; it was and would remain the metropolis of the state.

But the temper of the times was against large cities as seats of government. In Europe, a regional or national capital was usually the largest metropolis, a center of culture and finance as well as government. Not so in America in the 1840s, where the arcadian dream was still alive and many voters shared Jefferson's mistrust of cities. The American tradition of locating capitals outside large cities, close to geographic or population centers, was well established; the national capital and that of the neighboring state of Ohio stood as prime examples. As 1847 approached, the outcry against the "Detroit influence" and demands for "a healthier political climate" grew more strident. "The influence of 'quail parties' and 'quiet sup-

pers,' " said Levi Bishop of Marshall, "was often alluded to as the principal motive for the passage of many important acts of legislation."

Detroiters had miscalculated in delaying the capital selection until 1847, by which time the changing distribution of population in Michigan had reduced their relative power in the legislature. By 1847, the southern two tiers of counties outside Wayne contained three-fifths of the state's population; in the legislature of that year, they controlled 37 out of 65 house votes and 13 of 22 senate votes. For these legislators, the question was no longer a choice between Detroit and an interior location, but a matter of choosing among various interior locations, with Detroit out of the running.

In view of its enormous consequences for the Lansing area, the legislative history of the capital selection is worth examining in some detail. The matter was raised first in the house, where it was referred to a "select committee" that included members from Wayne, Calhoun, Genesee, Washtenaw, Monroe, and Ionia counties, with George Throop of Wayne as chairman. The select committee met, deadlocked as expected, and prepared three reports.

Wayne County, argued Throop in the first of these reports, was willing and able to provide buildings and capital grounds at no cost to the state. Placing the capital elsewhere, he warned, "would involve an expenditure of a very large sum of public money." He placed the cost of a move to the interior as high as $200,000—though, in point of fact, the actual cost of building a new capitol in Lansing was about $20,000.

The second report of the select committee, by John D. Pierce of Marshall in Calhoun County, raised strong objections to the permanent location of the capital in Detroit. Pierce, already well known as one of the creators of Michigan's highly praised school system, argued that Detroit "not only lies upon the frontier of the state, but of the United States, being ... in sight of a foreign territory." Ann Arbor, he said, was also too far east for a good capital site, and it "already had the University." Jackson, too, was too far east, and "had its share of public patronage in the penitentiary." Pierce concluded his report, recalled his committee colleague Enos Goodrich of Genesee County, "by advancing the claims of Marshall ... in glowing terms and well-selected argument."

"Last but not least," recounted Goodrich at an 1885 historical meeting in Lansing, "your humble speaker presented his solitary report." A capital located as far south as either Detroit or Marshall, or anywhere else in the southern two tiers of counties, he argued, "would be too remote from the geographical center of the state to have that *permanence* contemplated by the constitution." The state's population center, he noted, was shifting to the north and west. Goodrich discussed the route of the Michigan Central Railroad, which had figured also in the Throop and Pierce reports, and pointed out that "only a tenth part of the geographical surface of the state" lay south of it. A location north of the railroad would benefit the state "by giving impetus [to settlement] in a direction in which most of our state lands are located ... [thereby]

This scene, photographed near the Looking Glass River in Shiawassee County, typifies the kind of terrain found by early settlers. The surveyor's field notes show that some of the land in the Lansing area was swampy. The trees in this area are second growth. Photograph by author.

29

replenishing our treasury and populating our wilds." Goodrich cited the example of Ohio: "The legislative body of that state ... [with] considerable foresight, located the capital ... in the depths of a wilderness." The flourishing city of Columbus, he continued, "bears testimony to the wisdom of the measure." Goodrich concluded by strongly urging the selection of a point north of the Michigan Central Railroad, "the selection of which ... I would leave to the good judgment of the legislative body."

The select committee submitted its reports to the house without recommendation. At this stage, said Goodrich, "an organization was quietly and ... secretly formed, known and designated as the 'Northern Rangers.'" Its members included, in addition to Goodrich, House Speaker George W. Peck of Livingston County, Senator William Fenton of Genesee, and Senator Charles P. Bush of Livingston. Early in the secret meetings of this group, "there appeared upon the scene a quiet and unassuming character," a man "who had more to do with directing public opinion than most people imagine." The man was none other than James Seymour, then living in Genesee County, who had built a mill at what would shortly become North Lansing. In a letter to the legislators, Seymour offered not only to provide free land for the new capitol, but also "to erect on an adjoining lot, suitable buildings for the temporary use of the legislature and public officers, and lease them to the State without charge, till permanent buildings are erected." To show the central location of his proposed capital site, Seymour accompanied his letter with a map, on which he drew red lines to prominent points, with distances noted. According to Goodrich, "the map did more in directing people's attention to Lansing than any or all of the speeches in the halls of legislation."

Copies of Seymour's map, which Goodrich remembered as an ordinary "Farmer's map" of Michigan, with the accompanying letter, were placed on every legislator's desk. Seymour identified himself as "owner of a tract of land ... [in] Section nine of town four north range two west in the town of Lansing." His land, stated the letter, had the advantage of central location. The site proposed was 87 miles from Detroit, 86 from Monroe, and 91 from Mt. Clemens; it was 89 miles from the mouth of the Grand River and 86 from that of the Kalamazoo. The site was also equidistant from the southern boundary of the state and the northern line of Midland County.

In the course of the subsequent debate, the house voted on 13 sites in all. Ann Arbor was defeated 18-44; Byron, 27-31; Detroit, 18-43; Dexter, 17-44; Eaton Rapids, 27-34; Grand Blanc, 23-35; Jackson, 27-31; and Marshall, 29-32. At one point in the confused session, the village of Lyons won by 30-28, but the house later reversed itself. Finally, Joseph H. Kilbourne of Meridian Township in Ingham County proposed Lansing, which won by an initial vote of 35-27. The bill was ordered to a third reading by a vote of 40-24, and on the third and final reading, it passed by the decisive vote of 48-17. Motions to reconsider or substitute first Marshall and then Jackson were defeated, and Lansing emerged the decisive winner.

The house bill was then sent to the senate, where even greater confusion prevailed. Among the sites considered were Detroit, Ann Arbor, De Witt, Marshall, and Caledonia Township in Shiawassee County. Jackson, Marshall, and Lyons each received majorities that were subsequently reversed. In one day of debate, March 8, 1847, the senators voted 51 times without coming to a decision. Finally, on March 9, the exhausted senate approved the house bill, and with the signature of Acting Governor William L. Greenly (Governor Alpheus Felch having been elected to the U.S. Senate), the bill became law.

Both houses passed additional legislation fixing December 1, 1847, as the date on which the site in the Township of Lansing in the County of Ingham would officially become the "seat of government" of the state of Michigan. The governor was directed to arrange for offices for state agencies in the new capital, to move the state archives and library, "and to cause suitable rooms to be prepared for the next session of the legislature ... before the first Monday of January 1848." The governor was further directed to appoint three commissioners to designate the exact site of the capitol, which was to be named the Town of Michigan; and the commissioners were authorized to enter with private proprietors in a plat of the land. The legislature appropriated $10,000 for the erection of temporary buildings.

The tradition developed almost immediately that the selection of Lansing was a joke that somehow backfired. But if this were the case, the legislators had ample time to reconsider. The house did reverse one favorable vote, and the senate reversed itself three times. In fact, Lansing passed all three readings in each house by decisive majorities. It seems more likely that Lansing won because the embattled legislators could not agree on any of the more settled communities, whose mutual rivalries and antagonisms over the years had effectively diminished their chances for selection. In the end, the deadlocked legislators turned to a "dark horse" candidate.

The legislators of 1847 are generally seen as a contentious lot who chose a good capital site for the wrong reasons. Acting Governor Greenly, who signed the bill, thought that they had acted less "by any foresight ... of the immense benefits, which were ultimately to accrue to the state" than by sheer exhaustion, or "a desire to get rid of the whole subject." Yet the modern reader is struck by the eloquence, force, and cogency of the arguments put forward at the time, especially by Pierce and Goodrich. The parliamentary discord is in a sense deceptive, for it obscures the emergence of a genuine consensus that the capital ought to be removed from Detroit and placed in a northern location closer to the geographic as well as the prospective population center of the growing state. Seen in this light, the selection of Lansing appears less fortuitous than historians have generally assumed.

If the initial reaction in Detroit and elsewhere was decidedly mixed—incredulity, humor, anger, sadness—the reaction at Lansing itself was ecstatic. There, Mrs. Ephraim Ingersoll, whose husband had told Jacob Cooley what day of the week it was back in 1838, composed a

TOP: The *Ingham Herald*, a Whig newspaper, was one of the earliest newspapers in Ingham County. Tradition has it that irate citizens, angered that the paper appeared only intermittently and contained almost no local news, destroyed the building and hid the type and presses in an old "sink hole" near the present county courthouse. From the Wiskemann Collection.

CENTER: Established in 1846, the *Ingham Democrat* vociferously argued the Democratic party's point of view. The newspaper folded around 1850; very few copies of the paper have survived over the years. From the Wiskemann Collection.

Ingham Herald.

VOLUME I.]   MASON, INGHAM COUNTY, MICH., THURSDAY MARCH 6, 1845.   [NUMBER 11.

INGHAM DEMOCRAT.

VOLUME 2—NUMBER 44.   MASON, INGHAM CO., MICH., MAY 10. 1847.   WHOLE NUMBER 96.

These chairs were used in Michigan's first state capitol in Detroit, and moved to Lansing when the capitol of 1847 was built. Courtesy of Michigan State Museum.

31

song especially for the Fourth of July celebration of 1847. Sung to the tune of the Vermont anthem, *The Old Granite State,* it began:

The capital is coming, it is even now at hand,
Many immigrants are coming to populate our land.
Let those who've toiled in sadness now dismiss their former grief,
And raise a shout of gladness at the prospect of relief!

Chorus: Let the forest echo and the woods return the sound . . . Etc.

Meanwhile, on April 7, 1847, Governor Greenly's capital commissioners—James L. Glen, James E. Platt, and David Smart—assembled at the log house of Joab Page, by now a kind of primitive hotel for visitors. Augustus F. Weller, who traveled with the commissioners, remembered that it took three days to travel through the woods from Jackson, the nearest rail terminal, to Lansing Township. At Mason, they found that the swollen Sycamore Creek had washed out the bridge. A log was felled across the stream, but Smart refused to cross in that manner, and a raft had to be built. Between Mason and Lansing, recalled Weller, the road was "simply terrible." The last 10 miles "were nearly impassable by reason of the overflow of the streams"; in low-lying places, the logs of the corduroy roads were afloat.

The commissioners were subjected to pressures from all sides. Seymour urged them to choose a site in Section 9, promising to give the state free of charge "such suitable lot as may be selected" for building the capitol and to "erect on an adjoining lot, suitable buildings for the temporary use of the legislature and public officers." Seymour, who wrote more than half the letters received by the commissioners, made an additional offer of 185 acres in Section 9 as a village site.

Other landowners made similar offers. Justus Gilkey offered a 20-acre site for state buildings on his land in Section 5, and also offered the state half the lots in a village to be platted on an adjoining 40 acres. Henry B. Lathrop, who had donated the 20-acre site in Jackson for the state penitentiary, supported his friend Gilkey, offering the state $6,000 toward its capitol building fund should it select the Gilkey site.

Another landowner, Hiram Parker of Detroit, offered land for the capitol on the eastern boundary of Lansing Township, on the west side of Abbott Road near its intersection with Burcham Drive, in what is now the core of East Lansing's residential area. Had this site been chosen, it is unlikely that the legislature would subsequently have located the agricultural college on its present site, just south of Parker's land. Parker offered 20 acres for "public purposes," as well as every second lot in a tract of 70 acres to be donated to the state.

But the commissioners rejected all these offers and, after much deliberation and tramping through the woods, agreed that the capitol should be built on Section 16—the land set aside for the support of schools. They found it "in the main an excellent section of land exceedingly well timbered," with superior soil. Its center, said their report, was

"very handsomely elevated above the river, and that part of it adjoining the river forms a very desirable location for a village." The site "is nearly equidistant from the two water powers on Sections 9 and 21, at which point it is probable that extensive improvements will be made and at no distant day thriving villages spring up." To mark the site of the new capitol, the commissioners drove a stake in the middle of what became Block 115, a tree-covered eminence bounded today by Washington and Capitol avenues and Allegan and Washtenaw streets.

Of particular importance for the future of Lansing was the fact that Section 16 had been withdrawn from sale to speculators. All state-owned lands, including school sections in every township as well as other lands granted to the state by the federal government, were normally sold at state land offices to anyone who would pay the going rate of $4.00 per acre. While the legislature was debating the capital location, speculators had dispatched agents to buy land in many areas being considered. As soon as it appeared that Lansing had a real chance, however, Governor Felch sent an order to Judge Abiel Silver, commissioner of the state land office in Marshall, that Section 16 in Lansing Township be removed from sale.

Tradition has it that a speculator intent on buying Section 16 and reaping a huge profit was on board the same train that carried Felch's order from Detroit to Marshall. The train was delayed at Marengo and arrived at Marshall after the land office had closed. Felch's order, however, was taken to Silver's home, and when the speculator arrived at the land office the following morning, he was told the land was not for sale. The state eventually realized more than $100,000 for its "noble common school fund" from the sale of lots in the capital city, far more than the $2,560 it would otherwise have received.

Judge Silver and the three capital commissioners were responsible for platting the Town of Michigan. To these commissioners, wrote James P. Edmonds, for many years Lansing's unofficial historian, "we are indebted for our wide and beautiful avenues and streets and the many wide open spaces for public use." Few laws controlled town founding in this period. Plats were usually drawn by speculators eager for a high return; streets were generally narrow and lots small, with little land set aside for public purposes. But the Town of Michigan, whose plat was sworn before Justice of the Peace Gilkey on June 23, 1847, was different. The streets were planned on a grand scale—all were laid out "five rods" (82.5 feet) in width, except for Capitol, six rods (99 feet) wide, and Michigan and Washington, both seven rods (115.5 feet) wide.

The town plat covered an area of two square miles. To the one square mile of Section 16 were joined two contiguous private tracts, one on the north and one on the south, in Sections 9 and 21, respectively. Thus, the state, as owner of Section 16, became, along with James Seymour, George W. Peck, Samuel P. Mead, and William H. Townshend, a joint proprietor of the Town of Michigan.

Over the years, the town developed into three distinct areas, named for the direction of the river's flow: "lower town," north of the capitol on Seymour's land in Section

9; "middle town," near the capitol in Section 16; and "upper town," south of the capitol along Main Street. The name Main Street suggests the commissioners' belief that "upper town" would develop into the main business section. For a time, this was the case—some of the early hotels and businesses were located there—but in the early 1850s, most of the town's businesses became established near the capitol in middle town, and upper town became largely residential.

The commissioners also supervised the building of the state capitol. Theodore E. Potter, for whose family the village of Potterville is named, arrived in Lansing at the age of 14 on the day the frame was raised. "All the settlers around Lansing," recalled Potter, "were invited to the raising." Using many teams of oxen, a group of farmers from Delhi Township dragged a 50-foot log to the capitol site to form part of the structure. The large frames, or "bents," which had been assembled on the ground, were raised by ropes and pulleys pulled by a multitude of men, while sheep, venison, and beef roasted in large pits. The "raising" was complete by 3:30 p.m., after which food and whiskey (provided by Justus Gilkey—according to Weller, "the only man who had whiskey for sale within a reasonable distance from the capital") were consumed in enormous quantities. Only heavy timbers were available nearby; sawed lumber, nails, glass, plaster, and hardware had to be shipped by rail from Detroit to Jackson and hauled through the woods to Lansing.

Senator Charles Loomis of St. Clair, a member of the first legislature to meet in the new capitol was impressed with the building, declaring it "better than the one used for the same purpose in Detroit." The white-frame, two-story, 60-by-100-foot edifice, surmounted by a tin cupola and shaded by pine trees, looked more like a large Greek Revival house than a seat of government. The building stood on a slight eminence in the middle of the capitol square, a block diagonally southeast of the present capitol. A flight of six steps led to a gate, from which a wide plank walk led to the entrance. The national flag floated from a large "liberty pole" near the front entrance.

For a time, the new capitol housed all the state offices in Lansing. The lower floor contained Representatives Hall, the meeting chamber of the lower house, along with a legislative post office, clerk's room, "paste room" (the bindery for legislative documents), and the janitor's sleeping quarters. The second floor, reached by a broad, winding stairway, contained the Senate Chamber, committee rooms, and offices for the governor, his secretary, and the superintendent of public instruction. Furnishings were modest—legislators sat in high-backed, green-cushioned, cane-bottomed chairs at rosewood desks built for two. The furniture in the governor's office, the best in the building, was described by a Detroit reporter as "not finished with half the cost or magnificence of the business offices of many young lawyers barely started in their profession." The cellar was "devoted to the reception of wood," and a "fiery furnace" kept the temperature of the legislative chambers "at an unendurable pitch" during sessions. Ventilation, by all accounts, was terrible—"the many harebrained attempts to improve it having failed"—

The Republican of March 5, 1878, contained the following information about this photograph: "The artist Scotford has taken a photograph of the five gentlemen who located the capital in Lansing in 1847 as they stood on the steps of the old building at the last meeting of the state pioneer society." The men are, from left to right, Albert Miller of Saginaw; Daniel B. Harrington of Port Huron; Alpheus Felch, who resigned as governor on March 3, 1847, to take a seat in the United States Senate; Isaac D. Toll of St. Joseph County; and John J. Adam of Lenawee. From the Jenison Collection, Michigan State Library.

33

but the second-floor rooms were pleasant enough in summer.

The 88 members of the legislature of 1848 had considerable difficulty reaching the new capital. Most came by way of Jackson, and for some, the journey required four days. Upon their arrival, they found primitive conditions, the white-frame capitol somehow out of place, set incongruously in a gallows orchard of dead trees. Four hastily built hotels appeared; log stores and shanties lined muddy streets crowded, according to Senator Loomis, "with the stumps and hillocks always seen in a new clearing." Even though Loomis arrived four days early for the session, all the hotels were filled, "and there was not a room to be had in the entire town." He arranged board in a private home near the capitol, where he sat at table with the governor and other state officials, but he was forced to sleep in the capitol: "I have ... fitted me up a bed in one of the Senate Committee Rooms, and have another Senator as roommate. All the committee rooms in both houses are similarly occupied, and every house in town is full."

The legislature of 1848 is remembered as the "plank road" legislature because it removed legal obstacles that had previously hindered the construction of such roads. It is remembered also for changing the name of the capital from "Michigan" to "Lansing." Before the governor approved the name-change bill at the end of the session, the legislature considered a wide variety of names, including Pewanogowink, Swedenborg, Houghton, Harrison, Bushridge, Kinderhook, El Dorado, Thorbush, Huron, Marcellus, Fulton, Tyler, Cass, Lafayette, Washington, Franklin, and Okeema. The senate approved Okeema; a conference committee proposed Algoma. Finally, upon the petition of Joseph E. North, Jr., the legislature agreed on Lansing.

The new capital grew feverishly in 1847, in the manner of a booming frontier town. "When the fact was established," said the *Republican,* a newspaper which first appeared in 1855 "that the seat of government was to be located here, men of all classes, men with capital and men without capital, flocked here as to a land of promise." Courtland Bliss Stebbins, who edited the *Republican* in 1859, never forgot the rush of settlers when the state opened the sale of lots in Section 16. Speculation flourished; trade increased; "a village grew, as it were, in a day." But the initial boom was short-lived. The town's population—as reflected, in the absence of a census, in voting records and school-attendance figures—appears to have remained stable in 1848 and 1849.

Cautious investors and settlers delayed coming to the new capital. "There was no settled country nearby to create business," Stebbins recalled, "and the roads to the outer world were nearly impassable." The *Republican* noted the lack of an economic base: "It became apparent that something more than a state house was necessary to support the village." Medical problems did not improve matters; Stebbins reported that "fever and ague held the fort." The outbreak of a fatal epidemic of "brain fever," or spinal meningitis, caused an early adjournment of the 1849 legislature and the departure of many settlers.

Many people still believed that the choice of Lansing

was a "truce measure" and that once the excitement had died down, the capital would be placed elsewhere. Rival communities—Ann Arbor, Jackson, Marshall, even Detroit—hoped that the inconveniences of early Lansing—difficult access, limited accommodations, few amenities, "mosquitoes who presented their bills early and often," as well as disease—would cause the legislature to reconsider.

But the legislators, even while grumbling about the lack of amenities and the howling of wolves, found the area attractive, and many were sanguine about its prospects. Senator Loomis, despite his inability to obtain accommodations, declared that "the natural beauty of the location is very great and it will, in a few years, be one of the most beautiful villages of the land."

By all accounts, Lansing in the 1850s was indeed a handsome village on a lovely site. "Stand upon any prominent place," wrote an anonymous correspondent to the *Republican* in 1856, "and the points of interest that meet the eye are numerous." At either end of Washington Avenue the Grand River curved gracefully, presenting a majestic spectacle. Enormous red cedar trees overarched the Red Cedar River near its confluence with the Grand. From the steps of the Benton House, situated near the south bend of the Grand, one could view the high bank of the north bend, a mile and a half distant. The steps of the Benton House, a favorite hostelry of the early legislators, also afforded a fine view of Washington Avenue, which, "though somewhat undulating," wrote the same correspondent, "I doubt not is destined to be handsomely graded, to have broad and comfortable walks on either side ... and to become one of the delightful promenades of the state."

In order to keep the capital in Lansing, ordinary citizens outdid themselves in a flurry of preparation for the annual legislative sessions. Families provided room and board to supplement limited hotel space, and the town was generally spruced up. In December 1858, Rufus Hosmer, editor of the *Republican,* described the preparations for the coming legislative session. "The entire economy of life is disturbed," he wrote, "in order that six score of worthy men may fare well for a few days, and say a good word about the comfort, hospitality, and liberality of Lansing." New clothes were kept "till session"; delicacies were saved, houses painted, carpets beaten, woodpiles replenished, cellars filled, "for session." Even the churches "partook of the fever for improvement," with services occasionally canceled to permit painting and whitewashing.

During the constitutional convention of 1850, which met in Lansing, a motion by John D. Pierce to move the capital to New Buffalo was defeated by a vote of 80-0. The constitution of 1850, overwhelmingly approved by the voters, stated, "The seat of government shall be at Lansing, where it is established." This clause gave Lansing's hold on the capital a constitutional sanction, placing it beyond the mere discretion of the legislature. Another move to relocate the capital at the constitutional convention of 1867 found almost no support, and the seat of government remained firmly entrenched in Lansing.

LEFT: This photograph, taken in 1855 from the cupola of the 1847 state capitol, is possibly the oldest existing photograph made in Lansing. The Lansing House seen in this photograph is actually the second structure of that name. The original, a log structure built in 1847, was moved in 1848 and the three-story frame structure shown in this picture was completed. Courtesy of Michigan State Archives.

ABOVE: This building, completed in 1847, was the first state capitol built in Lansing. Before it was destroyed by fire in 1882, the building also served as a community hall. From the Jenison Collection, Michigan State Library.

RIGHT: "Michigan, Michigan" postmarks were used from the time the capitol was located in Lansing Township until the time that the name of the Town of Michigan was changed to Lansing in April 1848. Such postmarks are very rare and eagerly sought by collectors. The year of this postmark was most probably 1848. From the Wiskemann Collection.

ABOVE: The Everett House, as it looked in 1868. Originally, this building was the Benton House, named for United States Senator Thomas Hart Benton of Missouri. The Benton House was the most famous and colorful of Lansing's earliest hostelries. In 1857 Zachariah Chandler celebrated his election to the United States Senate with a banquet at the Benton Hotel. The hotel changed hands many times over the years and was razed in 1902 when R.E. Olds bought the property to build his mansion. Courtesy of the Michigan State University Archives and Historical Collections.

Chapter 4

The legislature of 1848 promoted religion and education in Lansing by granting to "all the religious denominations of professing Christians" and each regularly organized school district, one lot in the Town of Michigan, provided only that "a commodious house of public worship" or a schoolhouse be built. By 1853, eight lots had been granted to churches, including the First New Church Society, the First Baptist Church, St. Paul's (Episcopal), the Methodist Episcopal, Central Presbyterian Universalist, and Plymouth Church (Congregationalist). The first "pretentious" church, according to Cowles, was the First Presbyterian on Washington Avenue and Genesee Street, completed in 1852. The framed, spired building contained Lansing's first church bell, installed in 1856. "It rang cheerily for church services," said Cowles, "riotously for fires and tolled drearily for deaths and funerals." Few other "pretentious" churches were completed in the 1850s; one legislator complained that, despite the state's generosity, churches in Lansing were "like angel's visits—few and far between."

The first sermon preached in Lansing was delivered by Rev. Frank A. Blades—a Methodist circuit rider known as the "boy preacher"—in 1847 at the home of Joab Page. The Pages, devout Methodists, had organized themselves into "the First Methodist Class" in 1846. Lansing's first organized church services were held in a structure known as "God's Barn," on the north side of Wall Street between Center and Cedar streets. The barn, originally built by James Seymour, was purchased and remodeled as a church in 1848 by the Presbyterian and Methodist societies, who alternately held morning and afternoon meetings. The building was used for church services until 1865, when the Presbyterians built the Franklin Presbyterian Church at the corner of Franklin and Washington avenues.

Frank N. Turner, whose uncle was a Methodist trustee and superintendent of the Sunday school, remembered the first church as simple and devoid of ornamentation. "The walls were plastered. ... The pews were high back, home-made affairs that extended across the center aisle. Sometimes the pillars cut off our small boys' view of the pulpit and gave us a chance to nap or play tricks on the minister and deacon in front." A funeral, according to Turner, "was a great public attraction and divided its

honors of attendance with a political meeting." Many people attended funerals "out of idle curiosity to hear the funeral sermon and comment upon the grief shown by the mourners."

The first school in Lansing was organized quite casually. Its teacher, 17-year-old Miss Eliza Powell (later Mrs. John N. Bush), came to Lansing with her parents in April 1847. She remembered spending the first night in the "slab shanty" of one Zalmon Holmes in lower town; Eliza and her mother were given the only bed, while her father and 30 other men slept on the floor. At the request of Joab Page, Miss Powell agreed to teach school for $2.00 a week without board. Page hastily built a shanty, and school was held beginning in May 1847. Before the end of the three-month term, the original student body of 10 had grown to 40, and late in 1847, the crude shanty was replaced by a frame schoolhouse.

Lansing's second school was established by Laura A. Burr, who arrived in Lansing with her husband, Dr. Hosea S. Burr, in August 1847. Several families asked her to hold classes for their children, and "after having made several long benches under the canopy of trees our school was begun." In bad weather, classes were held in a small "board house" erected by Dr. Burr at the foot of River Street on the banks of the Grand. By Christmas, 80 pupils had enrolled in the River Grove School; Miss Delia Ward (later Mrs. Mortimer Cowles) assisted Mrs. Burr. But this promising effort was to prove short-lived. "In January, 1849, my school was brought to a close by the appearance of the epidemic ... of brain fever." The legislature hastily adjourned; Dr. Burr, "after a few weeks of unparalleled effort to cope with the disease," died in April; and the River Grove School went out of existence.

In spite of the difficulties and hazards of frontier life, the young capital grew appreciably in the decade before the Civil War. The federal census of 1850 showed 1,029 residents; the state census of 1855 counted 1,556, an increase of 51 percent; and from 1855 to 1860, the population climbed another 83 percent to 2,850. Lansing's economic base improved as the population of its hinterland grew; Ingham County more than doubled its population in the decade, growing from 7,597 in 1850 to 16,682 in 1860. With increased population came corresponding increases in the volume of business and assessed valuation.

By the end of its first decade, Lansing was dominating its hinterland and had become the regional trading center. Lesser trading centers existed in such thriving villages as Mason, Williamston, Dansville, and Leslie in Ingham County; Eaton Rapids, Charlotte, Grand Ledge, and Vermontville in Eaton; and De Witt and St. Johns in Clinton. But a plank road that gave Lansing a direct route to Detroit conferred an enormous advantage over these rival communities.

The legislature chartered plank roads between Lansing and De Witt, Mason, Portland, Ann Arbor, and Battle Creek as well as Detroit, but only the one between Lan-

The spire of the Plymouth Congregational Church, a short walk from the capitol at Townsend and Allegan streets, was a familiar Lansing landmark for nearly a century. The church, which was built in 1876, was destroyed by fire in 1971. From the Edmonds Collection, Lansing Public Library.

sing and Detroit was completed. This road—which covered the same route as the old U.S. 16, later Michigan route 43—was built by two companies: the Detroit-Howell Plank Road Company, which completed its segment in 1850, and the Lansing-Howell Plank Road Company, which opened its facility in July 1853. Mary Rix Dietz of Williamston remembered "the laying of the local section of the road." As the work progressed, "some movable buildings on wheels, equipped with a primitive housekeeping outfit, were moved from place to place." A sawmill had been built about two and a half miles east of Williamston; this small hamlet was known as "the Burg" and later "Podunk."

Well-maintained plank roads speeded up travel considerably. A journey of four, five, or even six days on dirt roads required only 10 to 12 hours on planks. Farmers could carry heavier loads without worrying about their wagon wheels sinking into the mire. There is little doubt that the plank road contributed enormously to the economic growth of the area. Plank roads, however, had their shortcomings. Annual repair of worn, rotted, or warped planks could cost 20 to 30 percent of the original investment, and the fixed costs of maintaining tollhouses and sawmills were high. In 1871, the Lansing-Detroit road replaced its planks with gravel.

John Whitely, a Lansing settler who arrived when the plank road was still new, remembered that the arrival of the stage from Detroit "was the event of the day to some Lansingites." The plank road acted as a sounding board, and the stage could be heard when it was still several miles out of town. The driver invariably arrived with a flourish, "with the long reins in his hands and his long whip cracking over the four prancing horses and often blowing a tin horn." Turner recalled that the stage depot was at "the old Butterfield Hotel" on the north side of Franklin Street (now Grand River Avenue) in North Lansing. The hotel, a yellow, two-story structure, had a long porch in front and a barn for the stage and horses alongside. The stagecoach was "of a type we now see in wild west shows . . . heavy wheels, body hung on leather braces, deep boot and driver's seat in front and trunk behind." There were three or four benches inside; the middle one was "extra wide so that four passengers could sit back to back." The stage could hold eight passengers comfortably, but "with some crowding twelve," obliging some passengers to ride backwards. The driver sat on a high perch; one or two passengers sometimes rode with the driver, but to do this "you must have a certain understanding with the driver as he is very particular in his choice of seatmates." When the driver was satisfied that all cargo was secure, he would take his place, grasp the reins, crack the whip, and the stage would depart.

Turner wrote a description of a journey from Lansing to Detroit on the plank road. The road began at the intersection of Franklin and Sheridan streets, where Tollgate No. 1 was located; the driver paid for the entire journey and received tickets for the other tollgates. Proceeding toward Detroit, the stage passed a number of familiar landmarks, including the farm of John W. Longyear, lawyer and sometime Congressman, and—after traversing a heavily

timbered area and descending a "stiff clay hill"—the agricultural college. The road passed through what is now the heart of downtown East Lansing on Grand River Avenue.

Continuing the journey, the stage passed the Marble sawmill and the home of Judge Mason D. Chatterton, one half mile east of which stood Tollgate No. 2. The stage then ascended the hill near the Okemos cemetery; from here, the spires of the Okemos Presbyterian Church could be seen. On this particular journey, the stage passed through Okemos without stopping, as there were no passengers to pick up and the driver "don't stop for the men to whet their whistles." The mail for Okemos was thrown off at Walker's store. At Tollgate No. 3, near Red Bridge and the residence of the surveyor John Mullett, the mail for Red Bridge post office was thrown off. Thus the journey continued to Williamston, where horses were changed and the passengers had lunch at the Lombard Hotel.

In the 1850s, stagecoaches rumbled daily into Lansing from St. Johns, twice daily from Jackson, three times weekly from Howell and Detroit, and twice weekly from Marshall. One September evening in 1856, there arrived on the stage from Jackson one George P. Sanford; then in his early 20s, he had come to teach at the First Ward School in North Lansing. A few miles south of Lansing, the stage encountered a dense, smoky fog, which an air inversion had caused to hang on for days. One passenger had to walk ahead of the stage with a lantern; the other passengers also had to walk, including a woman with a little girl. When the child tired of walking, Sanford recalled, "a gentleman of the party" carried her. "Tall, erect, with a benign and intelligent face, a deep, rich, cultivated voice, he was a man to be noticed in any place." Upon arriving at the Lansing House, the gentleman signed the register, "H. Seymour, Esq., Utica, New York." He was Horatio Seymour, soon to be Civil War governor of New York and a major national figure; he was the partner of his brother James in real-estate holdings in Lansing and elsewhere in Michigan.

The next morning, Sanford, with his friend John Horner, a teacher at the Michigan Female College, drove around Lansing in a rig. They found Washington Avenue still ungraded and dotted with stumps; a huge gully yawned in front of the Methodist Church. There was another gully in front of Alton's cooper shop, "from the bottom of which one could not see a block ahead or behind." Houses clustered closely together in lower, middle, and upper town, with few buildings in between. In lower town, James Turner lived in a frame house, the first in Lansing, built in 1848. As of 1856, there were only four brick buildings in the entire town: the Benton House, the Merrifield Building, the structure that later housed the Second National Bank, and the store of F.M. Cowles. There were no sidewalks.

The leading lawyers in town were John W. and Ephraim Longyear; Samuel E. Longyear and Rollin C. Dart studied in their office. George Washington Peck—who as speaker of the Michigan House had helped locate the capital in Lansing—"was a star of the time." Peck—a lawyer, Lan-

TOP: This bridge, built in 1855, had deteriorated in a matter of a few years. The city council was divided for a time on whether to repair or replace the bridge. It was finally replaced in 1871. Mayor John Robson, who demanded it be replaced, later wrote that "the timbers creaked and gave every evidence of weakness even when a dog trotted across, and as for heavy traffic, it was perilous." From the Edmonds Collection, Lansing Public Library.

CENTER: Ingham County's first courthouse, seen here as it looked in the early 1850s. Courtesy of Michigan State Archives.

BOTTOM: This building, built in 1855, served as Tollgate No. 2 on the Lansing-Howell Plank road. The building has since been restored and moved to a park in Okemos, where it now stands. Photograph by author.

TOP: The rear of the Turner-Dodge Mansion, facing the Grand River. This residence, built in the early 1850s, had been occupied by James Turner and Marion Monroe Turner, early Lansing settlers. Frank Dodge, Turner's son-in-law, and Abigail Turner Dodge, later occupied the residence. For some years the Great Lakes Bible College held classes in the building; it is now owned by the City of Lansing and used as a meeting place for cultural and historical activities. Photograph by author.

CENTER: Ingham County's second courthouse (1856-1902) had deteriorated badly by the 1890s.

BOTTOM: In the mid-1800s many dirt roads were covered over with planks to facilitate traveling. Plank roads, however, were found to be costly to maintain. In later years, planks were replaced by gravel. Courtesy of Michigan State Archives.

sing's first postmaster, one-term Congressman (1854-1856), and editor of the *Michigan State Journal*—was a Democratic party leader and fearsome orator. De Witt Clinton Leach, editor of the *State Republican,* was also a powerful orator; he defeated Peck in the congressional race of 1856. Both Lansing newspapers—the Democratic *State Journal,* founded in 1848 as the *Free Press,* and the *State Republican,* founded in 1855—were strongly partisan in the manner of the period. One of middle town's leading citizens was Orlando M. Barnes, who had just moved from Mason; he was county prosecutor and had just been defeated by Zachariah Chandler for the United States Senate. Barnes, lawyer, orator, and one-term mayor of Lansing, was one of the most popular men in town.

A few days before Sanford arrived in Lansing, a House of Correction for Young Offenders opened its doors on a 30-acre site just north of where Eastern High School now stands on Pennsylvania Avenue. The institution, one of the first of its kind and a source of considerable local pride, sought to provide a better environment for young offenders than the county jails or the penitentiary. In 1859, the legislature changed the name to the Michigan Reform School in order to lessen the stigma on its graduates.

For years the institution's Victorian buildings, only recently demolished, stood as a visible reminder of mid-19th-century ideas about dealing with juvenile offenders. In the early days, the inmates, dressed in prisoners' attire, worked hard to produce their own food and clothing in farms and shops kept by the school. Their daily regimen consisted of five hours of compulsory work, five and a quarter hours in class, an hour of military drill, and only occasional recreation in a high-fenced three-acre playground. From time to time, the boys were employed in such pursuits as manufacturing cigars (until 1875) and caning chairs for outside contractors. Over time, the institution was liberalized, and bars on the windows, high fences, and prisoners' garb gradually disappeared.

The Michigan Female College was established in 1855. Its founders, Abigail and Delia Rogers, came to Michigan from New York in 1847, taught at Albion College and the State Normal School in Ypsilanti, then came to Lansing to persuade the legislature to establish a college for women. Meeting with indifference from the legislators, the Rogers sisters opened their own college with 30 students and a faculty of five. The first classes were held on October 23, 1855, in Representatives Hall in the capitol; later, the college moved to the Ohio House, an early Lansing hotel that had fallen on hard times.

At first, the college admitted students of all grades and even a few boys. The school received donations of money from leading citizens, including James Turner and Zachariah Chandler, and the Rogers sisters built an impressive four-story brick building, the shell of which is now part of the main building of the Michigan School for the Blind. With its new building completed, the college expanded, broadened its staff and curriculum, and began accepting boarders as well as day students.

Abigail Rogers, a committed pioneer of education for women, was also firmly committed to the prevailing idea of feminine refinement. "The work of her needle," recalled a former student, "was as fine as her beautiful penmanship, and her love of order and her tasteful arrangement of her home were as noticeable as the thoroughness of her teaching and school day discipline." For her students, excellence in study was not enough; "their rooms must be in order and neatness so as to make them fearless of inspection." And "conversation was not merely *idle talk,* but a gift ... to be cultivated, and carefully improved."

A German immigrant named Weimann had a brewery and beer garden near the school, at the corner of Pine and Maple streets. According to Dr. Frank N. Turner, the Rogers sisters "objected to the smell of the brewery, the sauer kraut making," and the odiferous pens in which pigs fattened on waste malt. Moreover, the sisters' "delicate ears" could not "take in the beauties of ... 'Die Wacht am Rein' sung by a score of lusty Germans," especially at midnight. The Misses Rogers, temperance advocates as well as educational reformers, wielded considerable power in the community, and the brewery disappeared.

George Sanford lived in Lansing from 1856 to 1883; for much of that time, he was editor of the *Journal.* The Lansing he saw in 1856, "a raw, struggling village of perhaps two thousand people, reached only by stages ... was not yet the pride of the state." The only manufacturing enterprises were a gristmill and a sawmill, Parmelee's carding mill, and a foundry in lower town. But there were signs of improvement—the early log stores, which had carried "a little bit of everything and not much of anything," had given way to more specialized retail establishments.

The Lansing of 1856 changed quickly; an 1859 atlas and business directory, recently republished by the Historical Society of Greater Lansing, shows an astonishing array of stores, tradesmen, and professionals. The directory lists eight lawyers or law firms, as might be expected in a state capital. In addition, the community was served by two architects and seven builders, as well as blacksmiths, bricklayers, druggists, machinists, and a "phonographist" or stenographer. A farmer in town of a Saturday afternoon might imbibe at any of 10 different saloons, consult any of 12 physicians and surgeons, and park his horse at any of several livery stables. There were seven dry-goods and four hardware and stove merchants, and manufacturing—the eventual basis for the town's economic growth—was carried on in the production of saddles, trunks and harnesses, and sashes and blinds.

The late 1850s also saw the founding of the Michigan Agricultural College—which would become the first land-grant institution in what is now East Lansing. Precursor of the great Michigan State University, its beginnings were rather less than auspicious.

The Act of March 1837 that created the University of Michigan at Ann Arbor had provided for instruction in "practical farming and agriculture." The university had neglected this responsibility, however, apparently for lack of funds, and agitation for an institution specifically devoted to agricultural education began in 1849. In a speech at the state fair, E.H. Lothrop deplored the lack of agricultural education in a state in which "four fifths of the children ... will probably pursue agriculture as a profession."

Lothrop's speech induced the Agricultural Society to take up the cudgels. At its 1850 meeting, Bela Hubbard, a Detroit geologist, provided the rationale for a new kind of institution. "The day has gone forever," he declared, "when an enlightened liberal education was deemed useless for a farmer. No matter what might be a man's business, the more he varies his education the better, as he thus enlarges his mind and multiplies the sources from which he draws through life." Hubbard proposed that the new institution be "a labor school, in which actual work performed by the pupils would be passed to their credit, in the account for their instruction."

Both the University of Michigan at Ann Arbor and the State Normal College at Ypsilanti, now Eastern Michigan University, sought to become the site for the new school; to prove their commitment to agricultural education, both institutions began offering programs for farmers in 1853. At last, however, in a measure approved on February 12, 1855, the legislature established a fully independent Agricultural College of the State of Michigan, to be located within 10 miles of Lansing. The new college was authorized to teach "an English and scientific course" as well as "natural philosophy, chemistry, botany, animal and vegetable physiology, geology, meteorology, entomology, veterinary art, leveling and political economy, with bookkeeping and the mechanic arts which are connected directly with agriculture."

After examining areas near Holt, De Witt, Millett, and Haslett, the site-selection committee finally approved a tract of 677 acres in Meridian Township owned by Colonel A.R. Burr. This site, heavily forested except for two small clearings, was located on the Lansing-Howell plank road, along what is now East Grand River Avenue in East Lansing.

LEFT: **The Michigan Reform School band, circa 1870. The band frequently appeared in Lansing parades and rallies. Courtesy of Michigan State Archives.**

TOP: **This astonishing photograph, reproduced from a stereocard, shows reform school boys in jail cells. The boys were locked in these cells each night. Governor John Bagley put a stop to this practice in 1875. Courtesy of Michigan State Archives.**

ABOVE: **The main building of the Michigan Reform School, circa 1870. The institution sought to provide a better enviroment for young offenders than the country jails or the penitentiary. Courtesy of Michigan State Archives.**

LEFT: **The centennial medallion of Michigan State College. The design shows Beaumont Tower behind the old College Hall. College Hall was the first structure built for the teaching of scientific agriculture. Michigan State College had expanded so greatly over the years that in 1955 its name was changed to Michigan State University. Courtesy of Michigan State University Publications.**

The City of Lansing

Once the site had been selected, buildings were erected, a faculty was appointed, and the first students were admitted. Two main three-story buildings—College Hall, on the site of Beaumont Tower, and a residential hall known to later generations of students as "Saints' Rest," after a novel of the period—could accommodate about 80 students. The faculty consisted of Joseph R. Williams, president and director of the farm; Calvin Tracy, professor of mathematics; Lewis Ransom Fisk, professor of chemistry; Robert D. Weeks, professor of English literature and farm economy; John C. Holmes, professor of horticulture; and Enoch Banker, assistant in chemistry. Entrance examinations in standard school subjects were held on May 11, 12, and 13, 1857, and a dedication took place on May 13.

A circular of December 1856 described the program of the school at the time of its founding. Applicants had to be at least 14 years of age "and must have acquired a good common school education." Students were to devote "a portion of each day to manual labor, for which they will receive equitable remuneration." The "course of study ... will embrace a wide range of instruction in English literature ... mathematics, and ... Natural Science." Special attention would be given "to the theory and practice of agriculture in all its departments and minutiae."

Charles Jay Monroe, a student in the first class, found "a most desolate scene" when he arrived on May 10, 1857. Only a few acres had been cleared; near College Hall were "old stubs and partially burned trees." The students' first task was removing the construction debris and clearing the area near the buildings. By the summer of 1857, some 60 acres had been cleared, and the stumps pulled from 20. During the winter of 1857-58, more than 100 acres south of the Red Cedar River were cut into windrows and allowed to dry for burning the following summer.

The school day began with compulsory chapel exercises at 5:30, followed by breakfast at 6:00. The first group of students worked at farm duties from 6:30 to 9:30, when a second group reported for work. At 12:30 all students had lunch; at 1:30 a third group reported for farm duties. When not engaged in farm work, students attended class for three hours daily.

The college soon found itself in financial difficulties. Rising prices rapidly depleted its original grant, and small annual legislative appropriations barely covered costs. The early reputation of the college was uncertain; to many critics, it seemed that the college was mainly a training ground for the pioneer tasks of clearing land, and that agricultural education was suffering. Appropriations were cut even further, and the curriculum reduced from four years to two. Enrollment plummeted; in February 1860, there were only 19 students.

For a time, the legislature suspended classes while it debated the future of the college. The four-year program was restored, and in April 1861, 66 students enrolled. The Civil War intervened, however, and the senior class was excused to enlist in the Union army. Demands reemerged in 1863, 1865, and 1867 to relocate the college at Ann Arbor; not until 1869 was it clear that the Michigan Agricultural College would remain and prosper at its present location.

To the community of Lansing as a whole, however, the big year was 1859, for in that year Lansing was incorporated as a city. Hundreds of persons attended the official celebration on February 15, 1859; there were speeches, dances, and parties.

After incorporation, according to John Longyear, "the city began to assume metropolitan airs." A program of street improvements was undertaken almost immediately, beginning with the grading and leveling of Washington Avenue, which had the effect of lowering the surface of the roadway. "Some houses were left so high above the street," complained Longyear, "that it became necessary to construct flights of stairs from the sidewalks to the houses above." In the summer, the first fire engine arrived; the occasion was marked by a parade of 40 volunteer firemen in black uniforms and helmets, accompanied by martial music played by the city's brass band. Longyear also noted that a Mr. Webb of Delhi Township, "a super dangerous individual of the Buchanan persuasion," was the first person to be incarcerated in the city's new jail.

To deal with the problem of wandering livestock, the city established a pound and offered a reward of five cents for each pig and 50 cents for each horse brought in. On the day the pound opened, recalled Longyear, "the desks at the schoolhouses, generally occupied by boys, were notably vacant." Large droves of hogs, led by one or more boys, "were seen wending their way towards the place provided for all vagrant swine or horses." By noon the entrance to the pound was crowded with "hogs, horses, boys, and irate owners of livestock," and by nightfall "there were no more vagrant animals." Several boys, it seems, had opened enclosures and liberated additional livestock in order to collect the reward.

Under its new charter, the city included an area of seven and a half square miles, much larger than the two square miles of the original Town of Michigan. The charter provided one-year terms for the mayor, city clerk, and a council of seven aldermen, and the city was divided for electoral purposes into three (after 1861, four) wards. Other officials, apparently chosen by the council, included a four-member "city watch" and a town crier. Many years later, "Uncle" Dan Mevis, the original town crier, recalled that he "used to pace along Washington Avenue, ringing a bell lustily, calling attention to auction sales."

The city charter reflected the prevailing idea of short terms and frequent rotation in office. Of 23 mayors who served between 1859 and 1900, only 12 served more than one year. The mayors, a cross section of the city's elite, had a range of backgrounds, including banking and real estate (Hiram S. Smith, 1859); printing and publishing (John A. Kerr, 1860); shingle manufacturing and real estate (William H. Chapman, 1861-1862); medicine (Dr. Ira H. Bartholemew, 1863-1865); the ministry (Dr. William H. Haze, 1866); banking and milling (Cyrus Hewitt, 1868-1869); and physician turned businessman and temperance crusader (Dr. Solomon W. Wright, 1870). Only one—George W. Peck (1867), a powerful state Democratic party leader—was known primarily as a political figure.

LEFT: **Lewis R. Fisk was a professor of chemistry and acting president of Michigan Agricultural College from 1859 to 1862. Madison Kuhn once wrote that "he labored without authority and without the privilege of sitting in Board meetings to explain the college's problems to its members who seldom visited the campus. At the close of 1860, Fisk submitted a bill for five dollars 'for executive services,' perhaps to remind the Board of his anomalous position. The Board members were not amused." Courtesy of Michigan State University Archives and Historical Collections.**

ABOVE: **This painting by John S. Coppin, commissioned for the Michigan State University Centennial in 1955, depicts a father taking his son to register at the Michigan Agricultural College in the mid-1800s. Courtesy of Michigan State University Information Services.**

Chapter 5

135,000 SETS, 270,000 VOLUMES SOLD.

UNCLE TOM'S CABIN

FOR SALE HERE.

AN EDITION FOR THE MILLION, COMPLETE IN 1 Vol., PRICE 37 1-2 CENTS.

"   "   IN GERMAN, IN 1 Vol., PRICE 50 CENTS.

"   "   IN 2 Vols., CLOTH, 6 PLATES, PRICE $1.50.

SUPERB ILLUSTRATED EDITION, IN 1 Vol., WITH 153 ENGRAVINGS,

PRICES FROM $2.50 TO $5.00.

The Greatest Book of the Age.

Lansing came into being during a wave of religious revivalism, moral reform, and democratic ferment that swept the United States from the 1830s to the Civil War. Western New York State, from which many capital-region settlers had emigrated, was a center of religious revivalism. The reform movements—antislavery, temperance, common schools, women's rights, prison reform, humane treatment for the insane, and pacifism—made considerable headway in Michigan and nearby states. By the early 1840s, the distinctions among moral, religious, and political issues had blurred; for a time, a proposed sabbath-desecration law, which would have stopped railroads from running on Sunday, was the leading political issue in Michigan. Increasingly, however, antislavery began to overshadow the other reform crusades.

The abolition of property qualifications for voting and officeholding, early results of the reform wave, gave rise in the 1830s and 1840s to mass political parties organized down to the precinct level. By the 1840s, politics had become the most consuming popular interest, and strong party loyalties were inherited in the same manner as religion. "It was accepted as a matter of course," said Barber, "that partisan politics would descend from sire to son with unbroken regularity." At election time, politics were vigorously discussed, and strongly partisan eastern newspapers—Horace Greeley's New York *Tribune,* the Albany *Journal* or *Argus,* and others—were avidly read.

Capital-region settlers brought their politics with them. In Vermontville, Barber remembered, settlers from Rutland and Addison counties in Vermont voted as conservative Whigs, while those from Barrington were rock-ribbed Democrats. Although residents of Vermontville and the capital region opposed slavery, there were few abolitionists; Barber remembered only three in his village.

But all this would soon change. While the Michigan legislature wrangled over the location of the capital, there began a chain of events that would throw the entire political system out of balance and plunge the nation into a sectional crisis. The war with Mexico had begun early in 1846; on February 22, 1847, within days of the crucial house vote favoring Lansing, the heavily outnumbered troops of General Zachary Taylor stunningly defeated the forces of General Antonio Lopez de Santa Anna at the Battle of Buena Vista. In March, about ten days after Greenly signed the capital bill, the command of General Winfield Scott stormed into the city of Vera Cruz and began its march through rugged mountainous terrain to Mexico City. On September 8, in a remarkable military exploit, Scott's troops invested the fortified heights of

Chapultepec; on September 17, the Mexicans surrendered, the Americans occupied Mexico City, and the fighting ended as suddenly as it had begun.

The Mexican War, which received far more press coverage in Detroit than the capital bill, was one of the most unpopular in American history, widely seen in the North as having been fought to expand the area open to slavery. The war touched off a sectional crisis on the issue of slavery in the territories. The House of Representatives, divided along sectional lines, was unable to elect a speaker in its session of December 1848; before the crisis was eased by the Compromise of 1850, the nation hovered on the brink of war. In return for agreeing to the admission of California as a free state and the abolition of the slave trade in the District of Columbia, the South obtained a more stringent fugitive slave law. Both sides agreed that slavery in the territories would be decided by residents.

For a time, peace prevailed between the sections, but trouble arose again over the issue of fugitive slaves, a sensitive issue in Michigan. A famous incident occurred at Marshall, close to the capital region, in 1846, when a group of Kentucky slave catchers tried to arrest one Adam Crosswhite, a runaway slave, and his family. "Our citizens," reported the Marshall *Statesman,* "assembled in great numbers at the house. ... The news spread like wild-fire, and not an individual, of whatever age or sex, was indifferent. It was the loud and unanimous cry, 'The family shall never go back into slavery.' " One Kentuckian who flourished a revolver was arrested for assault with intent to kill; the others were charged with trespassing. In the excitement, Crosswhite and his family fled to Canada. There were other incidents, including one in Cass County, in which slave catchers were jeered by crowds, arrested, and charged with trespassing or worse.

The new Fugitive Slave Act, far more harsh than its predecessor, was strongly condemned in Michigan. An "underground railroad," which spirited slaves from the South to Canada and freedom, had been in operation for some years, and while details of its operations remain cloudy, there is little doubt of its support in the capital region.

The Fugitive Slave Act inspired a book—*Uncle Tom's Cabin* by Harriet Beecher Stowe—which had a remarkable effect on public opinion. In Vermontville, a visitor to the family of Robert Kedzie brought the first copy in 1852. Years later, Kedzie wrote to Barber that "food and earthly cares had little hold on us till wife and I, in tears and choking sobs, had read that wonderful book." Word got around Vermontville, wrote Kedzie, "that we had a book of wonderful pathos"; a neighbor asked to read it, and "soon thirty persons were on the list." The Kedzies did not see the book for two years, "and it came back the most worn and tattered book I ever saw."

Uncle Tom's Cabin sold more copies and circulated more widely than any other American book of the 19th century. Little Eva, Uncle Tom, and Simon Legree have become part of American folklore. By the end of 1852, 300,000 copies had been sold and eight power presses ran night and day to keep up with the demand. In countless log houses all over the capital region, the book was read aloud of an evening by the firelight. "Often some pathetic

This handbill advertising the bestselling novel of the 19th century, in America and abroad, reflects the intense response of Northerners to the slavery issue. *Uncle Tom's Cabin,* written by Harriet Beecher Stowe, sold out immediately. "So this is the little lady that caused the great war," Lincoln supposedly said to Mrs. Stowe when they met—not entirely in jest. Courtesy of the New York Historical Society.

incident," said Barber, "brought tears to all eyes." Repeated fugitive-slave incidents, widely reported in the North, seemed to confirm the portrayal of Southern life in *Uncle Tom's Cabin* and unleashed a wave of anti-Southernism.

The passage of the Kansas-Nebraska Act of 1854, which organized Kansas as a territory without excluding slavery, aroused fears of a conspiracy that sought not merely to extend slavery into new territories but to impose it on the free states as well. The act had the effect of destroying the Whigs and creating the Republican party. Almost spontaneously in the North, "fusionist" or "anti-Nebraska" rallies were held, including one at Jackson on July 6, 1854. This meeting, held at the call of 10,000 persons, was the first officially to adopt the name "Republican." The new party drew its members from the Free-Soilers, antislavery Whigs, and radical Democrats.

The new party gained strength as the sectional crisis continued. In Lansing, the *Republican*, which began publication on April 28, 1855, was founded for the specific purpose of advancing the new party in the capital region. Its founder, Henry Barns of Detroit, sold the paper—forerunner of the present Lansing *State Journal*—after its second issue. The paper changed owners and editors often; De Witt C. Leach, Rufus Hosmer, Cortland Bliss Stebbins, and Isaac M. Cravath were among those who edited the paper in its first decade.

The *Republican*'s early issues described the violence in Kansas, where armed pro- and antislavery bands stalked the countryside. Leach wrote a series of enraged, strongly anti-Southern editorials. The slave power, he declared in December, had "commenced a new series of outrages . . . surpassing in magnitude . . . any of its former acts, showing a reckless disregard for the feelings and rights of the people in the free states." In January 1856, the *Republican* asked whether "the scum of the whole South" should "scatter death and desolation over one of the fairest portions of our common country." The *Republican* desired peace, "but the only way to secure and preserve peace is to fill Kansas with true men and Sharp's rifles." The violence in Kansas reaffirmed the *Republican*'s implacable opposition to "popular sovereignty," supported by Cass and the Democrats, which would allow territorial residents to decide on slavery for themselves. Popular sovereignty could not work; "instead of affording the people of the new territories the right to form their own institutions in their own way, it has been construed by its authors to justify by force the establishment of the institutions [i.e., slavery] of another state."

Political excitement ran high in the capital region. There were Republican and Democratic clubs in all townships; candidates for local office stressed national issues. Large crowds heard stirring orations by Peck, Leach, Barnes, and other local leaders. The *Republican* began to accuse its rival, the *Journal*, of being in league with Southern extremists. During the frenetic campaign of 1860, the *Republican* gained an ally in the *Ingham County News*, published in Mason by David B. Harrington. This paper proclaimed itself "An Independent Journal, Neutral in Politics and Religion." But neutral papers got nowhere in this period; by the spring of 1860, the *News'* masthead bore the motto, "An Empire for Freedom, But Not Another Rod of Territory for Slavery." Harrington, announcing his change to Republicanism, complained that his Democratic subscribers had withdrawn their support; "this concluded our obligations of neutrality with them." The *News* joined with the *Republican* in denouncing slavery, Southerners, and Democrats.

The year 1860 saw the culmination of a decade of intense sectional and party strife. Local Republicans, who had supported Senator William H. Seward of New York for the presidency, followed the lead of the *Republican* and the *News* and approved their party's choice of the relatively obscure Abraham Lincoln of Illinois. Lincoln's nomination was "ratified," in the custom of the day, at a large rally in Lansing "by the roar of artillery, by bonfires, and by illumination." On September 6, 1860, there occurred one of the largest political rallies ever held in Lansing, part of a two-day visit to the capital region by Seward, who would become Lincoln's secretary of state.

Seward was something of a favorite son in Michigan. He arrived in St. Johns on the afternoon of September 5, where he was greeted by the "Wide Awakes" or Republican activists of Clinton County and their brass band. After a "sumptuous dinner" at the Clinton House, Seward and his party turned south to De Witt, three miles north of Lansing, where they were greeted by 100 mounted Lansing Wide Awakes. As the procession, by then a mile long, left De Witt for Lansing, the *Republican* later reported: "The scene was one of picturesque beauty. . . . The mounted Wide Awakes, in their separate detachments, with their long lances and flying pennants, the imposing array of carriages, bearing Lincoln and Hamlin flags, and the pealing strains of the cornet band echoing through the arches of the forest . . . altogether made a spectacle which our distinguished visitors . . . found equally novel and delightful."

The following morning, a two-hour parade of political floats, marching bands, and ordinary citizens in every kind of conveyance passed the reviewing stand on Washington Avenue. The students of the agricultural college marched behind a float drawn by "four fine farm horses" bearing the legend, "POPULAR EDUCATION: OUR PECULIAR INSTITUTION." Local military units—many of whose members would not live to see another presidential election—filed past, including the Williams Rifles, commanded by Captain John R. Price of Lansing; the Lansing Artillery, commanded by Captain Jacob R. Webber; the Curtenius Guards of Mason; the Lansing, St. Johns, and Eaton Rapids Wide Awakes; and the Grand Ledge Marching Band.

Democrats put on their own campaign in Michigan, which included speeches by Douglas in Detroit, Kalamazoo, and Jackson, but they had little chance of carrying the state. The capital region and the rest of the state went heavily for Lincoln and the Republican ticket. The *Republican* exulted over the victory: "We congratulate all lovers of their country, all good citizens and good men, upon this auspicious event." The paper then dismissed the possibility that the Southern states would actually make good their threat to secede from the Union if the "Black Republican" Lincoln were elected. "They have talked loud and big, to frighten us from voting for the man of our choice, and they will continue to bluster and talk of terrible deeds, to terrify our men now that they are elected."

But the Southern states did indeed make good their threat. On December 20, South Carolina seceded, followed by other states of the Deep South. They seized federal forts, arsenals, and customs houses. Lincoln's attempt to relieve Fort Sumter, one of two military installations still in federal hands, touched off the firing on Sumter and the secession of more states. When war came, it would profoundly affect the lives of people in the capital region as it did those in hundreds of other communities.

During the early spring of 1861, however, the standoff between the Lincoln administration and the Confederate government hardly made an impression on the local press. There was greater interest in the city charter elections, in which the Democrats did much better than expected, and in the untimely death of the popular Rufus Hosmer, publisher of the *Republican,* at the age of 45. But after the firing on Fort Sumter and Lincoln's call for volunteers, a wave of excitement swept the area. Lansing Mayor John A. Kerr called a citizens' meeting; a packed assemblage in Representatives Hall heard eloquent speeches by local leaders and pledged unanimously "to sustain the government in time of crisis." The legislature, called into special session by Governor Austin Blair, was in the city. By late May, there were so many flag raisings and other patriotic demonstrations that the *Republican* apologized for not reporting them all.

It had really come to war—the war so many had pre-dicted but few believed would happen. In May, ceremonies were held as the first Lansing contingent—the Williams Rifles, commanded by Captain John R. Price—prepared to depart. As the men stood rigidly at attention in the colorful parade-ground garb they would soon exchange for Union blue, Price, Peck, Leach, and other leaders made stirring speeches. Peck warned that—unlike the conflict with Mexico in which the enemy had inferior weapons—they were in for a long war. The Reverend C.S. Armstrong warned of the unholy temptations surely to present themselves to rural and small-town men far removed from home and church.

By December 1861, the *Ingham County News* could report that "Lansing has done as much for the war as any city in the state." Four companies had been raised—the Williams Rifles; "Elder's Zouaves," commanded by Captain Matthew Elder; "Stuart's Sharpshooters," commanded by Captain A.B. Stuart; and the "Lansing Rangers," commanded by Captain J.J. Jeffres—and two more were being prepared. Isaac M. Cravath, onetime *Republican* editor, raised a company known as "Cravath's Tigers." These units included some 600 men from Lansing and nearby areas; in addition, about 50 Lansing men served in other Michigan companies.

Before the war ended, the families of Ingham and Eaton counties had sent more than 3,800 men to serve in 20 Michigan regiments, 10 infantry and 10 cavalry, as well as other units; of this number, 560 were killed in action or died of wounds or disease. Capital-region soldiers fought in virtually every important military engagement in every theater of the war. The area took considerable pride in the fact that the overwhelming majority of its men had volunteered; the draft produced only 122 men, of whom 51

LEFT: **Senator William H. Seward, a favorite of Michigan, became President Lincoln's secretary of state. From Cirker,** *Dictionary of American Portraits,* **Dover, 1967.**

RIGHT: **John A. Kerr, a native of England, served as mayor of Lansing in 1860. Kerr was in the printing business and kept "open house" in his residence on East St. Joseph Street. He died at the age of 45. Courtesy of Lansing Public Library.**

BELOW: **The masthead of the first issue, April 28, 1855, of** *The Lansing Republican;* **forerunner of the present** *Lansing State Journal. The Lansing Republican* **was founded by Henry Barns, who wanted to create an antislavery, strong Republican newspaper in Michigan's capital. From the Wiskemann Collection.**

THE LANSING REPUBLICAN.

BY H. BARNS. LANSING, INGHAM CO., MICH. 1855. VOL. I.—NO. I.

were excused, presumably for medical reasons.

Political rivalry was by no means suspended for the duration. In March 1862, the *Republican* charged that even Northern Democrats were in league with secessionists. The local Democratic paper, the *Journal,* folded late in 1861 as a result of its unpopular stand on war issues. The demise of the *Journal* was brief, however; in May 1863, it resumed publication under the editorship of George W. Peck.

The war ground on, with the local Republican press reporting its events in fulsome detail and demanding its vigorous prosecution. Residents followed the war closely. When a Detroit newspaper arrived, recalled John Whitely, "Stephan Bingham or some other prominent citizen would mount a barrel ... and read aloud ... the latest war news to a large crowd of both men and women."

News of Lincoln's assassination reached the capital region on April 19, 1865; for some days, it was believed that Secretary of State Seward, who was well known in the capital region because of his campaign appearance of 1860, had been killed by the conspirators along with Lincoln. Governor Blair declared a period of mourning; the mayor ordered all businesses closed; Peck, Leach, and Bingham were chosen to "draft suitable resolutions" on behalf of the citizens of Lansing. Peck, who had disagreed often with both Lincoln and Seward, said in a moving address, "None felt more deeply [than I] the loss to the nation. ... One was an honest man and the other a great statesman." Leach, who described himself as "a political and personal friend of Lincoln," conceded that he had often disagreed with Lincoln "but in the end he proved wiser than I."

It was a Lansing officer, Lieutenant Luther B. Baker, Jr., who led the party that tracked down Lincoln's assassin, John Wilkes Booth; one of Baker's men, Sergeant Boston Corbitt, fired the shot that fatally wounded Booth. For years after the war, Baker and his horse, Buckskin, were conspicuous figures in local Memorial Day and Fourth of July celebrations. As late as the 1890s, Baker still appeared on the lecture circuit, giving a detailed description of the death of Lincoln, the pursuit, capture, and death of Booth, and the trial and execution of Booth's accomplices.

Shortly after the war, there occurred a tragic incident— the lynching of John Taylor, an 18-year-old black man, on August 23, 1866, in Mason. The incident can only be explained as an aberration, a result of the extraordinary pressures, tensions, and anxieties of the war and its immediate aftermath. "The hanging," wrote Mrs. Franc L. Adams of Mason in her *Pioneer History of Ingham County,* "has ever been a dark spot on Mason's escutcheon."

David B. Harrington, editor of the *Ingham County News* at the time of the incident, took "unusual pains to obtain and publish the facts." The victim, a former Kentucky slave, had become the camp follower of a Michigan regiment; at the end of the war, he came to Lansing. He planned to attend school in Owosso in the fall and "hired out" to a Delhi Township farmer to earn money for clothing.

When his employer refused to pay for his services,

Taylor left the farm; several days later, he returned to demand his money. As Taylor approached the house, according to Harrington, "fearing that [the farmer] would ... put some of his former threats into execution ... he picked up the axe with which to defend himself against attack." The house was dark, and the farmer was not at home. As Taylor groped about, "he aroused [the farmer's] eleven-year-old daughter, who began to scream ... [and] as she jumped from the lounge her head came into contact with the axe, making a slight wound." The screams alerted the farmer's wife, "and she pounced upon the negro, who then began using the axe to defend himself, making a slight wound." The woman's mother appeared, bearing a light; she also received a slight blow from the axe.

Taylor then managed to flee. The farmer organized a posse which captured him near Bath; he was lodged in the Ingham County jail in Mason in the custody of Sheriff Frederick P. Moody. At this point, ugly rumors began to spread. "The community in the vicinity ... was greatly excited, with people congregating at various places threatening vengeance. The most hair-raising and exaggerated reports were told and re-told, until the belief became general that the entire family had been murdered. That was the exact report which reached Mason the next morning."

Early the next day, Harrington went to the farmhouse in company with Dr. Wing and found that "not a drop of blood was spilled by those reported butchered except from the little girl, and as far as we could see no one was seriously injured." During the afternoon, "threats of vengeance and the stealthy appearance of strangers" aroused anxieties. A group of leading citizens suggested to Sheriff Moody that the prisoner be removed to Jackson or another safe place; the sheriff agreed that there was a danger, but maintained that he and his deputies could afford protection.

At 11:00 p.m. on the night of August 23, a group of about 100 men, some of them armed, approached the jail and demanded the prisoner. The sheriff refused, whereupon the men overpowered the sheriff and his deputies, broke through the jailhouse door, removed the prisoner, and dispatched him some distance from town. The reader is spared the details.

The incident had profound repercussions, having taken place close to the capital of a state that had abolished the death penalty in 1846 and whose citizens had often disparaged other sections of the country where summary justice was routine. "Mason got the blame," wrote Harrington, "notwithstanding [that] but two or three Mason men were connected with the outrage." Others besides Harrington have confirmed that the foul deed was the work of outsiders, for the rumor that the family had been butchered had spread far. Years later, James Toburn of Lansing recalled that he and another boy had stood near the Harper School and watched wagon load after wagon load of men heading toward Mason from the north; they were not sure of their "destination and errand" until the following morning. The incident caused great shame and embarrassment, and was deplored in press and pulpit for years.

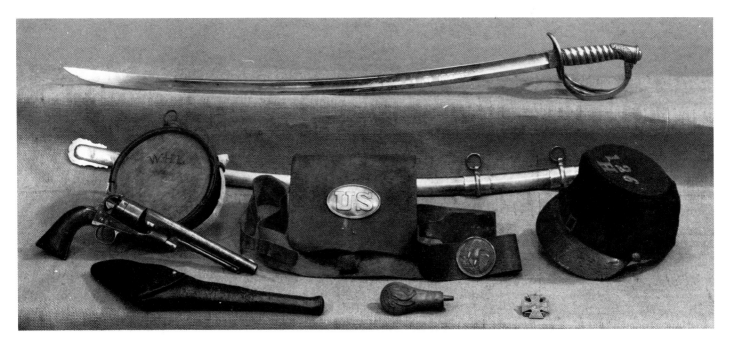

TOP: **Military artifacts of the type used by Michigan Civil War soldiers. Courtesy of Michigan State University Museum.**

ABOVE: **This scene, reproduced from a stereocard, shows a group of Civil War amputees playing croquet on the lawn of the state office building, which was razed when Lansing's present capitol was built. From the Edmonds Collection, Lansing Public Library.**

RIGHT: **Charles T. Foster served as Sergeant in Company "G," 3rd Michigan Infantry, under Captain John R. Price of Lansing. Foster was killed while bearing the regimental flag at the Battle of Fair Oaks, May 29, 1862. The Lansing post of the G.A.R. (Grand Army of the Republic) was named for him. From the Wiskemann Collection.**

Chapter 6

A Michigan State Gazeteer published in 1863—four years after Lansing's incorporation—analyzed the city's history and prospects. By now, the city's population had reached about 4,000, and its amenities included 11 churches, five hotels, two flour mills, three tanneries, two breweries, three sawmills, two sash and blind factories, two printing offices, several brickyards, and numerous "mechanic's shops." There was a stone quarry a short distance from town and a large annual trade in wool and grain. In addition to the Michigan Reform School, the Michigan Female College, and the Michigan Agricultural College—"all elegant structures that reflect great credit upon the city and State"—the city boasted the State Library, housed in the capitol, whose 16,000 volumes were open to the public, and whose collection included an original oil portrait of the Marquis de Lafayette.

Only the lack of rail transportation stood in the way of further growth. "The want of it retards the town," the *Republican* had complained in 1855, and "is the cause of the reproach upon our citizens, of all the sneers at the place." Getting to or from Detroit, the commercial metropolis, took 12 to 14 hours on the plank road; the citizen and visitor to Lansing, argued the *Republican,* ought to be able to cover that distance in two hours or less.

The first railroad to serve the capital region—the Amboy, Lansing, and Traverse Bay Railroad—reached Owosso, 28 miles from Lansing, in 1860. This road had received a generous grant of land from the state and had raised more capital by selling stock to such Lansing business leaders as Orlando M. Barnes and James Turner. Completing the line to Lansing, however, was terribly slow. Construction was delayed by Chandler's Marsh, north of Lansing, and for a time the line stopped at Bath Township, whence a stage shuttled passengers to and from Lansing. Many Lansing Civil War volunteers were transported to the Bath depot in lumber wagons. In November 1862, the road reached North Lansing; finally, in August 1863, the road was completed to a depot in the 400 block of East Michigan Avenue in Lansing. The city now had good rail connections to Detroit, Grand Rapids, and other points, since the road connected with the Detroit and Milwaukee Railroad at Owosso.

There were many jokes about this primitive railroad, which was called the "Ram's Horn" because of the shape of its route. The Amboy, Lansing, and Traverse Bay was also known by its passengers as the "Awfully Long and Terribly Bumpy" and "Almighty Long and Tremendous Bad." John Whitely complained that the poorly designed rolling stock and roadbed gave passengers "a terrible shaking," and that it was sometimes necessary for passengers to get off when the train reached "one of the high sand hills, so the locomotive could pull the empty cars up." John Longyear wrote that the trains sometimes moved so slowly that "anyone desiring to know which way the train was moving was obliged to get off and make a chalk mark upon the track."

The first locomotive—a wood-burning, "tea kettle" rig with one set of drive wheels and a whale-oil headlamp—was known variously as "the Black Swan," "No. 1," "Peggy," or "Short and Dirty." One engine blew up while crossing Chandler's Marsh; Edwin Todd, the conductor, reported that when the boiler exploded, "it shot straight up in a blinding flash which illuminated the countryside." The train crew was obliged to hike six miles to Lansing for assistance.

Whatever the limitations of the early railroads, the completion of the first railroad was greeted ecstatically in Lansing. "Since the walls of Jericho began to tremble," exulted the *Republican,* "no ram's horn ever created such a sensation." By the mid-1870s, four other rail lines served Lansing, distant markets were easily reached by rail, and the vast rural hinterland around Lansing became an area of prosperous farms. In 1874, Ingham County alone had 3,500 farms and a population of 29,193, of whom one fourth lived in Lansing. Ingham's production of wheat—the staple crop from 1860 to 1890, when the opening of the Dakota wheat farms forced capital-area farmers to diversify—climbed from 181,000 bushels in 1864 to more than 479,000 in 1874, a large proportion of which was sold and shipped from Lansing.

By the mid-1870s, Ingham County had several reasonably sized villages—Mason, Stockbridge, Williamston, Leslie, Dansville, and Webberville—which served as regional commercial centers. All except Dansville had railroad depots; all had gristmills and sawmills, blacksmith shops, grain elevators, and even hotels. In addition, three smaller hamlets—Aurelius Center, Bunker Hill, and Fitchburg—served as post offices and railroad stops. Other small hamlets grew up around storage and railroad facilities built by two of the railroads at six-mile intervals; these included Chapin's Station (now Eden), Delhi Station (now Holt), and Okemos.

Nowhere in the area was the dramatic effect of railroad transportation more evident than in Lansing itself. "With our railroads and shipping facilities," predicted the *Republican* in 1870, "there is no reason why Lansing should not ... [become] both the capital of a great commonwealth and the business heart ... [of] half a dozen counties." The *Republican* predicted correctly; by the mid-1870s, Lansing had become the largest wheat market in Michigan.

On a single day in September of 1875, more than 20 carloads of wheat were shipped from the Michigan Avenue depot of the Lake Shore and Michigan Southern Railroad; all the other roads in Lansing shipped wheat that day, too. During August and September, 1875, more than 300 carloads were shipped from Lansing at the going rate of $1.20 a bushel. Railroad and elevator crews worked night

A train arriving at the Franklin Street (now Grand River Avenue) depot of the Lake Shore and Michigan Southern Railroad, circa 1870. Courtesy of Michigan State University Archives and Historical Collections.

and day to keep up with business; superior handling facilities at the Michigan Avenue depot enabled a crew to unload a wagon of grain there in less than five minutes. In 1877, total wheat sales at Lansing reached a quarter of a million bushels, about double the sales volume of such other wheat areas as Kent, Kalamazoo, and Berrien counties.

With increased prosperity came visible changes in the city. "The ten years since the issue of the city charter," wrote John Longyear in 1870, "have seen an almost complete metamorphose of the place." Persons who had been away from Lansing for a few years were invariably surprised. The most noticeable changes dated from 1866, "when the three finest blocks [commercial buildings] were erected at a cost of over $250,000." A few of the old pioneer stores remained; they "forlornly stare at their new and imposing neighbors . . . [and] seem regretfully to look back to the time when they lorded it over the adjacent stumps and frog ponds." The only familiar landmark was "the old rookery dignified by the name of capitol," which "showed extensive ravages of time."

De Witt C. Leach, who had left Lansing in 1866 to edit the Traverse City *Grand Traverse Herald,* noticed striking changes in Lansing when he returned for a visit in 1873. First was the relative ease with which he was able to reach Lansing. In 1866, the 300-mile journey required five days of overland travel; in 1873, Leach could leave his Traverse City home at 8:30 a.m. and arrive in Lansing on the same day at 8:00 p.m. In 1866, only one railroad served Lansing, and "its reputation for speed, safety, or comfort was not of an enviable character." In 1873, the rail traveler could leave Lansing in any of six directions.

But more than rail travel had changed. When Leach left Lansing in 1866, there were few "good, substantial brick buildings." In 1873, he found a large number, and Washington Avenue had, for a town the size of Lansing, "an unusual number of fine stores." The Lansing House, described by Longyear as "the finest hotel in the North-West," reflected well on the city, as did Buck's Opera House. "If there is anywhere in Michigan, outside of Detroit," declared Leach, "a finer building than the Opera House, we have not seen it." While the city had few very expensive homes, there were many that indicated "a good degree of business success, and good taste and sound practical sense." Leach noted, too, Lansing's "admirable arrangement" of shade trees in residential areas. "Most of the streets have two rows of maples on each side, thus giving a row on each side of the walk." The wide streets platted by the capital commissioners had made it possible to plant four rows of trees on most streets "and yet leave ample room for travel or business." The street trees were newly planted in 1873, and Leach predicted that when they matured, "the State Capital will . . . be a city in a forest of the most beautiful trees." Some of these trees still stand today, stately and magnificent.

An array of colorful mayors governed Lansing during the 1870s. John Robson (1871, 1881) owned the city's largest furniture store. The popular John S. Tooker (1872, 1873, 1876), an ardent Republican who received the largest electoral majority of a Lansing mayor up to that time, later served as territorial governor of Montana. Daniel W. Buck (1874, 1875, 1886) began as a cabinetmaker, entered the furniture business, and eventually built the famous Buck's Opera House on the site of the present Gladmer Theater. Orlando M. Barnes (1877), a Democrat, Lansing pioneer, and for a time the wealthiest man in town, had served as Ingham County prosecutor; as a state legislator, he fought hard for prison reform. Barnes, who made and lost a good deal of money in lumbering, railroads, and banking, was an urbane and cosmopolitan man and arguably Lansing's leading citizen. Joseph E. Warner (1878) had a show-business background—for some years he had toured the world in search of curiosities for Barnum's circus. He settled in Lansing and served as city clerk, alderman, and police commissioner before his single term as mayor. William Van Buren (1879, 1880) fought hard for the purchase of a city-hall site on the corner of Allegan and South Washington, a move that was defeated by the almost unanimous opposition of residents of North Lansing.

The modern city, a product of the industrial revolution, was coming into its own as Lansing grew, and there was little experience in coping with the problems of a growing urban community. Problems involving bridges, illuminating gas, fire engines, and animal control became angrily debated political issues.

Bridges were essential in a city trisected by two meandering streams; by 1856, five wooden bridges spanned the Grand and Red Cedar rivers at strategic points. But wooden bridges have problems, including rot and decay; and flash floods in 1852, 1857, and 1860 had torn several bridges from their moorings and hurled them downstream.

John Robson, mayor of Lansing in 1871, remembered the "free for all" that ensued when he proposed replacing the old wooden latticed bridge on Michigan Avenue. "The timbers creaked and gave every indication of weakness when even a dog trotted across, and as for heavy traffic, it was perilous." The common council was divided—some members thought the old bridge needed only a few repairs, others that it should be replaced. Robson proposed an iron bridge. "Iron bridges," he said, "were a novelty in those days, especially in Lansing." No one had seen an iron bridge, and many believed it would be too costly for the city. Robson finally won, but only after a hard fight and a close vote. Ironically, the new iron bridge was swept from its piers in the spring of 1875 by large chunks of ice. The bridge was then moved from its original Michigan Avenue site and was used for many years over the Grand River at Kalamazoo Street.

The next controversy occurred over the question of illuminating gas, by then in use in many cities. The agent of an Ann Arbor gas company that "claimed to make the best gas that ever was gassed," said that its product, made from crude oil, "shone brighter and cost less than any other gas on the market." Robson was suspicious, and asked for the name of a town that used the apparatus; he was told that "some little town in Pennsylvania . . . was the proud possessor of the system." Robson, a merchant, occasionally traveled to New York, and he made a point of visiting the Pennsylvania town. He found that "all the bad

LEFT: **Dr. William H. Haze** was a Methodist Episcopal minister and mayor of Lansing in 1866. As a member of the legislature he was in favor of building Michigan Agricultural College, and in 1862 opposed a move to relocate the college to Ann Arbor. Courtesy of Lansing Public Library.

RIGHT: **Frank Robson** was mayor of Lansing in 1871 and 1881. Robson's administration is often remembered for political disputes over fire engines, illuminating gas, and bridges. Courtesy of Lansing Public Library.

LEFT: **John S. Tooker** was mayor of Lansing from 1872 to 1873, and again in 1876. In the early 1880s he was appointed territorial governor of Montana by President Chester A. Arthur. Courtesy of Lansing Public Library.

RIGHT: A bust of **Orlando Mack Barnes** (1824–1899) sculpted by Herman Wehner. Barnes, a lifelong Democrat, was one of Lansing's leading citizens. He served as mayor of Lansing from 1877 to 1878 and ran, unsuccessfully, for governor of Michigan (1878) and U.S. Senator (1883). He was a state representative from 1863 to 1864 and served as Ingham County Prosecutor. Barnes was also an attorney for the Jackson, Lansing, and Saginaw Railroad. He made and lost several fortunes in his lifetime. Photograph by author.

53

things they said about the gas company would fill a book and the book would be burned at the stake for unprintable epithets." The light emitted by the town's gas jets "looked like little lightning bugs, and the street lights were worse than nothing." The council decided against crude-oil gas, and the franchise went instead to the Lansing Gas Company.

"Then came the fight over fire engines," recalled Robson. The city's only fire-fighting equipment was one pumper with hand brakes. Improved apparatus was clearly needed, but the proposal to purchase a modern, steam-powered fire engine provoked no less furor than the iron bridge or illuminating gas. The opponents of the steam engine claimed that the heavy apparatus would sink into the mud of unpaved streets. Two companies offered fire engines, and agents for each drummed up public support for its machine. The Silsbury Company presented the common council with a citizens' petition in favor of its $6,000 machine; the Clapp and Jones Company had the support of the volunteer fire companies for its engine, priced at $4,500.

"It was a great fight," said Robson, "with no money in the city's jeans to pay for either machine." A secret test of the rival engines was arranged. The Clapp and Jones agent heated the water of his device the night before the demonstration. "His perfidy was discovered," said Robson, "and he was made to draw his water from the river." Although the tests showed the Silsbury machine to be "clearly superior," the Clapp and Jones agent put on a public display to gain more support, and Robson "was besieged by entreaties and later threats ... [to buy] the Clapp and Jones machine." Robson, in order to placate all sides, finally recommended that the city somehow find the money to buy both machines.

One of Lansing's ugliest gaslight-era controversies was provoked by the "wandering cow" ordinance of 1875. The issue arose when the common council, on the motion of Alderman Frederick M. Cowles, repealed one of the city's earliest enactments—that which required vagrant livestock to be confined in the city pound and released to owners only upon payment of a fine. Cowles hoped that the new policy would help the poor, since grazing land around the city had become expensive, and the depression that began in 1873 had caused a significant increase in the number of families on public charity. Cowles also hoped that the measure would help prevent the spread of fires, since the livestock would help keep down the dry grass.

A public furor began almost immediately. Under the heading "Havoc, Fear, and Filth in Lansing," the *Republican* published a letter from a "Thoroughly Vexed Woman" who complained that cows had destroyed the shade trees recently planted at public expense. The *Republican* agreed. "Where is the justice," it asked, "of taxing people to set out shade trees ... if cattle are permitted to run loose, and gnaw, rub, and push over these shade trees before they are properly rooted?"

For weeks, every issue of the *Republican* included at least one cow outrage. In May, the daughter of A.L. Bours, secretary of the state building commissioners, "was attacked by a vicious cow, and would have been killed but

for the timely intervention of a passerby." Three cows entered the barn of one J.H. Clements near the Grand River "and devoured a barrel of provender." In addition to the destruction of shade trees and gardens, the *Republican* reported that "little children and timid women were being frightened, and ... the sidewalks illustrated by bad pictures." Angry citizens scoffed at the idea that free forage for cows on city streets helped the poor or prevented fires. Finally, on a close vote, the common council repealed Cowles' wandering-cow ordinance.

Probably the most remembered incident of the 1870s was the disaster of April 1875, when rampaging ice and flood waters in the Grand River swept away all the city's bridges.

Trouble had been expected for weeks; a prolonged late-winter cold wave had caused a huge buildup of ice upstream, and spring was late coming. On March 9, the *Republican* reported "no sign of a thaw yet, and Lansing has many bridges in peril." A thaw came suddenly early in April. On April 10, with ice near the city breaking up, riders were sent to examine the ice upstream on both the Grand and Red Cedar rivers; they reported that a huge gorge of ice and flood waters would enter the city within hours. Persons living near the river were evacuated. Soon a tremendous roar was heard in the city as an immense ice gorge, studded with logs and other debris, broke under the pressure of water upstream and crashed into the Mineral Wells iron bridge. As hundreds watched, the Mineral Wells bridge, afloat on a cake of ice, was hurled downstream by the swift current into the Michigan Avenue bridge, which was lifted from its abutments. In a similar manner, all of Lansing's bridges were swept away; the old wooden Franklin Street bridge was discovered afloat in the river at Delta Mills, six miles downstream.

While the flood is remembered, its political aftermath has been forgotten. The manner of financing new bridges to replace those lost in the flood was a matter of great controversy, involving angry citizens' meetings, harsh words in the press, and four referenda to the voters.

Early in June, Mayor Daniel W. Buck and the common council proposed replacing all the bridges and selling bonds for $40,000 to cover the cost. A decisive popular vote defeated this proposition; many citizens, cautious about increasing the city's debt, demanded that only the most important bridge, that over Franklin Street, be replaced, and the cost defrayed from tax funds.

The common council continued to insist on all new bridges and $40,000 in bonds; the voters defeated this proposal a second and third time. When the common council scheduled yet another bond-proposal election in August, a public-indignation meeting was held in Representatives Hall. Leading citizens—including Schuyler S. Olds (no relation to Ransom E. Olds), Courtland Bliss Stebbins, Dr. Hulbert B. Shank, S.D. Bingham, and W.S. George, editor of the *Republican*—denounced the plan.

Bingham's address focused clearly on the issue of increasing the city's bonded indebtedness. "The whole bonded debt of Lansing is about $177,000," he said. "Let this bonding business be carried on, and in time we would stagger under as heavy a load as East Saginaw, which has a bonded debt of $680,000 on a valuation of perhaps $3,200,000." Interest alone on East Saginaw's debt amounted to $68,000 annually. "We would rather pay for these bridges," he declared, "than bond the city." The other speakers agreed. The persons at the meeting agreed that Lansing should sell no more bonds, that it should levy a tax sufficient to replace the Franklin Street bridge at once, and that the other bridges should be replaced out of general revenues when the city could afford to do so.

But the fourth vote carried the bonding plan, much to the consternation of the *Republican*. "The common council, by a system of scheming unparalleled in the history of municipalities," it lamented, "has forced the people to accept just what they said they must have in the commencement of the bridge controversy—all the bridges or nothing." The bridges were eventually rebuilt using funds provided by the sale of $14,000 in bonds, with the remainder of the cost met from general revenue.

The bridge controversy shows the highly cautious manner in which Lansing citizens approached matters of municipal finance. Lansing's bonded indebtedness was far lower than that of other towns of the period which mortgaged their futures with huge debts in a time of financial uncertainty; East Saginaw was only one of many small Midwestern towns that struggled for years to reduce an excessive debt. Traditionally cautious about overindebtedness, Lansing citizens also feared that a large debt might raise local taxes and discourage new business from coming to the area.

The city's growth placed a strain on its schools. When Lansing received its charter in 1859, the voters rejected a plan to consolidate the four school districts into one; but in 1861 the state legislature, in an unusual move for Michigan, disregarded local opposition and consolidated the schools into a single district. Thus was born the Lansing School District, still in existence, which operates the city's schools.

In order to keep the school district out of the bitter politics of the war years, it was agreed that school-board members would be elected on a nonpartisan basis and nominated at "union" caucuses open to voters of both major parties. Courtland Bliss Stebbins, who served briefly as editor of the *Republican* and for 20 years as deputy state superintendent of public instruction, himself often a school-board member, regretted the union-caucus arrangement. "The election," he said, "is really a farce. ... The election is made at the caucus, and it may be a 'packed' caucus." Nonetheless, Stebbins conceded, "the schools have been fortunate in the composition of the board"; James Turner, George W. Peck, Ephraim W. Longyear, and other distinguished citizens served on the first board elected under this arrangement.

In 1868, the school board, faced with an increase of 318 children in three years, took a number of remarkable steps for the time: it hired a superintendent, created a "high-school department," and began grading its classes. The last was seen as a particularly progressive step. Stebbins, a school-board member in 1868, thought that the new plan "placed Lansing's schools on a par with the best conducted schools of the state." School crowding continued to be a problem in the 1870s; at one time, 1,400 children occupied space designed for 600. Classes were held above stores, in church basements, "and even in an engine house." In 1871, the school board established a kindergarten, the first in Michigan; 60 children appeared at the first class and many more were turned away, as the budget allowed only one teacher. The kindergarten was abolished for financial reasons in 1873.

In 1875, a splendid three-story, mansard-roofed high-school building was dedicated with impressive ceremony. This building, designed by Elijah E. Myers, the architect of Michigan's present capitol, replaced a two-story wooden

LEFT: **Daniel W. Buck was mayor of Lansing from 1874 to 1875 and again in 1886. Buck was originally from Lansing, New York. He opened a small cabinet shop in Lansing and later added a furniture store. Buck also built the city's first opera house. Courtesy of Lansing Public Library.**

RIGHT: **Courtland Bliss Stebbins was an authority on school law and for many years served as Michigan Deputy Superintendent of Public Instruction. Stebbins served briefly as editor of *The Republican* and was also one of the founders of the Lansing Wheelbarrow Company. Courtesy of Lansing Public Library.**

structure built in 1868. Regrettably, according to the historian of the Lansing School District, the new building proved to be costly and unsatisfactory; the heating system, though expensive, never worked properly, and disputes with the contractors dragged on in the courts for years.

The new high school was the pride of the city; commencement exercises invariably drew a large crowd. The exercises of June 1875 were held at Buck's Opera House; Superintendent E.V.W. Brokaw presided over a program of inspirational addresses and "literary exercises," or student orations, judged for their eloquence and turn of phrase. A Miss Lou Hunter gave a eulogy for the recently departed Senator Charles Sumner of Massachusetts, who had appeared in Lansing—"a Washington in purity, a Luther in fervor, a Cromwell in persistence and greatness of soul."

By the 1870s, Lansing had become something of a cultural center. Literary and debating societies formed by the pioneers flourished in country schools until the 1880s. A short-lived Lyceum of Ingham County was organized in Mason in 1846; its 23 members started a library and debated such topics as whether civilization enhanced happiness. In the 1850s, a group known as the Capital Senate met in Lansing and debated similar topics. At the agricultural college, lyceums or literary societies flourished for years and served as centers of student activity until they were overshadowed by fraternities.

A Young Men's Association, organized by George W. Peck and others, began an annual series of lectures in 1866. This organization sought "to establish and maintain ... courses of literary and scientific lectures, a reading room, library, and other means for the promotion of literary and scientific pursuits." In 1866, Horace Greeley, editor of the *New York Tribune* and 1872 presidential candidate, was the leading lecturer; in 1867, the speakers included the explorer Bayard Taylor and Senator Charles Sumner of Massachusetts. At first, meetings were held in the Methodist Episcopal Church on South Washington at Ottawa; later, lectures were held in Capital Hall, a large meeting room over two stores in the 100 block of Washington. Later still, the society moved to Mead's Hall (later Mead's Temperance Hall), scene of many important cultural events.

There were other literary societies and a wide range of cultural diversions. A North Lansing Library and Literary Association met in the basement of the Franklin Street Church and avidly discussed "the expediency of the eight-hour system of labor" and "whether the elective franchise ought to be extended to women." Amateur theatrical performances supplemented those of professional players; in 1873, the Michigan Athenaeum presented the play *Six Degrees of Crime* with the popular Dr. Hulbert T. Shank in the leading role. The opening of Buck's Opera House in 1872—a magnificent 1,100-seat theater on the site of the Gladmer Theater—was celebrated with a performance of *Macbeth* with the famous actor Edwin Booth.

The Michigan poet William McKindree Carleton, better known as "Will" Carleton, often read his poems in Lansing in the 1870s and later decades. Carleton, nationally known then if forgotten now, read sentimental and inspirational poetry from his collections, *Farm Ballads* and *Farm Legends*, both published in 1875. His poems, written in plain language about plain people, evoked the simple virtues of the pioneer past. In 1955, Mrs. Nellie Zimmer of Lansing, then in her nineties, remembered that Carleton's reading of his most famous poem, "Over the Hill to the Poor House," left no eyes dry. This poem told of an aged woman sent to the poorhouse by indifferent children. Carleton, a master of histrionics, appeared in a shawl and imitated the old woman. Mrs. Zimmer recalled that Carleton sometimes followed this poem with a sequel, in which the old woman's scapegrace son heard of her plight, got religion, returned, and made his mother a happy home.

At least one cultural organization founded in the 1870s is still active today. The Lansing Woman's Club—founded in 1874 by Mrs. Harriet A. Tenney, the state librarian and the only major woman officeholder in Lansing, and Mrs. John A. Bagley, wife of the governor—arose as a result of limited educational opportunities for women. It grew out of the Lansing Library and Literary Association, founded in 1871, which operated a library for its members. Unlike the Young Men's Association, which mainly listened to lectures, the Woman's Club embarked on a program of weekly meetings with demanding preparation for each member. The members were divided into four "divisions"—art and literature, history, science, and education. Each division was responsible for one meeting a month; four papers were presented at each meeting, with time for discussion. Topics included "Europe and the Fall of the Roman Empire," "The Feudal System," "The Moors in Spain," "The Napoleons," "Life and Works of Hawthorne," "Divorce Laws," and "The Successful Woman and Man Compared." Each member was also required to bring "seed thoughts" to be read to the group in order that they might "hear for the first time their own voices in public." The activities of the Woman's Club have remained essentially unchanged over the years.

By far the most notable event in the cultural life of Lansing in the gaslight era was the appearance of Mark Twain in 1871. Twain, who had lectured in Lansing in 1868, based his well-received presentation on his forthcoming book *Roughing It,* a description of life in the Far West. The *Republican,* "thinking that perhaps his feelings might be hurt unless we gave him extended notice," printed Twain's lecture verbatim. While strolling around town, Twain encountered a Lansing booster who declaimed on the majestic breadth of Washington Avenue. "Yes," agreed Twain. "It is the broadest and deepest street I have ever seen."

Under President Theopholis Capen Abbott (1862-1885), the Michigan Agricultural College came into its own at last. With the aid of federal land-grant funds, provided under the Morrill Act of 1862, the college now had a secure endowment that made it less dependent on legislative whim. Abbott assembled a distinguished faculty, and the broad outlines of an agricultural education were worked out.

Henry Haigh of the class of 1874 left a reminiscence of

LEFT: **There is an interesting history behind Michigan Avenue bridges. This 1878 scene shows the second iron bridge spanning the Grand River at Michigan. The first iron bridge, built in 1875, was removed by the flood of April 1875, and later used at Kalamazoo Street. The sign above the bridge reads, "Five dollars for riding or driving this bridge faster than a walk." From the Edmonds Collection, Lansing Public Library.**

ABOVE LEFT: **This fire engine was purchased by the City of Lansing in 1858 and sold in 1871 to the City of Cheboygan, Michigan. The engine was discovered in a shed near the Cheboygan Water Works in 1915 by James T. Edmonds, who purchased it for $45 and brought it back to Lansing. This relic, which is now on display in the Michigan State Museum, was used by Torrent Engine Company No. 1. Courtesy of the Michigan State Museum.**

ABOVE RIGHT: **The Lansing High School was built in 1875. Designed by architect Elijah E. Myers, the building has since been remodeled and is now part of the central administrative building of Lansing Community College. Courtesy of Michigan State University Archives and Historical Collections.**

RIGHT: **Buck's Opera House and Furniture Store, 1880. Buck, an enterprising merchant, operated a grocery and clothing store on the premises of the opera house. The Gladmer Theater now occupies this site. From Durant, *History of Ingham and Eaton Counties*.**

student life in the first decade of the secure existence of the college. The students referred to the school as "the college," but Lansing residents referred to it as "the state farm school," in order to distinguish it from the state reform school. "But as to the inmates," said Haigh, "many made no distinction." The campus was beautiful— "an expanse of but recently timbered land along a pleasant stream"—with only two college buildings and four houses in Faculty Row.

The "stars among the faculty" were Abbott, "the tactful administrator, the cultured, kindly harmonizer"; Manly Miles, "the greatest teacher of practical agriculture of his time"; Robert C. Kedzie, "the great pioneer of practical chemistry"; George T. Fairchild, "the inspiring teacher of language and literature and belles lettres"; and Albert J. Cook, "the first graduate teacher [and] author of *Blessed Bees*."

In the 1870s, students continued to work on the farm, in the gardens, and on the grounds. "The small compensation," wrote Haigh, "came in handy to pay board bills which we thought were very high—$2.50 a week." The board, however, was good—quality meats, ample milk, cheese, butter, and eggs, and vegetables from the college farm. Honey was available from an apiary kept by Professor Cook, expert beekeeper. In winter, Cook kept his hives in the basement of Saints' Rest; some escaped to students' rooms. The bees, however, behaved well. "The professor," said Haigh, "by precept and example taught them not to sting. Blessed bees could hardly sting with any sense of self respect and such a name!"

Chapel services, daily and Sunday, and weekly Bible classes, were voluntary but well attended. Lansing ministers took turns holding Sunday services, with Abbott or a faculty member ready to fill in if necessary. Campus "red-letter days"—especially junior exhibitions and commencement exercises—attracted crowds; an eminent speaker often appeared at commencement.

Henry Haigh's memoirs also convey some of the "flavor of life" in Lansing during the mid-1870s. Haigh, who served as a clerk at the State Board of Health until he entered law school at the University of Michigan in 1876, boarded at the home of the celebrated Mrs. Sophie Knight, "who was at that time quite famous as a vocalist in Lansing." Governor John J. Bagley, who often visited state offices unannounced, was a familiar sight on Lansing streets. Mrs. Bagley, unlike other governors' wives, "entered into the social life of the little city to the great delight of local society." Social leaders of the day included many pioneer families—names such as Turner, Case, Dodge, Longyear, and Barnes. Barnes, who had moved from Mason to Lansing, had built "the most beautiful home in Lansing," on Seymour Street near the Grand River. Elected mayor of Lansing in 1877, he "became almost at once one of the most notable figures in the city," helping to cool the passions unleashed by the political conflicts of 1875. Barnes' "suavity and sweetness of demeanor made him a charming man to meet"; his home was "a center of refined social activity."

"No mention of Lansing in the good old seventies would be complete," wrote Haigh, "without mention of the four distinguished justices—Thomas F. Cooley, James V. Campbell, Isaac P. Christiancy, and Benjamin Franklin Graves—who made the Michigan Supreme Court second to none in this country, not even excepting those in Massachusetts and New York." Cooley, who had been dean of the University of Michigan Law School for 40 years, had a son who lived in Lansing with whom he stayed during court sessions. Campbell, who wrote one of the first histories of Michigan, lived in Detroit "but seemed to be around Lansing a good deal, in the State Library and in the Court." Haigh remembered "his attractive figure, classic countenance, and snowy white hair." Christiancy, who had a splendid Lansing residence, left the Michigan Supreme Court to succeed Zachariah Chandler, leader of the "Stalwart" faction of the Republican party, in the United States Senate. Graves was widely admired as a legal scholar.

The leading members of the Lansing bar were Schuyler Seager, Samuel L. Kilbourne, Edward Cahill, the Darts, and the Montgomeries. The *Republican*, then edited by W.S. George, state printer, "was really a fine newspaper of much power in the state." George P. Sanford, editor of the Democratic *State Journal*, was less popular; "he was regarded as a pessimist and a grouch and unable to see any good in the times and manners."

Lansing had become an interesting place by the 1870s. In addition to its increased wealth and extensive cultural life, the construction of the new capitol quickened the pace of life and drew many visitors.

For some years, all state government departments had used the capitol; in 1853, many of these moved to a "fireproof" brick office building on the site of the present capitol. As Michigan's population and wealth increased, the functions of government grew correspondingly, and both the capitol and the office building soon became inadequate. The office building, Governor Kinsley S. Bingham complained to the legislature in 1859, "was so badly constructed that . . . it was in danger of falling." To secure the building, "it was necessary to install iron bars, and even now . . . it shakes and trembles in every wind." The state archives, "housed in a building likely to fall," were unsafe; without sufficient space, the documents of the state "were poked in large boxes and stowed away in holes and corners . . . liable to deterioration by fire, mold, and vermin."

The capitol of 1847 had become an eyesore. In 1871, the *Republican* complained that it had become "an old rattle trap" and a "humiliation if not a positive disgrace" both to the people of Michigan and to the prosperous community that was emerging in Lansing. Longyear thought that "there were private dwellings in the City of Lansing that would sooner be taken for the capitol by a stranger than the shed actually used for that purpose." Maintenance was often deferred. One summer, the capitol received a long-overdue coat of paint; the clapboards were painted white, the blinds green, and the cupola a curious shade of pea green. "This was because," wrote a Detroit reporter, "some of the white paint . . . and the green paint . . . were left over; it was thought a pity to let it be wasted." The two colors were mixed and applied to e cupola.

On January 4, 1871, Governor Henry P. Baldwin proposed the building of a new capitol. The existing capitol, said Baldwin, had been built a quarter of a century before, when the state had "a population one fourth as large as the present time, and about one twelfth of the present taxable valuation." The "present and growing incapacity of the state buildings," the danger of fire, and the requirement of several years' time for construction made prompt action urgent. The legislators agreed, and on March 13, 1871, the governor signed a bill "for the erection of a new state capitol, and a building for the temporary use of the state officers." The act provided that the governor should appoint a three-member Board of State Building Commissioners, to be charged with the design and construction not only of the new capitol but of a temporary office building as well. The legislature appropriated $1.2 million for the new capitol, to be raised by a tax of about 16 cents a year on each Michigan resident.

The 1853 office building was razed to clear its site for the new capitol; a temporary building, which housed state government departments, the State Library, and the Supreme Court, was completed on the same block as the old capitol in November 1871. The Board of State Building Commissioners—Ebenezer O. Grosvenor of Jonesville, James Shearer of Bay City, and Alexander Chapoton of Detroit, with Baldwin as an ex-officio member—announced a design competition for the new capitol; they approved the entry of Elijah E. Myers, a well-known architect who had designed other state capitols and public buildings in the United States and abroad. On July 15,

Nehemiah Osborn and Company of Rochester, New York, was engaged as contractor, and late in August the work of laying the foundation began.

The celebration when the cornerstone was laid, on October 3, 1873, was so extraordinary that the building's dedication five years later seemed anticlimatic. "The weather," wrote a Detroit reporter, "was all that could be desired. Sun bright and clear, unclouded sky, air just cool enough to be bracing." The crowd was huge, the largest seen in Lansing since Seward's speech in 1860; it was probably about 30,000, but estimates ranged from 20,000 to 100,000. "Every train which reached the city was loaded to capacity," reported the Detroit *Free Press*, "and all the hotels and private residences were filled to overflowing." Reporters described Lansing's streets as "one moving mass of humanity" and "crowded with struggling, surging, crowds of people." Facilities were strained; to feed the huge crowd, the ladies of 11 churches commandeered empty stores and basements and served hot meals at reasonable prices. Room accommodations were another matter; the *Free Press* reported that "not a few ... were badly provided for in respect to lodgings ... from remarks made in the morning about 'sleeping on two straws' and 'roosting on the ridge pole.'"

The mile-and-a-half long parade began an hour late; its line of march went south on Washington Avenue past the reviewing stand in front of the old capitol, then along Ottawa and Capitol and back to Washington. The marchers, splendidly attired, included a detachment of Detroit police, 25 bands, 15 military companies, the Knights Templar, bedecked in plumes and swords and marching

The faculty of Michigan Agricultural College in 1890. The seated men are, from left to right, Henry G. Reynolds, Rolla C. Carpenter, Edward P. Anderson, Lt. W.L. Simpson, and William James Beal. The standing men are, from left to right, Eugene Davenport, Levi R. Taft, President Oscar Clute, Robert C. Kedzie, and Albert J. Cook. Courtesy of Michigan State University Publications.

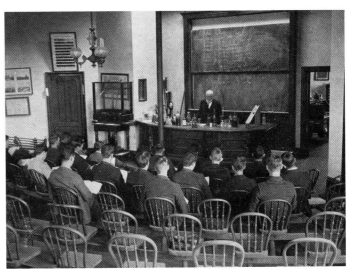

Michigan Agricultural College professor Robert Kedzie lecturing on petroleum, circa 1870. Courtesy of Michigan State University Publicatons.

24 abreast, and some 3,000 Masons and Oddfellows.

At 3:40 p.m., the cornerstone ceremonies began. Governor Bagley opened the exercises, dwelling at some length on what the new capitol would symbolize—that the pioneer period had ended and a new age of optimism and prosperity had begun. "Today we stand here as conquerors of forest and swamp, and can proudly say, 'If thou seekest a pleasant peninsula, seek it here.'" William A. Howard, the distinguished keynote speaker, compared the old capitol to the new: "Our present state capitol was built at a cost of $22,513.02. It used to be said in derision that Governor John S. Barry paid for it by cutting and selling the hay in the capitol yard." Howard observed that some persons in the crowd had helped raise the frame of the old capitol. "And now these same pioneers are gathered here with upturned faces, with looks of intent and glistening eyes, to lay broad and deep the foundations of a capitol worthy of their state."

A large copper box, containing a glass case of historical documents, was placed in a cavity in the cornerstone; the stone itself was raised to a height of 12 feet and lowered into place with three motions, each saluted by artillery, in a Masonic ritual. The entire gathering sang "Old Hundred," heard the benediction of the Reverend Noah Fassett and a salute of 37 guns, and the ceremonies were over.

Cornerstone Day put Lansing on the map; as the walls of the capitol began to rise, the railroads charged special excursion rates and brought a stream of visitors to the city. Construction materials from many parts of the world were used in the capitol—limestone from Illinois, sandstone from Ohio, granite from Massachusetts, marble from Vermont, tin from Wales, and plate glass from England. A Boston contractor installed a modern heating and ventilating system that included 32 miles of iron pipe; a system of batteries in the basement would spark the illumination of thousands of gas jets in the legislative halls and elsewhere in the building. The building boasted a steam elevator; its many ornamental features included the statuary over the east pediment. Glass panels etched with the seals of all the American states as well as the United States were installed in the ceilings of the legislative chambers.

The new capitol, its lighted dome visible on a clear night for many miles, is still downtown Lansing's most imposing structure, despite an enormous complex of modern state offices at its rear portico and skyscrapers nearby. The building, based on a five-part plan that includes three parallel rectangles joined by lesser elements, is surmounted by a narrower version of the national capitol dome.

The Lansing edifice was built during a boom in state capitol construction; New York, Kansas, Connecticut, Wisconsin, Texas, California, Illinois, Nevada, and Iowa all built resplendent "Gilded Age" statehouses at about the same time. Compared with these, in the opinion of architectural historian Henry-Russell Hitchcock, the Michigan capitol seems "a building of almost academic restraint." The Myers design was the simplest of all those entered in the competition; the runner-up was a kind of Second Empire design with a mansard roof and many towers. Guidebooks and tradition describe the style of the capitol as "Palladian," a mode named for a 16th-century architect whose buildings evoked the Roman style. But architectural historians dispute this classification. According to Professor Alexander R. Butler of Michigan State University, "no building could resemble less the work of Andrea Palladio than the Lansing capitol." Such features as "the use of the corner pavilion ... and decorative framing of the windows high on the dome, point to the French style of the mid-nineteenth century and not to sixteenth century Italy." The building lacks only a mansard roof "to complete the Parisian influence." Others have described the architecture as "American eclectic capitol architecture," since the building obviously evokes the national capitol and could not be taken for anything other than the capitol of an American state.

The dedication of the completed building took place on January 1, 1879, when some 2,000 persons crowded into the beautifully decorated capitol for moving ceremonies that included addresses by Governor Charles M. Croswell and five former chief executives—Alpheus Felch, William Greenly, Austin Blair, Henry Baldwin, and John Bagley. Felch, who had left the governor's office just before Lansing became the capital, said, "Hitherto the government may be said to have dwelt in tents—to-day it enters its permanent temple." The high point of the ceremony was the appearance of Ebenezer O. Grosvenor, vice-president of the building commissioners. "All hearts were melted," reported the *Owosso Press,* as he "presented the grand edifice in broken words to the Governor." As night fell, the capitol's gaslights were turned on; viewed from outside, "the building was all aglow as the light from thousands of gas jets gleamed forth." In the evening the Knights Templar appeared in the reporters' gallery to lead a promenade; at 11:00 p.m. a dance was in progress in the main hall. A snowstorm began before the party ended, "and the farmers who drove many miles had a tedious ride home."

The old capitol fell on hard times. The basement and first floor were occupied by the Piatt Brothers, manufacturers of handles and "bent work"; the Charles Foster Post of the Grand Army of the Republic, a Civil War veterans' organization, met in the Senate chamber. On December 16, 1882, the building caught fire. The fire engine proved unable to generate steam, and as thousands watched, the old capitol quickly disintegrated.

The old statehouse had symbolized Lansing's origins, and its loss occasioned a display of sentiment. A *Republican* reporter saw tears in the eyes of some of the older bystanders as the heavy timbers crashed into the flaming abyss; more than a few expressed guilt that the building had not been put to better use. A vital link to a simpler past was gone, and with it the pioneer period slipped further into memory.

If the old statehouse had stood as a visible reminder of the epic struggle of hewing a city out of a wilderness, its resplendent successor proclaimed a brave new world; for even as the old capitol burned, Lansing was laying the foundations of its modern industries.

LEFT: Though the cornerstone for Michigan's capitol bears the date 1872, the ceremonies were actually held on October 3, 1873. From the Jenison Collection, Michigan State Library.

BELOW LEFT: A view of the state capitol under construction, circa 1876. Note that the iron supports for the capitol dome have been installed. The Plymouth Congregational Church, completed in 1876, may be seen at the left. Courtesy of Michigan State Archives.

ABOVE: Cornerstone Day, October 3, 1873, attracted the largest crowd Lansing had ever seen; the dedication of the completed capitol five years later seemed anticlimatic. The Knights Templar, seen here, played a major role on this ceremonial occasion. They marched 24 abreast during the parade. From the Jenison Collection, Michigan State Library.

BELOW LEFT: The dedication of the new capitol, held January 1, 1879, drew a crowd of nearly 2,000. The ceremonies included addresses by Governor Charles M. Croswell and five former chief executives. From the Jenison Collection, Michigan State Library

Chapter 7

THE RISE OF INDUSTRY

Lansing's economy in the post-Civil War years benefited from a fantastic boom in the market for farm implements. In these years, hundreds of millions of acres in the trans-Mississippi West were settled; in a single generation, almost half a million acres, equal to the land area of all of western Europe except Spain, were put to the plow in the United States alone, and there were comparable agricultural booms in Canada, Australia, Russia, and Brazil. An amazing number of the plows used in this extraordinary expansion of agriculture were made in Lansing, which by 1890 emerged as a world center for the manufacture of plows and other agricultural implements.

There was every reason for Lansing to grow along these lines. The area still had magnificent stands of hardwood trees, an essential raw material of farm tools; it was well served by railroads; and its entrepreneurs had long dealt with farmers and understood their needs. The first Lansing firm to tap the new market in an important way was the Bement Company, which began manufacturing agricultural implements in Lansing in 1868. Its founder, Edwin Bement, had operated a small foundry in Fostoria, Ohio; the Lansing operation began in a River Street building known as the old Houghton foundry. Bement died in March 1880, and his two sons operated the reorganized company in two new buildings at Grand River and Ionia streets. The firm's diverse product line included farm tools of every description—plows and harrows in their many varieties, road scrapers, cauldron kettles, cultivators, seeders, round heating stoves, and bobsleds. The value of its annual production, reflecting the pace of settlement of western lands, jumped from $4,000 in 1870 to $30,000 in 1875 to $125,000 by 1880, when its products were sold all over the United States.

The Bement Company continued to grow during the 1880s; by 1885, the firm employed between 700 and 800 people and was by far the largest industrial firm in Lansing. Its plant occupied two full city blocks; its facilities included machine and blacksmith shops, a foundry, and warehouses; its products, diversified to include cooking and heating stoves, included the famous "Palace" cooking stove, and the quality of its products was widely respected. The Palace stove, reported the *Journal,* was a considerable improvement over old-fashioned devices that simply "held fire that was at least one-half wasted." The new stove conserved energy and heated evenly. "It is as far ahead of stoves of fifty years ago," wrote the *Journal,* "as the railroad is ahead of the stage coach."

A second firm that sparked Lansing's industrial growth was the Lansing Wheelbarrow Company, known in later years as the Lansing Company. A wheelbarrow, which was made by blacksmiths in a time-consuming and expensive manner before the advent of the factory-made product, is an essential agricultural device. The wheelbarrow company, managed after 1885 by Arthur Courtland Stebbins, was the largest consumer of wood in the Lansing area; residents became accustomed to the sight of logs used in its products floating down the Grand River to the company plant on Saginaw Street. "Experience soon taught," reported the *Journal,* "that the elm logs became so heavy from lying in the water that a large number escaped their destiny ... [and] floated down the Grand River to Grand Rapids, where they were doubtless taken out and made into furniture." The firm learned to season its lumber and, under Stebbins' leadership, diversified its product line; in addition to wheelbarrows—about 10,000 annually by 1890—its products included "Reynolds' Improved Warehouse Trucks," "Herbert's Patent Horse Pokes," and rubber-tired wheels. Its president, Edward W. Sparrow, was one of Lansing's leading citizens.

A bird's-eye-view map of Lansing in 1890 shows the extent to which it had become a factory town. The limits of the city were Pennsylvania Avenue on the east, Main Street on the south, Logan on the west, and Willow on the north. These were the limits of housing; beyond them in all directions was a vast rural hinterland. Industrial firms clustered along the banks of the Grand River, spanned in 1890 by bridges at River, Shiawassee, Saginaw, and Franklin streets and Michigan and Washington avenues.

Three blocks from the iron bridge at the foot of River Street, near the south bend of the Grand, were the buildings of Pliny F. Olds and Sons, manufacturers of gasoline engines. This firm, destined to play a crucial role in the development of Lansing's industries, had difficulty remaining afloat in its early years; in 1885, Olds saved his company with a timely loan of $1,500 from Professor Robert Kedzie of the agricultural college. The firm's first business was that of repairing steam engines, by then widely used in industry and agriculture; by the late 1880s, it had begun to manufacture its own vertical steam engines of three, five, and 10 horsepower. A "gasoline engine" of that period was actually a gasoline-fired steam engine, not an internal-combustion engine.

Two blocks upstream, at the foot of Washtenaw Street, stood the plant of Clark and Company, manufacturers of carriages and farm wagons. This firm, founded in 1881 by Albert and S.E. Clark, had operated Lansing's first large factory; by 1890, it was turning out about 5,000 carriages annually, including the "No. 1 Extension Phaeton," whose features included steel axles, oval-edged steel tires, hand-buffed leather top, English broadcloth cushion and back, and grain leather on fenders and dash. Two blocks north, just east of the Michigan Avenue bridge, stood the huge yard and sawmill of the Lansing Lumber Company. From Shiawassee to Ottawa, also fronting on the river, were the impressive works of the Bement Company, which occupied two full city blocks.

Two additional wagon companies—the Bush Road Cart

Workers outside the Bement Plant. The company, founded in 1868, manufactured stoves and agricultural implements. From the Wiskemann Collection.

63

Company and the Lansing Wagon Works—occupied adjoining sites three blocks north of the Bement works. The Bush Company made a specialty of its "fine phaeton cart," whose features included "upholstered cushions, spring back and leather dash, front and back sides being entirely enclosed, thus excluding mud." The firm also manufactured a "very fine, light, speedy track cart, weighing about seventy-five pounds." The Lansing Wagon Works, which had been founded in 1875, grew more rapidly for a time than the Bement Company; it kept a constant stock of two million board feet of lumber for its line of farm and team wagons, carriages, and buggies.

Other firms—some destined to future prominence—dotted the landscape. The Lansing Iron Works, later Jarvis, Barnes, and Company, founded in 1872, manufactured stationary steam engines; the Lansing Wheel Company, founded in 1885 by W.K. Prudden, made wheels for vehicles of all kinds, "from the lightest sulky up to farm wagons, drays, and omnibusses."

The Lansing of 1890 changed quickly. Shortly before his death in 1928, J.W. Bailey—long active in Lansing real estate—remembered the city as it appeared in that year. "There was a horse car in town when I started business here," he wrote, "just one horse car, and that was all." Electricity was little used; there were few telephones and no public sewer system. The six-story Hollister Building, then the Capital National Bank Building, was the tallest in town; the Downey Hotel still kept a stove in the middle of its lobby. The city hall and post office had not yet been built; city business was conducted from the second floor of what later became the Consumers Power Building at 110 West Michigan Avenue. A tintype gallery, and later a "fried cake shop," which peddled its wares all over town from a three-wheeled cart, occupied the future site of the Hotel Olds. Peace was kept by the town marshall, as the police department did not come into existence until 1892.

During the decade that followed, the city would acquire not one but two rival and competing telephone companies, and not merely more horsecars but a system of electric streetcars that grew at the end of the decade into part of a comprehensive interurban system of electric street railways serving a large area of central Michigan.

Telephone service was the first of these modern conveniences to reach the city. There is a bit of local lore in early telephone history; a Lansing dentist and inventor, Dr. George H. Richmond, had perfected a voice transmitter, and succeeded in transmitting a human voice over a 230-mile loop of telegraph wire between Lansing and Detroit. Richmond obtained his patent about a year after that obtained by Alexander Graham Bell, but he was unable to raise capital in Lansing to finance a telephone venture, and his device languished. Telephone service came to Lansing, however, in 1880. The manager of the Jackson branch of the Telegraph and Telephone Construction Company agreed to construct an exchange in Lansing if 50 people subscribed; 60 signed on, and the service soon expanded to 100. The first commercial telephone was at the Lansing House. In 1893, the Citizens' Telephone Company appeared, and until the Bell system

absorbed its competitor in 1923, Lansing was served by two competing telephone companies. In the early days, telephone service operated only from 7:00 a.m. to 10:00 p.m., except for emergencies. The city's first telephone directory, published in 1893 by a Boston firm, contained names but no numbers.

The city's municipally owned water system had its origins in the 1880s. In 1883, Mayor William Donovan appointed a committee of distinguished citizens to discuss the possibility of establishing a waterworks. The committee, whose members included Edward W. Sparrow, George Ranney, James Turner, and A.O. Bement, hired a Kalamazoo civil engineer, W.R. Coats, to recommend a system. Coats found that the city stood astride a natural basin with an ample water supply that could easily be tapped by a system of deep wells. Coats also reported that the natural water pressure of a pipe driven into the ground was "greater than anything in this country or Europe," and that the water had "unsurpassed flavor." The committee, after visiting waterworks in other communities, finally recommended a privately owned system. But Mayor Donovan and A.O. Bement insisted on public ownership, a principle approved by an overwhelming vote on January 26, 1884. The city thus created the Board of Water Commissioners, and in April 1886, the board began pumping water through 16 miles of mains.

Since the public water system worked well, sentiment grew for a publicly owned electric service. Electricity had been generated in Lansing since 1883, when the Piatt Brothers, who had operated an illuminating-gas company, set up the Lansing Electric Light and Power Company which provided limited service in the downtown area. When it was found that the city was paying $104 annually to power each of its 90 streetlights, compared with an average of $75 paid by 25 other communities, the movement for municipal power gained headway. Mayor Bement strongly urged municipal ownership in his May 1892 inaugural address. The issue was debated vigorously, and at a special election held in July 1892, the voters approved the city's purchase of the Lansing Electric Light and Power Company. Electric service was placed under the management of the Board of Water Commissioners, which then became known as the Board of Water and Electric Light Commissioners, and later as the Board of Water and Light.

Even after public ownership, there were complaints about electric service. In September 1893, the *Republican* criticized the "penny wise and pound foolish" practice of shutting down electric service after 10:00 p.m. The city had 3,000 convention visitors, reported the *Republican*, who were camped on the state fairgrounds; "should one of them have cause to come downtown after dark, the chances are that, unaccustomed to the streets, he would hardly find his way back to the campgrounds." Some citizens threatened to build bonfires for illumination. "It is high time," concluded the *Republican*, "that [Lansing] lay aside her village ways and assume metropolitan customs."

Important advances in public transportation occurred in the 1890s. Beginning in 1866, a series of horsecar companies, none of which survived very long, offered service

BELOW: **Clarence E. Bement, son of Bement Company founder Edwin Bement. The Bement Company, which manufactured agricultural tools, grew to be the largest industrial firm in Lansing in the mid-1880s. Courtesy of Lansing Public Library.**

BOTTOM: **Gasoline-powered steam engines being shipped from the Pliny F. Olds and Son Gasoline Engine Works on River Street, Lansing, circa 1895. The Olds Engine Works sold 2,000 of these units in just five years. Courtesy of the Michigan State University Archives and Historical Collections.**

CENTER: **William Donovan, an engineer by profession, served as mayor of Lansing from 1884 to 1885. Courtesy of Lansing Public Library.**

TOP: **Workers assembling spoked wheels at the Lansing Wheelbarrow Company, circa 1900. For several years the wheelbarrow company was the largest consumer of wood in the Lansing area. Courtesy of Michigan State University Archives and Historical Collections.**

ABOVE: **A.O. Bement headed the Bement Company, Lansing's first large industrial firm. Bement was active in public affairs and served as mayor of Lansing from 1892 to 1893. Courtesy of Michigan State University Archives and Historical Collections.**

65

along Washington Avenue. In January 1886, a reliable company, the Lansing City Railway Company, received the city's franchise for horsecar service. In 1890, H.L. Hollister and M.D. Skinner bought the company and electrified its line; the first trial run of the electric line took place on August 26, 1890. The firm was acquired by absentee owners in 1892, and service began to deteriorate. While the introduction of the electric cars had caused a sensation, the equipment soon became dilapidated, and Lansing's streetcar service became known as the worst in the state.

The 1890s began with good economic news, and the prospects for continued economic growth seemed excellent. In July 1892, the *Journal* reflected on the sound and steady growth that had characterized Lansing's economic history. "Lansing has not boomed," it said, as had many other Michigan towns. "But her growth has been steady and sure, until she has taken rank among the first commercial centers in the interior of the state, making her future assured beyond peradventure." Early in 1893, the *Republican* reported the previous year "the brightest ever known in Lansing's history." In 1892, Lansing's population had increased more than that of any other city in the state. Employment was high, "for nearly every manufacturer ... has been forced to extend the capacity of his workshops and build new capacity to meet the demands." And several new industrial firms—including the Lansing (formerly Ionia) Pants and Overall Company—had recently moved to Lansing.

But despite the upbeat economic reports of the press, the clouds of depression were lowering. Community leaders were making every effort to bring new businesses into the city. A Lansing Improvement Association, successor to an organization of the same name in the 1870s, accumulated a cash reserve in a real-estate transaction and began offering inducements to business firms to locate in Lansing. In January 1893, the association sent 4,000 letters to firms in Michigan and neighboring states asking, "Are you satisfied with your present location and business advantages? If not we will furnish you with a site and erect suitable factory building thereon." The letter pointed out the advantages of Lansing, including "four big railroads at your door" and a site "within one half-mile of the business center of the city."

Such inducements brought at least two new firms to the city: the Lansing Pants and Overall Company in August 1892, and the Hammell Cigar Company in April 1893. With the arrival of the latter company, Lansing became a national center of cigar manufacturing and also acquired one of its more colorful business and political figures, James Hammell, who became famous for lighting his cigars with dollar bills as he strolled into his favorite watering place on Michigan Avenue.

As the depression deepened, the cigar industry became one of the few bright spots in the city's economy. A *Republican* report of October 1893 gives a sense of the scale of cigar manufacturing in Lansing, one of the forgotten aspects of the city's industrial history. "The largest consignment of leaf tobacco ever brought to Lansing," reported the *Republican*, "was delivered to the Hammell

Company by the Grand Trunk Railroad." The 50,000 pounds of tobacco—two full carloads—were loaded on six huge wagons and paraded down Washington Avenue; each wagon "bore a banner informing the public of the character and contents of its load." The tobacco in that consignment was used only as binders for the company's cigars; the finished product would require an equal quantity of fillers and wrappers.

In the spring of 1893, a banking panic occurred in Lansing. On April 18, the Central Michigan Savings Bank suspended operations, and a run began on the city's remaining five banks. Banking leaders met at the Hotel Downey and agreed to demand the 90-day notice allowed by law for the removal of savings deposits. At the opening of business on April 19, a large crowd gathered at the Ingham County Savings Bank and there began, as reported in the *Republican*, "one of the most savage onslaughts ever experienced by a Lansing bank." By 10:00 a.m., the crowd had reached such proportions "that it was evident that steps would have to be taken to quell the excitement." Theodore C. Sherwood, the Michigan Banking Commissioner, left his office to assure the crowd that "the Ingham County Savings Bank was built upon rock and capable of paying every dollar of liability." Sherwood denounced one of the bank's leading stockholders who, "frightened by the supposed danger, had withdrawn several thousand dollars and precipitated the run." The crowd cheered Sherwood frequently; when he finished, "the throng dispersed quietly and contentedly, and during the rest of the day nothing more than the usual banking business was done."

Despite Sherwood's assurances, however, the Ingham County Savings Bank closed on August 6, 1893. Two Lansing banks had closed within four months; in July 1896, a third—the People's Savings Bank—also wound up its affairs. The bank failures had a devastating effect on community morale and helped inculcate a "depression mentality" in some persons for years afterward. The remaining assets of the failed banks were placed in the hands of receivers. In April 1898, the depositors of the first failed bank, the Central Michigan, received 86 cents on the dollar; those of the Ingham County and People's Savings Banks received 60 and 59 cents, respectively.

Some Lansing firms continued to do well until 1895, and upbeat reports still appeared in the press. "Despite the financial stringency," reported the *Journal* in April 1893, "the development of this city has been phenomenal." The Bement Company apparently fared well; in January 1894, it shipped "the largest consignment of goods ever made by an establishment of this city"—a solid trainload of cars loaded with plows and harrows that attracted a crowd of visitors. In a five-day period, the company shipped 24 carloads of agricultural implements, "without perceptibly disturbing the storage room at their factory."

The Lansing Wheelbarrow Company did less well. "Yes, the dull times have affected us some," conceded its manager, Arthur Courtland Stebbins; "we are at present with only half a force, and I really see little if any encouragement before next year." The bank failures seem to have placed Lansing squarely in the grip of the depression; there was little good economic news until a national upturn became apparent in 1898. In addition to the banks, the leading local casualty of the depression was the Lansing Lumber Company, which was forced into bankruptcy.

The failure of the banks, the heavy unemployment, and other economic problems inevitably led to recriminations. In January 1898, the press reported the conviction of one Christian Breitsch, a director of the People's Savings Bank, on the technical charge of having falsely sworn that "he was the bone fide owner of ten shares of stock unpledged to any other debt as required by the state banking law."

The *Journal* regretted the prosecution of Breitsch, as he had had no part in the tangled management of affairs that caused the failure. The banking system—badly in need of overhaul—and the climate of "flush times" before 1893, argued the *Journal*, were the real culprits. Lansing's banks, it charged, had "too much faith in the profit-making capacity of some of our local industries, in founding and developing which much of the money of the banks was swallowed up." The bankers, before 1893, "took things too easy" and allowed matters to run along "as long as deposits kept up and the 'cash on hand' was sufficient to meet legal and banking requirements."

The year 1896—the low point of the depression—was memorable for the completion of city hall and a dispute over the adoption of standard time. "As nearly everyone in Lansing noted," said the *Republican* in April 1896, "the new city hall began striking the hours yesterday and struck them on standard time." Standard time had been introduced by the railroads early in 1896, but some locals continued to use "sun" or local time, which varied 20 to 25 minutes from standard time. To complicate matters further, Lansing was near the western edge of the eastern time zone, and for a time some local firms insisted on using central standard time. Eventually, eastern standard became the legal time.

The election of 1896—the last of the exciting political campaigns of the 19th century—pitted Democratic-Populist candidate William Jennings Bryan against Republican William G. McKinley in a debate on gold versus silver. The money issue had split the Democrats; the *Journal*, which normally supported Democrats, upheld gold and opposed Bryan. Despite the opposition of both the *Republican* and the *Journal*, Bryan carried Ingham County by 500 votes. In August, Bryan visited Lansing; a parade to greet him formed near the Michigan Central station and reached as far west as the Grand Avenue bridge. Bryan spoke to enthusiastic Lansing crowds at the Star Theater, the old post office, the Downey Hotel, in front of the capitol, and in a big tent at the corner of Cedar and Michigan avenues.

Two novels of the late 19th century, both by local authors, were set in the Lansing area. A. Arnold Clark's *Beneath the Dome*, published in 1894, is a period piece that recounts the failure of its hero, a young legislator named Oliver Arkwright, to persuade the Michigan legislature to pass reform legislation in line with the single-tax theories of Henry George, then very much in vogue and obviously favored by Clark. *Chronicles of Break O'Day* by E. Everett Howe, originally published in 1893, is a capital-region example of the "local color" movement in American literature. Howe's main character, a Major Ratke, farmed land in a desolate part of Ingham County that local residents recognized as the area around Johnson's Swamp, about four miles west of the present city of Leslie. Many of the incidents in the novel were based on actual events of the 1870s, including the peddling of "Bohemian oats"—seeds that would allegedly quadruple a farmer's yield per acre. The "Bohemian oats" scandal, in fact, gave rise to a series of lawsuits that ultimately reached the Michigan Supreme Court.

A third and rather more significant Lansing writer of the late 19th century was Sarah Ellen Van De Vort Emery, the subject of recent research of Professors Pauline Adams and Emma S. Thornton of Michigan State University. Mrs. Emery, who was involved in many of the reformist crusades of the late 19th century, published two books—*Seven Financial Conspiracies* (1887, 1892, and 1894) and *Imperialism in America* (1892). The large sales of both volumes—400,000 and 50,000, respectively—attest to her wide influence among her contemporaries.

Seven Financial Conspiracies fed the growing debate on currency that culminated in the bitterly fought election of 1896; the fact that William Jennings Bryan, the Democratic-Populist candidate, carried Ingham County despite the opposition even of the local Democratic newspaper suggests that Mrs. Emery's writings did have considerable local influence. Mrs. Emery was also one of the founders of the State Equal Suffrage Association in 1884, served as a delegate to the Michigan Greenback Party Convention of 1884 and the first National Labor Union Convention in 1887, and edited a monthly eight-page Populist newspaper, *The Corner Stone*, from 1893 until her death in 1895.

In the midst of the economic distress—perhaps, in part, because of it—rivalry between Lansing and other communities in its hinterland heightened and occasionally became strident. Rivalry was especially acute between Lansing and Mason, 12 miles to the southeast, the seat of Ingham County since 1840. It seemed incongruous to some Lansing residents and to both newspapers that the "metropolis" of the area and capital of the state should not also have the county seat.

Typical of this thinking was a January 1893 editorial in the *Journal*. "The seat of government is coming to Lansing sooner or later," it argued; erecting an adequate city hall and county building "would greatly hasten the day." The *Journal's* additional arguments must surely have offended the citizens of Mason. Many residents of that community, it claimed, would actually prefer not to be "encumbered" with the county seat. The *Journal* attributed to Mason businessmen the position that "the uncertainty which surrounds the location of the county seat disturbs property values in the city, and upsets calculations generally." In fact, the *Journal* claimed, "the effect of depending solely on the court house to boom the town is just what is consuming many Michigan towns with a dry, consuming rot." In neighboring Shiawassee County, Corunna, the county seat, was languishing, while Owosso forged

67

The Rise of Industry

ahead, secured manufacturing enterprises, "and became a town of importance." And in Eaton County, Grand Ledge "has nearly doubled in size," while Mason "has lingered in the old rut." The sooner Mason gets rid of the courthouse, concluded the *Journal,* "the better off her citizens will be."

The issue of locating the county seat in Lansing had hung fire for years. In 1877, 500 persons had crowded into a meeting hall as the county board of supervisors failed to garner the required two-thirds majority to place county-seat location before the voters. With the completion of Lansing's city hall in 1897, the issue arose again; the press reported an informal discussion of the advantages and disadvantages of locating in Lansing as the county board visited Lansing's new city hall. The supervisors from Mason had voted against accepting the invitation to visit the new city hall, denouncing it as "the entering wedge by which Lansing men hoped to start the movement in favor of removing the county seat."

During the informal discussion, John Robson, A.O. Bement, Judge Mason D. Chatterton, and M.D. Gilkey presented Lansing's case, pointing out the many advantages of locating the county seat in the capital city. The city would offer the county space in its new city hall on attractive terms; the county would be relieved of the expense of returning prisoners to Mason after trial in Lansing. George Sanders of Mason defended the existing location, also in economic terms. "It would be necessary to build a new sheriff's residence and jail in Lansing; the cost would be $25,000 in Lansing but only $10,000 in Mason," the difference reflecting higher land values in Lansing. While many of the supervisors favored placing the county seat in Lansing, their constituents did not, and a motion to place the issue on the ballot failed to obtain the needed two-thirds majority. Both Lansing papers engaged in an ugly dispute on the county-seat issue with the *Ingham County News,* the Mason weekly founded in 1859 by David B. Harrington. "The tales of an aged fishwife are marvels of veracity," claimed the *Republican,* "when compared with the county seat stories published in the *News.*"

A proposal to enlarge Lansing's membership on the county board led to a list of "remonstrances" against Lansing, submitted to the board by Mason Supervisor J.T. Campbell. "Giving Lansing more supervisors," one remonstrance read, "would be dangerous for the county." Lansing was ambitious, said another, "which is not only a detriment to the county but to itself." Campbell pointed to Lansing's huge municipal debt of $490,000, insisting that out-county residents "do not want the city to have a representation on the board ... which will involve upon us debts or enormous expense." And some felt that giving Lansing more power on the board would make county politics, normally relatively peaceful, as quarrelsome as those of Lansing. "Lansing fights with everybody," said Supervisor Walt of Delhi Township, "including its street railway company, and its citizens are always protesting against its common council."

Lansing Mayor Russell C. Ostrander dismissed the remonstrances as contemptible. "You know how petitions or remonstrances are secured," he said, "they are dictated

by the county seat." The fact is, he continued, "that Mason is in its decadence; ... people in that city know that, and in fact everybody knows that." Such rhetoric did not endear Lansing to the out-county area, and the city did not get additional representation on the county board.

In the midst of the county-seat crisis and an uncertain economy, Lansing celebrated the 50th anniversary of its selection as state capital. The subdued celebration evidently reflected the mood of the citizenry, who were all too aware of Lansing's reputation as a "bankrupt city." Mayor Ostrander's moving address omitted the customary boosting of the city and dealt instead with the "undefinable yet tangible manner" in which having the capital had made Lansing a unique community.

"A community is not to be judged alone," said Ostrander, "by its wealth, its manufactures, or the size of its population." Lansing was a political town. Since the capital was located here, 30 legislative sessions and three constitutional conventions had met in the city, and 16 (actually 15) United States Senators had been chosen. The State Supreme Court had held its annual sessions in Lansing since 1858; and Lansing men and women "first gave benediction and God speed" to Zachariah Chandler, Austin Blair, and other hallowed figures of the recent past.

All this, continued the mayor, "has a direct effect on the inhabitants of the community." There had been in Lansing "a quickening of the mental and moral atmosphere ... [that] leavens the intelligence of the inhabitants, as in university towns." Ostrander described a phenomenon familiar in other capital cities and even county seats. "The doors of the legislative process have been open to the people," he said. "There has been the personal watching of contests, the actual contact with the actors." Lansing was still a relatively small town in 1897; the legislature and courts were often the best show in town. Legislative sessions and court trials often drew crowds; many ordinary citizens either worked for or had frequent contact with legislators or saw them in hotels and restaurants; judges, governors, and other public officials were familiar figures on the streets. Both local papers covered state affairs more fulsomely than any others in the state, no doubt reflecting the interests of their readers. Visitors often remarked that ordinary citizens were astonishingly familiar with the intricacies of legislative and judicial matters and public policy generally.

Early in 1898, a slow recovery began, and plans for expanding streetcar systems all over lower Michigan into "interurban" systems were discussed in the press. A system that would link Lansing to many of the villages and small towns in the area would confer an enormous economic advantage, a fact not lost on Lansing's commercial interests. "We have passed through the slough of the despond," wrote an anonymous contributor to the *Journal* in January 1898, "and when those new electric roads commence to be built, I shall be very much surprised if the old town doesn't experience something strangely like a boom."

Later in January, franchises for electric car lines from Lansing to St. Johns and Ann Arbor were awarded; to some small-town merchants, the news was the crack of doom. "The time is fast approaching," warned the *Portland Observer,* "when ... small towns ... will be like the four-corner settlements of thirty or forty years ago in this state." The electric roads were coming—"it won't be long before these roads will be laid through the farming country as thick as the railroads are now"—and trade "would then go away from small places like Portland and Mason and go to Lansing." A few years later, the interurban line from Lansing to St. Johns was completed, and it had precisely the effect anticipated: in the early years of the 20th century, Lansing's wholesale and retail trade increased at a rate far in excess even of its manufacturing industries.

The decade ended with an economic upturn and a mood of optimism. The Spanish-American War of April to August, 1898, one of the most popular in American history, diverted attention from local problems. The outbreak of the war inspired patriotic effusions in the capital region that evoked memories of 1861; Henry R. Pattengill, editor of the Michigan *School Moderator* and a popular speaker, gave a memorable patriotic address at the armory. Lansing's own Company E of the 31st Infantry was mobilized in April; the regiment trained at Camp Eaton near Island Lake, and was later sent to Chickamauga, Tennessee, and Macon, Georgia. In January 1899, after the war had ended, the 31st was ordered to Cienfuegos, in southern Cuba, where it lost 14 men to yellow fever. The unit did not see combat.

In February 1898, the *Journal* published the replies of businessmen and citizens to the question, "What is the best thing that will make Lansing grow?" One F.B. Johnson proposed "an adjustment of the defunct bank matters"; George W. Stone suggested "confidence and loyalty—stand by one another—patronize local industry." F.M. Alsdorf urged a major campaign to advertise Lansing's advantages and attract capital. "We know what the city was when the wheel works, the iron works, the Lansing lumber works, and many other idle plants, were operating at their full capacity. Get these things started up again and Lansing will grow."

One "anonymous influential business man" displayed a remarkable prescience. He noted that while the economy had picked up somewhat during the previous year, it was still sluggish. But things had improved, and "Lansing is now at the point where a move in the right direction is sure to get things moving at a lively rate and bring good results." What Lansing needed was "something to get things going, and then the town will grow. I don't pretend to know what that thing is, but I'd like to find out."

"Something to get things going" was indeed in the offing. Before very long, the city would emerge as the national center of a completely new industry, and would experience growth and prosperity on a scale beyond the wildest imaginings of 1898.

TOP LEFT: **Admiral George Dewey, who commanded the victorious American fleet in the Battle of Manila Bay during the Spanish American War, received a hero's welcome in his tour of American cities. Dewey and other dignitaries may be seen to the left of the group of women who formed a "living" American flag on the capitol steps. Courtesy of Michigan State University Archives and Historical Collections.**

ABOVE: **Russell C. Ostrander served as mayor of Lansing in 1896. Ostrander later became chief justice of the state supreme court. Courtesy of Lansing Public Library.**

FAR LEFT: **The Thoman Milling Company, 125 East Ottawa Street, Lansing, was built by Frederick Thoman in 1869. Courtesy of Michigan State Archives.**

ABOVE: **James Hammell, a cigar manufacturer, was one of the city's most popular men. Hammell served as mayor of Lansing from 1900 to 1903. During his term the city began replacing board sidewalks with crushed stone and gravel bases. Courtesy of Lansing Public Library.**

Chapter 8

TOP: **This model of the 1897 Olds horseless carriage was the first gasoline-powered vehicle produced in Lansing. Courtesy of the Oldsmobile Division, General Motors.**

CENTER: **Manufacturers often promoted early automobiles with photographs of celebrities riding in them. In this photograph, Mark Twain is seated directly behind Roy D. Chapin. Chapin, who was born in Lansing in 1880, was employed by Olds and later became the president of Hudson Motors. Courtesy of the Oldsmobile Division, General Motors.**

BOTTOM LEFT: **The first Reo Roadster, built in October 1904. Courtesy of Michigan State University Archives and Historical Collections.**

TOP: **The curved-dash Oldsmobile was placed on the market in 1901. Courtesy of the Oldsmobile Division, General Motors.**

CENTER: **Oldsmobile's entry in the 1908 Glidden Tour. The Glidden Tours, held annually from 1905 to 1913, demonstrated the reliability of automobiles. Courtesy of the Oldsmobile Division, General Motors.**

BOTTOM: **Oldsmobile 1915 Touring Car, No. 2. Courtesy of the Oldsmobile Division, General Motors.**

RANSOM E. OLDS AND THE HORSELESS CARRIAGE

The neighbors and friends of Pliny F. Olds, proprietor of an engine shop on River Street in Lansing, often warned him about his younger son, Ransom Eli. Young Olds was an inveterate tinkerer, and more than one neighbor told his father "that kid of yours will blow his head off one day."

The Olds family had moved to Lansing from Parma, Ohio, in 1864. Young Olds apparently left school in the tenth grade; while still in school, he served as an apprentice in his father's shop. He would arise at 5:00 a.m., light fires at home and in the shop to have steam ready when work began, attend school, and return to work in the shop at 4:00 p.m. In 1883, he completed a six-month course at Bartlett Business College in Lansing and was later employed in the family business as a bookkeeper and machinist. When Wallace Olds, the elder of Pliny Olds' two sons, decided to sell his half share in the family business in 1885, Ransom gave his father $300 and a promissory note for $1,100 and became a partner.

The engine shop had had difficult years. For a time, its main business was repairing steam engines, but it had made a small beginning in manufacturing. When Ransom Olds became a partner, the firm began concentrating on the production of gasoline-fired steam engines, a device especially useful to those who required intermittent engine power, as its "flash boiler" could generate steam in about five minutes. The device caught on; the firm sold 2,000 units in five years, enlarged its plant, and began to prosper.

Sometime in the summer of 1887, apparently in an effort to find new uses for his company's steam engines, Olds began to experiment with a horseless carriage. Olds' first carriage, a three-quarter-ton, rear-axle-driven, tiller-steered contraption, was powered by his company's gasoline-fired steam engine. The three-wheel design, Olds later wrote, made steering easy; he had obtained "the finest cut gears made" to avoid noise; and on a summer day of 1887, Olds started the engine as a crowd watched. Olds "realized that I had a colt on my hands, and did not care to have too many spectators." The next morning at 3:00 a.m., he "got up steam ready for a start"; at 4:30, the doors of the River Street engine works were opened, Olds operated the lever, and the vehicle moved slowly out. It picked up speed going down a ramp, but balked at a slight rise near the pavement. Olds dismounted, "gave the vehicle a push to be remembered, which did the business," and the vehicle ran a whole block before it stopped again. By then it was getting light, and Olds was anxious to avoid curious onlookers. "I secured two pushers from behind," he remembered, "and together with the engine, got it back without accident, which ended my first trip in a horseless carriage."

Olds continued to experiment with the horseless carriage for the next three or four years while carrying on his duties at the engine works. He replaced the one-horsepower engine with one of two horsepower, which also proved inadequate. Olds dismantled the carriage and built a second one in 1892, this time using a four-horsepower engine. The new vehicle performed well on good roads but "had no back gear for hill climbing"; Olds recalled that he "dreaded the sight of a hill." The 1892 model, considerably more advanced than the 1887 machine, looked like a surrey; its up-front seat concealed water and gasoline tanks adequate for a run of 10 or 15 miles. Two connected steam engines powered the device; it ran quietly and, according to an observer, "emitted no steam as a result of an ingenious contrivance of the inventor." With the vehicle's machinery concealed, there was nothing about it "to scare horses," said Olds; they "did not seem to mind it any more than an ordinary carriage."

Olds was only one among many inventors tinkering with horseless carriages, and the Scientific American sent an observer to examine the machine. "Mr. Olds states that his machine never kicks or bites," reported the observer, "and never tires out on long runs, and during hot weather he can ride fast enough to make a breeze without sweating the horse." This national publicity led to the first export of an American self-propelled vehicle; the Francis Fine Company, a London patent-medicine firm, asked that the car be shipped to its offices in Bombay, India. It is not certain that the vehicle ever arrived at its destination—one account claims that the ship containing it was lost at sea, and another that the vehicle arrived safely and gave good service for a number of years—but the episode is significant, for it was not merely the first export of an American automobile, but the first to be sold anywhere.

Olds did not manufacture this vehicle in quantity, in part because he recognized the limitations of steam engines, and also because the engine company demanded his time. The internal-combustion engine, perfected by Gottlieb Daimler in 1885, seemed to promise far more reliability than the steam engine, and Olds immediately understood its implications for the horseless carriage. Boiler problems and the delay in generating pressure made steam engines far less flexible than internal-combustion devices, which had already begun to replace steam engines in industry and agriculture.

By 1892, Olds—with the assistance of his brother Wallace, who had returned to Lansing, and Madison F. Bates, a skilled machinist at the Olds engine factory—had devised his own internal-combustion engine. The Olds company needed capital to manufacture the new device, and several Lansing business leaders, including Edward W. Sparrow and Samuel L. Smith, purchased shares in the engine company. For several years, Olds continued to spend his time manufacturing stationary gasoline engines; not until 1896 did he resume experimenting with a self-propelled vehicle.

In an article in the Michigan Engineer's Annual in 1898, Olds described his third vehicle, which was powered by an internal-combustion engine. This vehicle "was always ready at a moment's notice"; there was no

Ransom E. Olds and The Horseless Carriage

delay in generating steam. To start the device, "all one has to do is turn the motor over and draw in a mixture of gasoline and air, which is ignited by an electric spark." The engine would then run continuously, "and the driver needed only to throw the lever to different points to back, stop, or start the carriage without any reference to the motor or mercy on the horse." To stop the engine, it was necessary only to throw a switch.

The vehicle, "in constant use during the past one and one half years," weighed half a ton, including its 400 pounds of machinery. It carried three gallons of gasoline and had a cruising range of between 25 and 50 miles, depending on road conditions. It could attain a speed of 12 to 15 miles an hour, and required "little more care than an ordinary carriage." The vehicle could be stopped "by turning the speeding lever to the backing point, without any reference to whether the motor is stopped or not." Since 12 miles an hour was then considered a terrifying speed, Olds assured his readers that the vehicle could be stopped in a distance two or three times its length, "as the reverse can be used in addition to the brakes." Collisions, said Olds, were less likely on city streets than with horse-drawn vehicles, "as the [horseless] carriage is always under perfect control and [is] not like a horse which may get frightened or shy at some passing object."

The new vehicle was a handsome contraption. Olds had its body constructed by Clark and Company, wagon manufacturers, whose works were a few blocks north of the engine shop. A *Republican* reporter inspected the vehicle and went for a ride with Olds. "The first thing that strikes the eye is the beauty of the vehicle," he wrote. The dark green, red-trimmed, leather-upholstered body was "finished in the highest state of the carriage builder's art." It performed splendidly—"hill climbing and other severe tests being successfully met by the motive power"—and the reporter did not doubt "that the much mooted question of the horseless carriage has been successfully solved by Messrs. Olds and Clark."

But there was no possibility of manufacturing a significant number of the vehicles, as the engine company was swamped with orders for its popular gasoline engines. Olds concluded that additional capital and a new organization were needed, and he invited a group of Lansing investors to join him in forming the first company organized in Michigan for the specific purpose of manufacturing motor vehicles. On August 21, 1897, a new firm—the Olds Motor Vehicle Company—was organized in the offices of Edward W. Sparrow, who was already a stockholder in Olds' engine company. The first meeting of the directors of the new company produced a document that has become famous in the history not only of Lansing but of the automotive world. For years a plaque inscribed with the following entry from Arthur Courtland Stebbins' minutes of the directors' meeting was displayed on the wall of the coffee shop of the Hotel Olds:

It was moved by Mr. Stebbins that R.E. Olds be elected manager for the next eleven months. Carried.

It was moved by Mr. Stebbins that the manager

be authorized to build one carriage in as nearly perfect a manner as possible and complete it at the earliest possible moment. Carried.

The new company announced that it would use the premises of the engine company until a suitable factory could be built, and that it would manufacture only engines and transmissions and purchase bodies and wheels from other firms. The automobile company, however, did not prosper. A dispute arose when many of the engine company's employees joined the machinists' union, which demanded better wages and working conditions; the company apparently met some of the demands but refused others. When Olds learned that his brother Wallace, manager of the engine company, sided with the workers, he dismissed him and purchased his stock. Richard H. Scott, who would become a major executive in Olds' automotive enterprises and a leading citizen of Lansing, succeeded Wallace Olds as manager of the engine factory.

The engine company did well after the autumn of 1898, even as the automobile company faltered. The engine-factory workers objected to the dismissal of Wallace Olds, and for a time a slowdown reduced production; but business improved considerably in 1899 and 1900, as the market expanded and more engines were made and sold. Meanwhile, the automobile company produced only six cars; Olds, believing that a fantastic market existed for his machine, sought to raise additional capital to expand manufacturing facilities. But local investors, who were willing to invest in Olds' engine ventures, were skeptical about automobiles, and Olds was forced to look elsewhere for capital to save his faltering automobile company.

He began negotiating with investors in Detroit, Buffalo, Newark, Chicago, and Indianapolis, and finally accepted the offer of Samuel L. Smith of Detroit. Smith, who had lived in Lansing and had been familiar with Olds' work on horseless carriages from the beginning, agreed to a complicated transaction in which a new company, the Olds Motor Works, absorbed the stock of both the Olds Gasoline Engine Company and the Olds Motor Vehicle Company. Olds agreed to locate the new company in Detroit, and by August 1900 a new factory on Jefferson Avenue near Belle Isle was ready for production.

But even the new company's start was not promising. The first vehicle produced, a $1,250 "improved model" of the 1896 carriage, sold poorly, and Olds spent much time experimenting with 11 different cars, including electric vehicles that were sufficiently perfected to cruise up to 35 miles on a battery charge. Seeing that a relatively expensive automobile would not sell, Olds began to plan a simple-to-operate, inexpensive-to-maintain vehicle that could sell for substantially less than $1,250.

Sometime in the fall of 1900, Olds went to the office of his engineer, Horace F. Loomis, and told him that "what we want to build is a small lowdown runabout that will have a shop cost of about $300 and sell for $650." Olds sketched a car body with a curved dash; Loomis "cleared his desk" and drew a plan of the car. Milton Beck, a design engineer, planned an engine, and Loomis designed a planetary transmission, "getting the idea from a small water-meter mechanism which I had picked up."

By October 1900, the first curved-dash car was ready for testing. The two-seat vehicle, started by a crank on the driver's side and powered by a rear-mounted, one-cylinder, four-cycle engine, was steered by a tiller and rolled on wire-spoked, pneumatic-tired wheels at one reverse or two forward speeds. The vehicle was undoubtedly a winner, but Olds was still uncertain whether the car developed by his design team would be a commercial success. The company had been moving toward electric cars, and the curved dash was only one among many models it offered for sale in 1901.

Then occurred a fortuitous incident that changed everything. On Saturday, March 9, 1901, fire struck the factory; within minutes, the walls of the building collapsed. Tradition has it that one curved-dash vehicle was the only car rescued from the fire, thus forcing Olds, when production resumed, to concentrate on that model. Whatever its origin, the decision to concentrate on manufacturing the curved-dash car was a fortunate one. As Fred A. Smith—son of Samuel L. Smith and, for a time, an associate of Olds—later wrote, the decision to concentrate on the curved-dash car "put an end to experimenting and chasing after strange electric gods and led to the mass production of a successful motor vehicle."

With its factory destroyed, the company needed new facilities; and the Lansing Business Men's Association—predecessor of the present Chamber of Commerce—saw an opportunity to attract Olds back to Lansing. Harris E. Thomas, president of the association, visited Olds in Detroit and offered a 52-acre tract, the old state fairgrounds, as a factory site. Olds accepted. In August 1901, he agreed that construction of an assembly facility would begin immediately, with a foundry and other buildings to be added later; 400 workers would be employed at

first, with the number gradually reaching 1,200. Olds moved back to Lansing to supervise the construction of his factory, and at the same time to arrange for the building of his mansion on South Washington Avenue, a Lansing landmark for many years until its demolition in 1966 to make way for I-496. Within four months of the agreement, the new factory was in operation, and by the end of 1901 an astonishing 425 curved-dash runabouts had rolled out of the factory. Olds production techniques—in which the cars moved on rolling platforms through the assembly process, with parts bins placed where needed—anticipated the assembly line.

Olds was a genuine pioneer of the automobile industry. His cars, named Oldsmobiles in 1900, did much to popularize the motor car with the American public and to "democratize" automobile ownership, previously limited to the very wealthy. Olds established a network of dealers to facilitate distribution, and his insistence on cash sales helped stabilize the automobile industry in its early chaotic years. Olds also stressed advertising. Ads that appeared in the national press after 1902, featuring slogans such as "nothing to watch but the road" and "the best thing on wheels," helped popularize the Oldsmobile and promote sales. Races and endurance runs—including the famous California to Detroit jaunt of Eugene Hammell and L.L. Whitney—drew public attention to the car. In 1902, the company turned out 2,500 cars, and in 1903, 4,000 vehicles were produced and sold. Wealthy and prominent persons, as well as ordinary citizens, bought curved-dash Oldsmobiles.

The company prospered. Within three years of its founding, the Olds Motor Works became the leading American automobile manufacturer, and Lansing the center of the automobile industry. Discord arose, however, between Olds and Fred and Angus Smith, sons

ABOVE: **Curved-dash Oldsmobiles on parade, 4th of July, 1904. Courtesy of Michigan State University Archives and Historical Collections.**

RIGHT: **Ransom E. Olds became a partner in his family's engine business in 1885. Mr. Olds is shown here at the peak of his automotive career, circa 1908. Courtesy of Michigan State University Archives and Historical Collections.**

Ransom E. Olds and The Horseless Carriage

of Samuel L. Smith, the majority stockholders in the Olds Motor Works. Olds and the Smiths apparently disagreed about what kinds of cars the company ought to produce. By 1903, the popularity of family or touring cars, which could carry luggage and four or five passengers on long trips, became apparent; the curved-dash Oldsmobile, which looked like a horseless carriage, was becoming obsolete. Disagreement first arose when Olds, in charge of the Lansing plant, learned that the Smiths were making major company decisions in Detroit without consulting him. At the January 1904 meeting of the board of directors, Olds, having been passed over as vice-president and general manager, resigned from the board and sold his stock. After his resignation, the Olds Motor Works did not do well, and in 1908 it was acquired by General Motors.

Olds did not remain "unemployed" very long—his name was already a household word, and his connection with any automotive enterprise would go far toward ensuring its success. In August 1904, a new company was incorporated; it was announced that construction of a new Lansing factory building would begin in a month, and that by January 1905, 1,000 men would be employed. The new firm took the name "The R.E. Olds Company." The Olds Motor Works protested at once. "In our opinion and in that of our attorney," complained the Olds Motor Works, "the use of the name 'Olds' by you in any automobile company, is clearly an infringement of our rights." Olds denied "that I sold them my name" and insisted that the name "R.E. Olds Company" would never be mistaken for the Olds Motor Works. After much discussion and to avoid legal difficulties, however, the name was changed to the Reo Car Company.

Early in September 1904, factory construction began on a Washington Avenue site south of the Grand Trunk Railroad depot. Soon three production buildings and an office were completed, and by mid-October an experimental Reo, as the new cars were to be called, was completed. The new $1,250 crank-started touring car was powered by a two-cylinder, 16-horsepower, double-opposed engine and equipped with heavy wooden artillery wheels, a steering wheel, and a concealed radiator. The company also produced a scaled-down version for $650.

After some initial difficulty in creating a dealer network, the company began to prosper; by March 1905, a new Reo was rolling off the assembly line every 40 minutes. In 1906, the company delivered 2,458 cars and paid a 35-cent dividend on every share of stock as well as a 50-percent stock bonus. In 1906, Olds and his associates—E.F. Cooley, Edward W. Sparrow, C.B. Wilson, R.H. Scott, and Horace T. Thomas—organized the National Coil Company to manufacture jump-spark coils for gasoline engines. Later that same year, Olds organized and became president of the Michigan Screw Company; Hugo Lundberg of the Detroit Screw Company became its general manager. The Atlas Drop Forge Company, another Olds enterprise, was also organized in 1906.

The Reo Car Company continued to do well, despite the sharp recession of 1907—one casualty of which was the Bement Company, the firm that had paced Lansing's industrial growth in the 1880s. Reo produced about 4,000 cars in 1907 and continued to grow until 1910, despite the early demise of many automobile companies. In 1911, Olds purchased the remaining assets of the Bement Company. The Reo Motor Truck Company, organized by Olds in 1910, began operations in the old Bement plant and produced more than 900 trucks in 1911; by 1916, truck production had increased by 300 percent.

While the truck company did well, the Reo car, basically unchanged since 1904, began to lose popularity. In 1911, Olds, compelled to make major changes in his car line, announced the "Reo the Fifth." Olds described the new vehicle as his "farewell car," claiming that it could never be improved upon. The car, which sold for $1,195, was equipped with a windshield, top, and self-starter. Despite the new model, the company never recovered its share of the market, and Olds, increasingly involved in his Florida real-estate holdings and other ventures, left the management of the company to Scott.

Olds had established two successful automobile companies as well as several firms in the automotive-parts field, a considerable achievement in view of the abbreviated careers of many automobile companies. By a recent estimate, more than 1,000 American companies manufactured automobiles at one time or another; few survived for any length of time. Even in Lansing, there were several abortive automobile ventures. In 1899, Madison F. Bates, a former Olds employee, along with James P. Edmonds and J. Edward Roe, began the Bates Automobile Company. The company produced only 25 of its $2,000 touring cars; its slogan, "Buy a Bates and Keep Your Dates," did not help sales. The company continued to manufacture engines as the Bates and Edmonds Engine Company. In 1903, Frank Clark of the Clark Carriage Company, who had supplied automobile bodies for Olds, began production of the Clarkmobile, a one-cylinder runabout; the company produced about 1,000 units before folding its automobile business. Two of Clark's associates—William H. Newbrough and Harris Thomas—manufactured about half a dozen New Way cars before deciding to concentrate on engine manufacture. There were several other abortive Lansing auto ventures about which little is known, including a car called the Greenleaf by Smith Clauson, an engineer.

In June 1944, at a large municipal tribute to R.E. Olds on his 80th birthday, Frank N. Arbaugh, one of the founders of Lansing's first complete department store, reflected on what Olds and the automobile industry had done for Lansing. Olds, by then a venerated automobile-industry pioneer, had established two successful Lansing automobile factories "even before the vehicle was called an automobile." Arbaugh did not doubt that "this was the great epoch in the industrial life of Lansing," and that the modern industrial history of the city had begun. Arbaugh, in a litany familiar to a Lansing audience, mentioned some of the firms that had arisen in the city as a direct result of Olds' influence—among them, the Auto Body Company, National Coil Company, Motor Wheel Company, National Screw Company, Atlas Drop Forge, Lansing Stamping Company, Dail Steel Products, Capital National Bank, and the Lansing Lawn Mower Company.

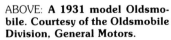

LEFT: **A curved-dash Oldsmobile in front of the Downey Hotel just before its departure for an endurance run. This vehicle was shipped to California and driven to New York in 1904. Courtesy of the Oldsmobile Division, General Motors.**

BELOW: **The Olds straight-dash body shop in 1905. Courtesy of the Oldsmobile Division, General Motors.**

ABOVE: **A 1931 model Oldsmobile. Courtesy of the Oldsmobile Division, General Motors.**

RIGHT: **An Oldsmobile 1922 Sportsman's Roadster. Courtesy of the Oldsmobile Division, General Motors.**

Chapter 9

THE AWAKENING OF LANSING

The advent of the automobile industry abruptly ended the torpor and uncertainty of the 1890s. So swiftly did new factories appear where there had been vacant land as to leave local residents incredulous. Benjamin Franklin Davis, president of the City National Bank, wrote in 1905 that the Reo Car Company "seemed to rise out of the ground a year ago," and new factories and enlargements of old facilities were going up everywhere. "I fancy if some of our quiet citizens should see some of these activities ... they would rub their eyes and wonder how they had slept through such a noise." The *Journal* assured its readers that "the prosperity that was lost has returned, with redoubled vigor." Not only was Lansing's old reputation as "bankrupt city" forgotten, but the city was becoming "the central point around which revolves the entire business of central Michigan."

Although a large share of the city's industrial output consisted of automobiles and automotive parts, the economy was nonetheless quite diversified. The *Republican*, in its 50th anniversary issue of 1905, listed 59 products made in local factories. "The variety of Lansing's manufactured products," it said, "is one of the greatest sources of satisfaction." In addition to automobiles and accessories, Lansing's 1905 labor force of 4,300 workers produced products that included stoves, mirrors, wax models, tents and awnings, rugs, cement blocks, cigars and cigar boxes, electric coils, low-water alarms, showcases, castings, windmills, water tanks, veneered doors, and cream separators. And with the city's preeminence in automobile and general manufacturing came a major advance in jobbing and the wholesale trade.

The city took great pride in the scale and sophistication of its modern factories and its newly won prestige as the dynamic center of a major new American industry. "A trip through the huge plant," wrote a *Republican* reporter after a tour of the Olds Motor Works, "impresses one with the immensity of the efforts that the American people can invoke." The Olds factory covered one million square feet, employed 1,500 workers, and assembled cars with 1,300 parts, "each of which must move in perfect unison with its 1,299 relatives." The *Journal* published, as though for incredulous readers, every fresh proof of the city's growing stature as a progressive and prosperous manufacturing town. "It is remarkable the prestige the city has acquired," wrote the sales representative of a Lansing automotive-parts firm in 1905. "At place after place at which I called, as soon as I stated I was from Lansing I was given much more consideration." Lansing automobiles, he said, "have a great reputation, and the city is closely watched for new things in the automotive field."

With the economy on the black side of the ledger and signs of prosperity everywhere, a new confidence crept into the boosting of the city. "Time was," admitted the *Republican* in 1907, "when Lansing people felt called upon to apologize for their city. ... But it's different now." A new municipal slogan—"A Larger, Livelier, and Lovelier Lansing"—was adopted, apparently at the suggestion of the Lansing Business Men's Association, and the phrase "Greater Lansing" was used for the first time— not in its modern sense of a large market area, but of a Lansing great in stature and prestige.

In 1905, the *Journal* proudly described the city's advantages for the benefit of firms contemplating relocation. Lansing offered not merely "magnificent city and state institutions," but a new $150,000 post office, a superior school system with 14 "ward schools" and two parochial schools—one German Lutheran and one Roman Catholic—and a total of 23 churches. The city had two banks, the City National and the Lansing State Savings; these "had weathered many storms, are on a solid basis, and are officered by some of our keenest business men." There were two telephone companies, express and telegraph offices, a new Carnegie Library, a fine opera house, and the newly opened Bijou Theater. The city also had "well equipped police and fire departments," publicly owned water and electric service, more than 60 fraternal organizations, and "no rival as a convention center."

The city's growth strained credulity. From 1890 to 1900, Lansing's population had grown from 12,202 to 16,845, with most of the increase apparently occurring early in the decade. By 1901, population reached 18,000, and by 1905, it was 29,000. In the five years preceding 1905, Lansing's industries—which included 82 incorporated companies in 50 different industries—doubled their work force and increased the value of their output by 134 percent. "Lansing today," concluded the *Journal*, "is the center of a hard-working, prosperous and enterprising set of manufacturing, retailing, and professional institutions, with new enterprises springing up as if by magic." Moreover, Lansing continued to be an attractive city with a high proportion of homeowners. "To the strangers within our gates," the paper continued, "a surprising impression greets them in viewing the fine, clean, and wholesome aspect of the houses ... in every direction of the city." There was "no sordidness," except in isolated cases, and most streets were "well paved and shaded by foliage."

That life in Lansing moved to a new beat is evident in a

A view of the state capitol from Michigan Avenue near Washington, circa 1915. The six-story structure on the left is the Prudden building, which was destroyed by fire in 1920; the Bijou theater, down the street on the left, burned down in 1924. The City National Bank building was razed and replaced by the Bank of Lansing, which was completed in 1932. Courtesy of Michigan State University Archives and Historical Collections.

The Awakening of Lansing

1905 *Journal* description of a new phenomenon in the city—the evening rush hour. With most of the new factories clustered around downtown and the work force recently doubled, there was considerable traffic congestion. Shortly after 5:00 p.m. "the crowd invades the street with a rush," and from then until 6:00 p.m. "it eddies and flows in a din and confusion." Most streetcar passengers carried dinner pails; throngs of office and store employees stood at every corner of downtown; huge wagons, rushing by with their last load of the day, and "impatient automobiles," which did not yet dominate the traffic even of this automobile city, heightened the "hustle and bustle" of downtown and the surrounding area. To the reporter, the evening rush hour was "a glorious picture of industrial thrift"; each person who carried a dinner pail had "the satisfaction of being a breadwinner in a city that is pushing to the front in every way."

A greatly improved system of streetcars and interurban lines eased access of workers to factories, increased Lansing's share of retail trade, and integrated the economic and social life of the community. "Lansing's street car service has not always been all that could be desired," wrote Davis in 1905, recalling the problems of the 1890s, "but all this is changed and now the equipment and service compare favorably with other cities." In April 1906, the Michigan United Railways, a syndicate that owned city and suburban lines in other areas of Central Michigan, acquired the Lansing city and suburban lines.

The Michigan United Railways improved facilities and service. Parts of Michigan and Washington avenues were double-tracked, and the company built a large repair facility at Shiawassee and Cedar streets. In addition to providing regular and fast service to St. Johns and intermediate points, as well as service within the city, the company operated two "streetcar resorts"—one at Waverly Park in Lansing and another at Pine Lake, now Lake Lansing, in Haslett. Waverly Park, reported the *Journal*, "is pleasantly situated on the Grand River, about three miles southeast from the city ... on a piece of wooded land, gently sloping down to the river." Its facilities included a hotel, refreshment stands, music pavilions, playing fields, and boating facilities; special attractions included balloon ascensions, band concerts, and dramatic performances.

The easily accessible streetcar resorts drew crowds from a wide area; a total of 6,000 persons attended the opening day of Pine Lake resort in July 1905. "Many who wanted to go to Pine Lake were disappointed," reported the *Journal*, "because they could find no place on the cars." Later in the decade, crowds of 10,000 persons at both resorts were not unusual.

The streetcars made large gatherings possible and created a new kind of community life in Lansing, especially during the summer. Memorial Day, the Fourth of July, and Flag Day were invariably celebrated by parades attended by thousands; a new holiday, Labor Day, first observed during the 1890s, began to rival the Fourth of July as a community observance. If in recent years Labor Day has marked a mass exodus from the city for a final summer fling in distant resorts, in the early 20th century the holiday had the opposite effect and drew a crowd. An esti-

mated 10,000 persons attended the Labor Day celebration of 1905 despite bad weather; a parade of union members—carriage makers, building laborers, carpenters, glass workers, moulders, plumbers, painters, printers, electrical workers, butchers, bricklayers, cigar makers—took an hour to pass the reviewing stand.

Three miles to the east of downtown Lansing stood the agricultural college. Its fortunes had improved dramatically with the return of prosperity, and it was now a source of considerable local pride.

For two generations, the college, its campus surrounded by a high board fence, had lived in splendid isolation in the midst of a vast agricultural region. The community that was to become the city of East Lansing—the professors and their families—lived in Faculty Row, a campus cluster of nine homes built between 1857 and 1885. Today only Faculty Row No. 7, for years the home of Professor William James Beal, the distinguished botanist, still stands; it is now Cowles House, the residence of Michigan State University President Cecil M. Mackey.

The faculty, whose interest in scientific agriculture made them agrarian fundamentalists or celebrants of rural life, found isolation congenial. The faculty, and especially the faculty wives, were eager to set the students an example of righteous living, and the distance from Lansing made access to its saloons and worse temptations difficult. But as the area grew and prospered, the macadam road to Lansing and the trolley line ended the isolation, and increased enrollment at the college forced many younger faculty members to seek housing off campus.

The first move off campus was a real-estate venture of Beal and Professor Rolla C. Carpenter. Their subdivision, an area of 15 acres near Michigan Avenue and Harrison Road, was known as Collegeville. It did not provide water or sewer service and attracted few faculty members. In the next decade, other subdivisions—College Delta, Brooks' Addition, and Oakland—were platted and sold, and a community began to grow. In 1903, with the platting of the College Grove subdivision, the new community began to spread east of Abbott Road.

The first step toward the creation of East Lansing was not the chartering of the city, but the organization of a community school district—a problem complicated by the fact that Abbott Road, the dividing line between Lansing and Meridian townships, ran through the community. Children in the western portion of the community attended the Brickyard School of Lansing Township, while those in the eastern part of the community attended Marble School, operated by Meridian Township. The opening of the new Central School entailed legal and political battles, with some adherents of the Marble and Brickyard schools in bitter opposition. Finally, the legislature authorized a new school district for the college community, and in December 1901, the Central School opened on West Grand River Avenue in what is now East Lansing.

The community continued to grow, demands for city services increased, and in time a movement developed for incorporating the college community as a city. In March 1907, a bill to incorporate the "City of College Park" was

RIGHT: **Races and endurance runs were an important means of promoting early automobiles. Two Oldsmobile racers, ready to depart, are seen here in front of the Hotel Downey in 1910. Courtesy of the Oldsmobile Division, General Motors.**

CENTER LEFT: **Lansing Fire Department in front of the Central Fire Station in 1912. The department acquired its first motorized fire engine in 1908, but chose to retain one horse-drawn apparatus. Courtesy of Michigan State Archives.**

LEFT: **Lansing's Department of Public Safety in 1912. The man standing toward the front in the center of the group is Chief Alfred Seymour. Courtesy of Michigan State Archives.**

ABOVE: **Workers of the final assembly division at Olds Motor Works, 1910. The "assembly line" consisted of sawhorses. Oldsmobile's 1910 Limiteds, with 42-inch wheels and huge engines with five by six-inch cylinders, were produced at a rate of six per day. Courtesy of the Oldsmobile Division, General Motors.**

The Awakening of Lansing

submitted to the legislature.

A hearing before a committee of the Michigan House of Representatives showed that some residents strongly opposed incorporation. At the hearing, according to the *Republican*, a "physical clash" nearly occurred between Charles B. Collingwood, postmaster of the college and leader of the incorporation forces, and L.B. Gardner, an attorney retained by the opposition. Gardner had argued that a recent postcard poll of residents on the issue of incorporation was invalid, since "the cards were withheld from those who opposed incorporation." Collingwood objected, and, in a heated exchange, each called the other a liar. Beal and John Deloss Towar, an agricultural scientist and early historian of East Lansing, joined Collingwood in leading the movement for incorporation.

The opposition included one Horace B. Angell, who, with his partner Charles H. Chase, owned 97 acres of choice residential land in the heart of what is now East Lansing. Angell and Gardner proposed a new plan—annexation by Lansing. Among the advantages of such a move, they argued, would be "public water and sewer systems, sidewalks, and . . . a government conducted for the benefit of the community." The college would be "belittled," said Gardner, by placing it in a small town of only 500 people when it could as easily be a part of Lansing.

The argument continued at a second hearing before the house committee on city corporations. Residents favoring incorporation, said Collingwood, were heavily in the majority, with 81 taxpayers in favor and only 26 against. The house committee, still doubtful that the little community ought to become a city, apparently changed its mind after the appearance of the college president, Jonathan L. Snyder. Snyder declared that the sanitary conditions of the village were such that the college would soon be forced to stop admitting students it could not accommodate on campus, and that the college authorities strongly favored incorporation. Snyder's views carried a great deal of weight, and the committee reported in favor of incorporation.

Other hurdles remained, however, before the new city could begin its official life. The house committee, displeased with certain features of the proposed city charter, insisted on changes. The committee was unable to support charter provisions that called for a popular referendum on all city ordinances, conferred great powers on the mayor, and, most important, outlawed the sale of liquor not merely in the incorporated area but for some distance around it. The amended charter created two wards instead of one, resulting in a total of four aldermen instead of two. There would be no popular referendum on city ordinances, and liquor sales could be prohibited only within the incorporated area.

The name of the proposed city was also a matter of some debate. President Snyder urged "East Lansing," on the grounds that a College Park already existed in Maryland, and post office approval was unlikely. The *Republican*, which supported incorporation, also endorsed "East Lansing," as the name would "doubtless expedite the handling of mail, and give people generally a better idea of the location of the agricultural college." The house, however, rejected "East Lansing" and approved "College Park." A deadlock ensued when the senate approved "East Lansing"; Governor Frank M. Warner suggested the compromise name of "Bird Center." In the end, both houses agreed on East Lansing.

There were still further legal complications. The charter bill had inaccurately described the city's boundaries, and an amended bill had to pass both houses, creating another two-week delay before the city could elect officers and create an administration. Finally, on June 15, 1907, residents of the city of East Lansing held their first nominating caucus, on the front lawn of the schoolhouse. On June 18, the voters supported the unopposed slate of candidates, and Clinton D. Smith became East Lansing's first mayor.

While the residents of East Lansing wanted an effective city government to provide water, a sewerage system, and police protection, the issue of liquor seems to have been decisive. Lansing had saloons and all the problems associated with the traffic in liquor; East Lansing citizens, overwhelmingly sharing the social values of sobriety and righteous living of early-20th-century progressives, were determined to exclude demon rum. In fact, East Lansing remained dry until 1968.

Some of the original charter provisions—such as the one that required a popular referendum on all city ordinances—reflected the progressives' suspicion of politicians and their determination to return the control of government to the people. And incorporating rather than accepting annexation by Lansing was a symbolic act, in a sense retaining some of the isolation, the sense of apartness, that had characterized the life of the college community since the 1850s. Very early in its history, East Lansing conceived of itself as a special place, a unique community. As Lawrence Kestenbaum, East Lansing's historian, has written, "A headquarters for scientific agriculture, an academic enclave, and a self-proclaimed exemplary residential community, East Lansing was convinced of the possibility of a better world and determined that the first steps be taken at home."

About two weeks before East Lansing elected its first officers, the agricultural college celebrated its 50th anniversary. (The college elected to celebrate the anniversary of its opening in 1857 rather than its founding in 1855.) The week-long celebration culminated in a visit by President Theodore Roosevelt on May 31, 1907, an event that drew an even larger crowd than Cornerstone Day in 1873; it was observed as a celebration not merely of the college but of Lansing and the entire capital region.

Many years after the event, Dr. LeMoyne Snyder, son of Michigan Agricultural College President Jonathan L. Snyder, wrote that as early as 1900 his father had begun planning the celebration of the semicentennial. "Now Dad was a great admirer of Theodore Roosevelt," said Snyder, "and what could be better than to have President Roosevelt come . . . and deliver the Fiftieth Anniversary Address to the graduating class?" In the spring of 1906, when LeMoyne Snyder was nine years of age, he accompanied his father to Washington to visit Roosevelt. After getting their shoes shined by a bootblack outside the Willard Hotel, Snyder and his son took a horse-drawn hack to the White House, where they were greeted by House Speaker "Uncle Joe" Cannon and ushered into Roosevelt's office. Snyder "extended the invitation to Roosevelt," and he accepted on the spot.

The plans for the semicentennial proceeded. "This was such a tremendous event," said Snyder, "that I believe it is perfectly safe to say that it has never been duplicated before or since." As May 31, the day of Roosevelt's visit, approached, the press reported a flurry of preparations. The Olds Motor Works and the Reo Car Company agreed to provide 10 cars for the use of Roosevelt and other dignitaries; Secretary E.V. Chilsom of the Lansing Business Men's Association, anticipating that hotels would be crowded with visitors, arranged for private homes to receive the overflow. Factories and many businesses announced that they would remain closed on "Roosevelt Day."

The semicentennial provided the occasion not only for a presidential visit, but also for a series of meetings that assessed the state of the college and the plight of agricultural education. It was obvious that the college, at the time of its golden anniversary, had succeeded; that agricultural education, which it had done so much to create, was a highly respected and well-established endeavor; and that Michigan Agricultural College enjoyed widespread support among the citizens of the state. In contrast, Beal, in a retrospective address, remembered his arrival in May 1870 to teach a summer course in botany.

He got a ride with a farmer, "and on the way soon learned that many farmers within twenty miles placed a low estimate on the value of the state farm, as it was then called." At that time, the college was "young, poor, and small." No faculty member had a chair to himself, "but a whole settee"; the professor of botany also taught history.

The week-long celebration began on Sunday, May 27, with a baccalaureate sermon by the Reverend Matthew Henry Buckham, president of the University of Vermont, in the college armory, which was decorated for the occasion in the college colors of green and white. The college officials, reported the *Republican*, spared no trouble to make the campus live up to its reputation as the most beautiful in America. The reporter noted "a general well kept appearance" in the drives and walks, flower beds, "the absence of dead foliage on the trees," and "the inviting velvet-like appearance of the grass." An open-air platform for Roosevelt's speech had been placed just east of Snyder's house; the platform, on a slight eminence, looked out over a natural amphitheater, affording anyone within half a mile a good view of the speaker. The main campus buildings—the library, Williams Hall, the Abbott Halls, and the new Women's Building—had been outlined with light bulbs, and a string of lights was placed in the trees near Faculty Row. "The effect of the illumination," wrote the reporter, "is very brilliant ... and it will call forth admiration from all who witness it."

On May 31, Roosevelt's train arrived at the Lake Shore Depot on East Michigan Avenue at 9:59 a.m., nine minutes late; he was greeted by Governor Frank Warner,

Jonathan L. Snyder, president of Michigan Agricultural College from 1896 to 1915, favored the incorporation of a college city in 1907. He urged the legislature to call this city "East Lansing," rather than "College Park." The name "East Lansing" was eventually agreed on by both houses of the committee. Courtesy of Michigan State University Archives and Historical Collections.

Benjamin Franklin Davis, for years one of Lansing's most respected and influential citizens. He was one of the founders of the City National Bank in 1886. From the Wiskemann Collection.

The interior of the Lansing Grand Trunk-Western Railroad Depot on South Washington Avenue. The depot, completed in 1905, was praised by city planner Harland Bartholemew as being Lansing's finest railroad depot. The railroad discontinued passenger service in the late 1960s, and the depot has since been remodeled for use as a restaurant. Photograph by author.

The Awakening of Lansing

Lansing Mayor Hugh Lyons, and Snyder. After an informal reception, Roosevelt and the other dignitaries drove three blocks to the capitol through densely crowded streets; Roosevelt stopped to commend some of the soldiers on their smart appearance. At the capitol, Roosevelt addressed the legislature, the first president to do so; he readily agreed to address a large crowd from the balcony.

The party then drove to the college, with Roosevelt riding in a Reo car driven by R.E. Olds, accompanied by Snyder and his private secretary, William Loeb. Roosevelt agreed to the automobile ride, a novel gesture at the time, as a way of bringing attention to the Lansing automobile industry; upon learning of the rivalry between the Reo Car Company and the Olds Motor Works, Roosevelt suggested that he return to the depot in an Oldsmobile. At 11:45 a.m., the presidential party approached the west entrance of the campus, toured the grounds, and parked on the lawn near the speaker's platform. A luncheon was served at Snyder's flag-bedecked house; the guests included President Horace B. Angell of the University of Michigan, the members of the State Board of Agriculture, and several legislators.

Thousands of persons had arrived on the campus before the presidential party; at 1:30 p.m., a formation of gray-clad cadets performed evolutions in front of the speaker's platform. As the vast crowd awaited in eager expectancy, Roosevelt and the dignitaries "issued from the house," and a tremendous cheer went up "in unison with the waving of flags, banners, and handkerchiefs." After an invocation by the Reverend E.N. Lake of the First Baptist Church of Lansing and a musical selection by the Bach Orchestra of Milwaukee, Snyder introduced Roosevelt, whose long address, interrupted often by cheers and applause, extolled the dignity of manual labor and the mission of agricultural education. At 4:15, Roosevelt boarded an Oldsmobile for his return to the Lake Shore Depot.

"Roosevelt Day" was an extraordinary success and has become one of the most remembered events in the history of the area. For years afterward, the Reo Car Company distributed large copies of a photograph of Roosevelt, Snyder, Loeb, and Olds in a Reo car. It seemed that everyone from miles around came to Lansing or the campus to see Roosevelt, and Cornerstone Day was no longer the gauge of a Lansing crowd. "Today a new standard was established," said the *Republican,* "and 'the day that Roosevelt was here' will serve for comparison for all crowds that come to Lansing in the future."

Perhaps the most extraordinary municipal event ever held in Lansing was the mass basket picnic of July 5, 1915, which celebrated the gift of Potter Park to the city. Judge Edward Cahill suggested the picnic; Mayor J. Gottleib Reutter enthusiastically supported the plan and appointed a committee on arrangements. The press and the committee were determined to make the event a publicity stunt—"the largest basket picnic ever held in the United States." The committee proposed to mark the event as a novel one by transporting the entire population of the city to the park in automobiles. The *State Journal,* in repeated editorials, urged car owners to "give a lift for Lansing."

The plans for the picnic included a band concert, balloon ascension, a dedication ceremony, logrolling contests, and a gigantic tug-of-war between teams representing the "north side," as North Lansing came to be called, and the east side. The *Journal* of July 3 published a photograph of a formidable north-side team, captained by Art Leonard, an employee of the Auto Body Company, which "had broken two ropes and was testing a third." Leonard said that "his biggest worry" was getting a rope strong enough to pull "Doc" Cochrane, captain of the east-siders, "out of the mud." Cochrane, a dentist, was reputedly the strongest man in the city.

The picnic was even more successful than expected; a total of 25,000 people attended despite the coldest July 5 in memory. A high wind swept the "aeronaut" through the treetops as he began his ascent; the east-side team apparently won the tug-of-war. The dedication speeches of W.K. Prudden, B.F. Davis, Judge Edward Cahill, and Mayor Reutter left no doubt that the purpose of the gathering was to celebrate the city's prosperity. "For those who recalled the troubles of 1893," said Davis, "the growth of Lansing to its present proportions is especially significant, and its possibilities almost immeasurable."

As though the extraordinary mass basket picnic, which attracted national attention, were not enough, a "municipal barn dance and moon light festival" celebrated the completion of the roof over the Farmer's Market later in July. And in addition to these special events and holiday attractions, there were such recurring summer attractions as the circus and chautauqua. The June 5, 1915, parade of the Barnum and Bailey Circus was three miles long. The circus paraphernalia arrived on five trains with a combined length of one mile, and its 28 tents covered 14 acres.

The traveling or circuit chautauqua, a successor to the lyceum of the 19th century, was from 1910 to 1917 a regular feature of summer life in Lansing. The traveling chautauqua offered a three- to nine-day program of musical and dramatic events in communities on its circuit. The chautauqua got off to an uncertain start in Lansing; that of 1910 appears to have been poorly attended. In 1911, however, the Lansing Chautauqua Assembly presented a nine-day program, from June 24 to July 2, in a tent at a ball park at Kalamazoo and Walnut streets. Senator Robert M. La Follette of Wisconsin spoke on "Popular Government," President George E. Vincent of the University of Minnesota on "The Larger Unselfishness," and the labor leader John Mitchell appeared. The most popular chautauqua lecturers were "inspirational"; Russell Herman Conwell's "Acres of Diamonds" was delivered 6,000 times in chautauquas all over the United States, including Lansing. In 1912, William Jennings Bryan, three-time presidential candidate and soon to become secretary of state, appeared in what may have been the high point of Lansing's chautauqua. Tickets for Bryan's appearance were sold out three weeks in advance.

A somewhat less edifying form of entertainment was the carnival. Carnivals were occasionally sponsored by fraternal organizations for fund-raising purposes, in which case they were exempt from the customary city fee of $100—a

LEFT: On May 31, 1907, President Theodore Roosevelt visited Lansing in celebration of the Michigan Agricultural College semicentennial, drawing a crowd even larger than that of Cornerstone Day in 1878. College President Jonathan L. Snyder and Roosevelt are seated in the rear of the car; R.E. Olds and Roosevelt's secretary, William Loeb, are seated in the front. Courtesy of Michigan State University Archives and Historical Collections.

ABOVE: The executive board of Lansing Business Men's Association, 1912. The association, predecessor to the Lansing Regional Chamber of Commerce, had pursuaded R.E. Olds to return to Lansing after the Detroit fire. Courtesy of Michigan State Archives.

RIGHT: J. Gottlieb Reutter served as a member of various governmental boards and commissions for 48 years, and served as mayor from 1912 to 1917. During World War I, Reutter guided the city in a period of anxiety and unrest. Courtesy of Lansing Public Library.

The Awakening of Lansing

policy that sparked some controversy. "The city would be better off without any entertainments of this sort," claimed the *Journal*, "for as a whole they are neither elevating nor instructive and the influence they exert is anything but beneficial." The *Journal* wondered how the city attorney could possibly construe carnival companies, with their snake charmers, hamburg vendors, and "man-eating lions," as coming under the heading of "municipal concerts or fairs."

Far more controversial was the issue of "demon rum," which in the early years of the 20th century revived and became one of the capital region's epic political battles.

As a result of the temperance crusade of the 1840s and 1850s, Michigan had passed a prohibition law; it was not enforced, however, and in 1875, Michigan repealed prohibition. The Women's Christian Temperance Union and the Prohibition party kept the issue alive, but not until the formation in the 1890s of the Anti-Saloon League, which worked mainly through churches, was there an effective anti-liquor crusade.

Saloons and breweries had long thrived in Lansing, often in conflict with the authorities. In 1893, Mayor A.O. Bement, a factory owner concerned with the drinking habits of some of his employees, vigorously enforced city ordinances regulating the hours during which saloons might operate, as well as state laws that outlawed liquor sales on Sundays, holidays, and election days. The saloon keepers fought back. In February 1893, the *Republican* reported a secret meeting of "Lansing Saloonists," who had raised "the black flag of war" against Bement. The mayor, the saloonists complained, had persisted in enforcing the law, with the result that "at present all bars are closed promptly on time and no liquor is sold during the time prohibited by law." Later that year, the mayor, angered over increased arrests for drunkenness and a wave of fights in certain bars, warned saloon keepers that "an accurate tab" would be kept on future incidents and that owners who wished their licenses renewed should keep their premises in better control.

As the city's economy and population grew after 1900, so did the number of bars, and the Anti-Saloon League emerged as a powerful state organization with a paid staff and headquarters in Lansing. Securing "local option" or prohibition in Lansing, the organization believed, would go far toward advancing the cause of prohibition in the state and nation. The "drys," who organized their campaign down to the precinct level, secured local option in 1910; in 1912, the "wets" won the local-option election, and the saloons reopened. In 1914, the drys revived the issue, and the saloons were closed a second time.

But the issue would not go away. In 1915 and 1916, the wets regrouped and forced the issue to a fourth vote. A heated campaign, in which no one could remain neutral, preceded the largest vote in the city's history on April 3, 1916. The Ingham County local-option fight took on national proportions as the Ingham County Local Option Committee, on behalf of the drys, announced that "Ingham County is to be the center of an anti-saloon fight that will reach through Michigan between now and April 3 and extend to every Congressional district in the land." The

drys organized their campaign around school districts. Committee leaders listed every voter as wet, dry, or doubtful, and exhorted the "pronounced drys" to win over the "doubtfuls" with "a pitch of enthusiasm which will bring them to the polls regardless of weather."

Lansing's elite, reflecting its New England origins, and most of the city's churches were strongly dry. Clarence Bement, then manager of the Novo Engine Company, joined other business leaders at a dry rally at the Franklin Avenue Presbyterian Church. "I defy anyone," said Bement, "to point out one thing the city has lost by being dry." Bement claimed that there was far less drunkenness, despite the presence of "blind pigs" which dispensed liquor illegally, and that "Lansing as a city is far more orderly and temperate than when the saloons were wide open."

Of all the Lansing dry leaders, none achieved the effectiveness of Henry R. Pattengill, one of the city's most admired citizens. Pattengill, at a dry rally at the Reo plant, asked how liquor could make "a larger, livelier, and lovelier Lansing." Harris E. Thomas, a Reo executive, argued that the return of booze "would be the worst thing that could happen to the large industries of Lansing." In addition to its adverse effect on employees' personal lives, alcohol would promote accidents. Factory machines needed steady hands, and liquor would cause an increase in the cost of liability insurance.

The Liberty League, organized by the wets, matched the drys in the organization and intensity of its campaign. The appearance at a wet rally of the Reverend Wallace M. Short of Iowa City, a wet Congregationalist minister, was something of a triumph. The Reverend Mr. Short, speaking as "a Christian minister and American citizen," denounced prohibition "as a wrong means of achieving temperance." Short claimed that he was "born a prohibitionist" but saw the light and gradually changed his views. Former Senator Edgar F. Hansen of Maine, speaking at the same rally, described the failure of prohibition in his state. Prohibition, he said, had the effect of substituting illegal for legal access to liquor, with disastrous results. "Throw out one saloon," said Hansen, "and a dozen blind pigs, speak-easies, and blind tigers come into being."

As the day of decision neared, Walter S. Foster, an attorney and member of the local-option committee, challenged the wets to a public debate on the topic, "Shall the manufacture of liquors and the liquor traffic be prohibited?" After lengthy negotiations, the two sides agreed on a set of rules and scheduled the debate for March 31 at the Prudden Auditorium.

The rules give a sense of the intensity of the issue. "The price of peace at the coming debate," reported the short-lived *Lansing Press*, "is a set of rules as long as a motorcycle will run on a gallon of gasoline." So that neither side would pack the house, tickets were distributed evenly; wet and dry adherents were to sit on opposite sides of the auditorium. Each side agreed not to misquote the other; a stenographer was to make a verbatim transcript of the proceedings for later publication. It was announced that Pattengill would speak for the drys, and Congressman J.C. Meeker of Iowa, a famous orator, would represent the

LEFT: The issue of prohibition was bitterly debated in early 20th century Lansing. This placard was displayed during the fourth and decisive vote on local option, held on April 3, 1916. From the Wiskemann Collection.

BELOW: The chemistry building of Michigan Agricultural College, 1912. Courtesy of Michigan State University Archives and Historical Collections.

ABOVE: Henry R. Pattengill (1852–1918), one of Lansing's leading citizens, was editor and publisher of the *Michigan School Moderator* and served as Michigan Superintendent of Public Instruction from 1893 to 1896. A fearsome and popular orator, his favorite topics included education, temperance, and patriotic themes. Pattengill Street and Pattengill Junior High School are named for him. From the Wiskemann Collection.

RIGHT: The second Wells Hall (1906–1966) replaced an earlier structure which had burned down in 1905. This building, first a men's dormitory and later an office structure, was divided into six separate parts to reduce the danger of fire, decrease noise, and discourage the practice of running down long corridors. Courtesy of Michigan State University Archives and Historical Collections.

85

The Awakening of Lansing

wets.

"While waiting," reported the *Press*, "Henry R. and Meeker were chinning over President Woodrow Wilson's handling of the Mexican question and the submarine issue." Promptly at 8:00 p.m., the "two gladiators," each followed by about 40 adherents, made their way to the stage. In Meeker, Pattengill found a worthy adversary; the *Press* reporter described him as "considerable of a platform speaker—eight years he's been at it for the wet side." Meeker knew the arguments, had a fine speaking voice, stage presence, "and a whole bagful of tricks."

In the end, the debate seemed anticlimactic, with both sides claiming victory. Those who came to see a sharp conflict were disappointed; Meeker and Pattengill apparently liked each other. In a sense, they did not debate. "Congressman Meeker," said the *Press*, "talked about all the world except Ingham County, and he won, without opposition"; Pattengill "talked about Ingham County, and he won, without opposition." The 3,300 persons who attended "were just about where they were when the session started."

As the campaign peaked, each side became more strident. Thousands attended a dry parade on April 1; the procession included 30 truckloads of Sunday-school children under 10 years of age. On April 2, both Lansing dailies published a full page of pictures of liquor deliveries to Lansing saloons in the benighted days when they were open. The Liberty League, for its part, published full-page advertisements warning voters that prohibition would not create temperance. "The blind pig and the bootlegger," claimed the Liberty League, "are worse than the saloonman ever dared to be"; outlawing alcohol would merely have the effect of replacing one method of dispensing liquor with another.

A remarkable "dry" document, which sheds considerable light on the thinking of the period, appeared in the *Press* at the height of the campaign. Aleta Estes Munger, a reporter, told her colleagues in the newspaper office that it was perfectly safe for unescorted women to go about a dry Lansing after dark. The editor said, "Prove it," and assigned Miss Munger to start out at 7:00 p.m., "go to any place where a self-respecting Lansing woman would want to be," ride streetcars, see a movie, go to a railroad station, walk back at 11:00 p.m., and write what happened.

"I did a daring thing last night," wrote Miss Munger, "at least in the opinion of the mere men on the office staff." Miss Munger went first to the Hotel Wentworth on West Michigan Avenue, past a group of stores "where saloons once filled the air with horrible smells and filled the sidewalks with leering, bleary men who made remarks and spit tobacco juice upon the sidewalk." She visited the capitol and then walked several miles to the home of a friend on Logan Street. After a short visit, she boarded a streetcar and then saw a movie at the Orpheum Theater.

"In the old days of saloons," said Miss Munger, "a careful woman would take an aisle seat. We Lansing women nowadays sit quite indiscriminately; without the fear that a man with a distillery breath is going to sit next to us and make himself obnoxious." At the Orpheum were large numbers of women, many alone. Miss Munger left

the theater about 10:00 p.m. and meandered over to South Washington Avenue and Washtenaw, looking at window displays. Groups of young men, "having a corking good time," ambled by; none spoke to her. "It was by this time, mind you, 10:15—the hour when formerly men came reeling along the sidewalks, swearing and cursing, sometimes fighting; the hour when the 'flip youths' who had had a few friendly rounds were brazenly hailing any and every woman who had the termidity [sic] to be out so late as 10:15."

The business district was dead. "To me a dead town at 11:00 p.m. means a town in bed and asleep—a decidedly 'live town' at 6 or 7 o'clock in the morning, when the men and women set out for their day's tasks." To Miss Munger, a confirmed dry, a town without liquor meant "bright eyes" in offices and stores, "steady hands" at the machines and factories, "happy children and joyous mothers."

The vote was decisive—the drys carried every precinct by a larger majority than in 1914. Of a total county vote of 9,186, the drys garnered 5,800, or 63 percent; the most lopsided result was in East Lansing, where the wets obtained only 78 votes out of 318 cast. The *Press*, in an election postmortem, attributed the dry victory to the fact that the voters, having tried local option, preferred it. "The wets fought a clean, above-board fight," said the *Press*, "and did their best against long odds. The facts, however, were in favor of the drys." Statewide prohibition came in 1918 and national prohibition two years later, and the issue was laid to rest for the time being.

International events—the Mexican crisis and the outbreak of the First World War—affected life in the capital region. After Mexican irregulars, apparently led by Francisco Villa, attacked Columbus, New Mexico, in March 1916, President Woodrow Wilson ordered a column of cavalry under General John J. Pershing to enter Mexico and pursue Villa. In June 1916, after a skirmish between Pershing's cavalry and the troops of the Mexican government, Mexico and the United States hovered on the brink of war, and Wilson ordered 100,000 National Guard troops to patrol the border between the two countries.

Thus began a long period of military service for several hundred capital-area men. Company E of the 31st Michigan Infantry, now a field-artillery unit, served on the Mexican border from June 1916 to March 1917. Upon its return from border duty, it was organized into the First Batallion—Batteries A, B, and C—of what would soon become the 119th Field Artillery, 32nd Division.

The American declaration of war against Germany had been expected for some time, and its announcement on April 6 seemed anticlimactic. The Mexican border units—their ranks filled with enlistments—were called back into federal service and left the city on August 17, 1917. From June to November, 1918, as part of the 119th Field Artillery of the 32nd Division, the unit saw almost constant front-line duty in the final major Allied offensive of the war. A total of 3,025 Ingham County men, including the 119th, and 27 women served in the military forces during the war.

The First World War was a difficult period for Lansing

With many of its young men and some women in the armed forces, the city outdid itself in support for the war effort. One "Victory" and four "Liberty" loans were oversubscribed; an Ingham County War Committee, headed by Walter S. Foster and Benjamin F. Davis, coordinated war-bond sales and other patriotic activities.

"Patriotism ran so high," reported the *State Journal* in its 1955 commemorative issue, "that half-hearted participation in activities supporting the war—particularly if the reluctant one was of German ancestry—became highly suspect and some incidents of violence occurred." Americans had taken sides with one or the other of the warring parties since the war began in 1914; when the United States entered the war, zealous patriots, including many in Lansing, intimidated persons whose patriotism they considered wanting, including many persons of German ancestry. The *State Journal* reported that "tar and feather parties were held mysteriously." Persons known as "pro-German" were taken from their homes and brought to the vicinity of the country club, where "they were given the treatment." Many who were "guilty of no more than having a German accent" were branded as " 'those German butchers.' "

Lansing was fortunate in having as its mayor J. Gottleib Reutter, a German-American and one of the city's most respected leaders. Reutter, whose patriotism was beyond question, did all he could to calm the anti-German hysteria. "There was a general bitterness against Germans," Reutter recalled later, "and I worked day and night to keep them [the local Germans] out of trouble, counseling them to keep their opinions to themselves."

The German-Americans, who had been an important presence in Lansing from its founding, were by no means the only immigrant group in Lansing during the early 20th century. The local automobile industry had considerable numbers of immigrants on its payroll, and during the war it began a program of Americanization. Of 3,759 Reo employees in April 1917, 947 were foreign-born, including 35 percent of its "conscription age" workers. In addition to many persons of German or Austro-Hungarian birth, there were significant numbers of Poles and Syrians, many of them recent immigrants. Reo and other companies cooperated with the Lansing School District in offering classes and promoting citizenship. The Americanization program continued for a decade after the war, until immigration restrictions reduced the numbers of immigrants and made the program obsolete.

During the war, the city, along with the rest of the nation, experienced food shortages. Flour and sugar were often unobtainable. A fuel shortage coincided with the blizzard and cold wave of January 1918, one of the worst in memory. The most serious wartime problem—the epidemic of Spanish influenza—began in October 1918; by December, the city had 2,557 cases and 140 deaths.

ABOVE: **Michigan Avenue Bridge, as seen from the north, 1912. Wooden bridges built in earlier years decayed rapidly and often collapsed during flash floods. John Robson, mayor of Lansing in 1871, proposed that iron bridges be built. Though most people in Lansing had never even seen an iron bridge, Robson's proposal was, after great debate, accepted. Courtesy of Michigan State Archives.**

RIGHT: **In March 1916, the engineering building at Michigan State College burned down. R.E. Olds, who remembered that his father had borrowed $1,500 from chemistry professor Robert C. Kedzie in 1885, donated $100,000 towards the construction of what became Olds Hall, a replica of the burned structure. Courtesy of Michigan State University Publications.**

87

Chapter 10

The war ended for Lansing on May 12, 1919, when the 119th Field Artillery arrived at the Grand Trunk station for a hometown parade before mustering out. Although Lansing men and women had served in all military branches, and some were still on duty with the Siberian Expedition under General William S. Graves, the city had a special feeling for the men of the 119th. These men, said the *State Journal*, "had borne Lansing's colors throughout the war," and their return had been eagerly anticipated. The city was ablaze with color as a huge crowd watched Colonel Chester B. McCormick parade his men smartly up Washington Avenue and down Capitol. A *State Journal* reporter recalled that on August 17, 1917, "a crowd of laughing boys" had begun the first leg of a journey that would take them first to Texas, where they were formed into the 119th, and then to England, France, and Germany. The 119th had been in the thick of the final Allied offensive that broke enemy resistance on the western front and ended the war; and it was "a more grim, older crowd" that filed from the cars on May 12, 1919.

The men returned to a city confident that the war had merely interrupted the extraordinary economic growth of the past generation. Only a month earlier, Edward VerLinden, president of the Olds Motor Works, had announced a seven-building, million-square-foot factory expansion and the need for 2,000 additional workers. Other city industries announced similar plans; the *State Journal* reported that Lansing industries had deconverted quickly from war work and that "practically every plant in the city has made or is making plans for expansion."

While the city did indeed resume its economic growth during the 1920s, the immediate postwar years were difficult for Lansing. The return of "normalcy" was delayed by wartime inflation, the lack of an orderly transition to a peacetime economy, and a brief but sharp business recession in 1920-21. By the spring of 1919, the wartime moratorium on residential construction had created a national housing shortage—a shortage particularly acute in Lansing, where homes had been in short supply since the advent of the automobile industry. Wartime inflation had cut deeply into the profits of the city's gas and streetcar companies; their demands for rate increases touched off one of the city's most bitter political disputes. And the city's bridges, sewers, and streets, poorly main-

tained during the war, began to show signs of neglect and arouse complaints.

By the spring of 1919, Lansing's housing shortage had become a crisis. Rental housing was unavailable at any price, and there were few homes for sale. The *State Journal* reported a "house famine"; mail carriers, asked to count all the city's vacant houses, found only 152, mostly substandard shacks "hardly fit to be called dwellings" and concentrated in those areas brought into the city by the annexations of 1916 and 1917. Theodore G. Foster, a real-estate dealer, said that returning soldiers alone would take "every one of the 152 houses that can be called dwellings," and he wondered how the city could possibly house the families of additional workers brought in by plant expansions. A minimum of 250 homes, said Foster, ought to be under construction; he found only 50. Frank N. Arbaugh, the department-store owner and president of the Chamber of Commerce, predicted that Lansing would soon have a "tent city" if building contractors, "without a vision of the future," held back.

To meet the crisis, and to assure builders that houses built on speculation would find a ready market, the *State Journal*, the Lansing Real Estate Board, the Chamber of Commerce, and city officials began a nine-day "own your own home" campaign in April 1919. "A supreme effort is being made," said the *State Journal*, "to pledge for Lansing enough homes to properly house its families" as well as new arrivals. The warning of William C. Durant, president of General Motors, that "Lansing must match the expenditure of millions by General Motors with adequate housing for its workingmen" heightened the intensity of the campaign. The "own your own home" crusade became a regular feature of *State Journal* editorials and advertising supplements for months after the planned nine-day effort. By the spring of 1921, the crisis had eased, as new residential subdivisions appeared all over Lansing and East Lansing and city officials reported record numbers of building permits.

Housing was not Lansing's only postwar crisis. A proposal for rate increases by the city's gas and streetcar companies, both providing service with outmoded equipment and compelled by their franchises to charge prewar rates, gave rise to a bitter and protracted dispute. A polemic newspaper, *The Gas Mask*, opposed rate increases for both companies and demanded public ownership. An opposing single-issue newspaper, *The Square Deal*, argued that state-imposed bonded-debt limits would not permit public ownership, and that the proposed increases were reasonable. Although the issues of utility rates and public ownership recurred sporadically throughout the decade, an ominous public letter by VerLinden forced the issue. His company, he said, needed gas; he sought "to impress upon city officials and the community at large the absolute necessity of solving the controversy with the gas company." Were this not done, he warned, the Olds Motor Works would "of necessity alter our plans of expansion . . . to meet conditions as they exist." VerLinden also demanded an accommodation with the streetcar company, which needed to extend its service. VerLinden complained that his employees had to walk five blocks to his factory after reaching the end of the streetcar line.

The quality of city services also became an issue. In March 1919, heavy rains caused sewage—still dumped raw into the Grand River—to overflow into the city's water system; hundreds became ill, and schools and factories were forced to close. City officials feared an outbreak of typhoid and warned residents to boil drinking water. At first, only one main appeared to be contaminated; the contagion, however, soon spread to the city's entire water system. The Merchant's Bureau of the Chamber of Commerce complained that Lansing's streets had never been "in such disgraceful condition" and that the city's negligence "was menacing the health and happiness of a prosperous citizenship."

The *State Journal* echoed the merchants' complaints. "No town, city or village," it claimed, "has worse streets and few of them rank so low." To prove its point, the *State Journal* dispatched a reporter on an automobile tour of the city. "There is little need of a seat," wrote the reporter, "because the never-ending ruts and bumps keep the driver and his party up in the air most of the time." Few streets were in good repair; Morton Avenue near Jerome "left an impression that could be compared only to the bounding main." In wet weather, huge pools of water stood on the streets, and flooding was common even after a light rain because of the practice of sweeping dirt into catch basins.

Even garbage collection—which has a curious history in Lansing—became an issue. In 1916, at the suggestion of Mayor Reutter, Lansing emulated Flint and Battle Creek and began disposing of its organic garbage at a "piggery" or hog farm. Since the city charter did not permit spending money for garbage collection, Mayor Reutter purchased pigs, garbage cans, and equipment with his own money; the pigs were fattened on the city's garbage and sold on the hog market. "The piggery developed into a big project," Reutter wrote many years later. "We had an average of 1200 pigs all the time, selling them in car lots." In 1920, the *State Journal* described the city's piggery as "an interesting place"—the several hundred hogs "were well shaped and present a fine sight as they roam over the farm." Reutter and Superintendent of Public Works Ward Hill spent a lot of time at the piggery, and "we were making money on every car we shipped—for the city."

As houses were built near the area, however, fastidious neighbors complained of stench and filth, and the piggery was much ridiculed. The city was eventually forced to relocate the piggery, first in neighboring Delta Township and later in Portland. Neighbors complained of huge swarms of flies that compelled them to keep doors and windows closed in warm weather; in a heat wave, the stench would sometimes force nearby residents to leave their homes.

Many community leaders, aware that Lansing stood on the brink of a new spurt of growth, were becoming concerned with the city's appearance and apprehensive about the consequences of another generation of uncontrolled expansion. Lansing, if the truth be told, looked more like a factory town than a state capital. "Every town or city," urged the *State Journal*, "should have its civic association, part of whose duty should be to keep a city beautiful." Restrictions on buildings were necessary, for without controls "factories creep into residential districts . . . and the hideous, ill-constructed building rises next to the city hall or Masonic Temple." A "civic association"— which apparently meant a planning commission—could assist in zoning the city into areas suited for residential, commercial, or industrial uses; it could educate public and private taste, urging "that public buildings be just as useful as they are beautiful, as it would cost no more to erect a beautiful building than an ugly one."

Various "piecemeal" planning measures had been discussed for years. As recently as 1916, Professor Edward Lindemann of Michigan Agricultural College, in a well-publicized lantern-slide lecture, had proposed a system of inner and outer boulevards. According to Lindemann, Lansing had made "relatively few mistakes in planning," and a dual system of boulevards, leading to parks and "beauty spots" on Lansing's periphery and to important public buildings in the civic center, was all that was required.

Farsighted persons realized that coping adequately with such matters as the city's appearance, health, sewage and garbage disposal, mass transit, building standards, and even recreation and the quality of life, required a comprehensive and not a piecemeal approach. A city plan was needed that would take far more into account than easy access to beauty spots and public buildings. In 1920, Mayor Benjamin A. Kyes agreed with the need for a comprehensive plan and appointed a "city plan commission," the first in the city. Its members included such community leaders as Richard H. Scott and Alfred H. Doughty of Reo; Otto Eckert, the city engineer; H. Lee Bancroft, the city park and cemetery commissioner; former Mayor Reutter; and Mrs. Martha L. Baker. The commission strongly urged a comprehensive plan and on June 14, 1921, the city council engaged the firm of Harland Bartholemew, a city-plan engineer of St. Louis, Missouri. Bartholemew was charged with making a detailed study of the city; identifying areas suitable for residential, commercial, and industrial use; and making recommendations on a broad range of issues including street-plan changes, mass transit, housing, recreation, and "civic art."

Bartholemew's report, published as *The Lansing Plan*, is a useful description of the city as it stood on the brink of a new wave of industrial expansion and population increase.

Bartholemew agreed that the city had excellent prospects. He noted the recent population growth—more than 80 percent in each of the preceding two decades— and described Lansing's "remarkable power of expansion." He doubted that "the vigor of previous years would persist," but was certain that Lansing "would never become sluggish." The city had many attributes to attract yet more industry, including excellent transportation facilities (80 freight trains entered the city daily), readily available hydroelectric power, ample coal and iron resources within easy reach, and a close proximity to the iron- and steel-producing areas along the south shore of Lake Michigan. For all these reasons, as well as the quality of the city's labor force, continued growth seemed assured.

But if the city had excellent prospects, Bartholemew also found much to criticize. "The present city," he wrote, "shows evidence of haphazardness, carelessness, and un-coordinated effort. The best city that could have been built on the site has not been realized." Much of the natural beauty of the river front—"undoubtedly impressive in the early days of the community"—had disappeared. The ordered, rectangular street layout of the Town of Michigan had not been followed as the city grew; streets too often varied in width, jogged, or ended abruptly, "all without apparent reason." The city had too many dangerous railroad grade crossings; the industrial Belt Line of 1905 "was ill advised with reference to tendencies of growth and an orderly residential expansion"; the street railway system had been poorly planned. The creation of parks lacked any plan and "relied too much on the generosity of individual citizens"; as a result, the city had too few parks "to soften its pronounced industrial character." In the area of housing, Lansing was more fortunate, "but still the standards and safeguards were imperfect."

Bartholemew saw Lansing's deficiencies as the direct result of "undirected, uncontrolled growth." The city in 1921 appeared as "a strange mixture of factories, stores and homes with certain individual units of each type preempting space properly belonging to another use."

The downtown area was "without distinction," exhibiting a miscellaneous assortment of architectural styles and building heights and a "motley display" of street signs and antiquated streetlights. In its post office and city hall, the city had attempted "something of an unusual and distinctive building group," but the buildings were too close together and their effect was diminished by inappropriate surroundings. The city's other buildings—especially its schools—"had fallen short of a standard which Lansing has a right to expect." The school buildings were "cheap in architectural effect [and] cramped for exterior space." The public library and high school occupied the same block, "none too large for the latter alone"; the intermediate school on Lenawee was "huge and factory like." The streets outside the city's core had too few trees and too many wires, poles, and billboards.

Lansing had ample time in which to improve its appearance, said Bartholemew, if the city would improve its street plan, control building heights, eliminate dangerous grade crossings, demand varied architectural styles in its new subdivisions, concentrate commercial centers at strategic points, and encourage good landscape gardening. Bartholemew urged public ownership of the river front and "a more dignified tone in the business district," which could be achieved by removing projecting business signs, modernizing street lighting, and prohibiting sidewalk obstructions. A "modern plan of streets" would make possible a number of squares, parks, and plazas in residential and commercial districts. In keeping with the "city beautiful" movement, of which Bartholemew was a part, he also urged "more commemorative statues, memorial shafts, and other features" expressive of the capital city.

Bartholemew also suggested that Lansing consolidate its railroad and interurban passenger terminals just west of Larch Street on Michigan Avenue, a location that would afford a fine view of the capitol. "A passenger terminal in this location," he wrote, "offers ... a much more impressive portal to the city than may possibly be secured by the building of several stations." And persons who arrive on the interurban, he said, "deserve better treatment than being dumped out on the street."

Bartholemew understood that the long-range future of downtown Lansing would depend largely on the future building policy of the state. "The State of Michigan," he predicted, "is not always going to find its present capitol adequate and is very likely in time to need an additional office building similar to that on Walnut Street." Urging that the state group its future buildings to maximize their effect, Bartholemew proposed a breathtaking "suggested new capitol group"—a cluster of four Second Empire or Beaux Arts state office buildings, with formal gardens and a memorial shaft, to the west of the capitol. It was a magnificent conception, showing the influence of the Champs-Elysees and the Place de la Concorde in Paris, as well as the mall between the United States Capitol and the Washington Monument. Bartholemew's proposal disregarded the 1921 state office building; this structure "has been shunted off to the side and so located as to be without setting commensurate to its size."

But the state of Michigan, still proud of the relative simplicity of its capitol, was not ready for the soaring pretension of Bartholemew's opulent building group. The "city beautiful" movement was waning—critics in Lansing and elsewhere scoffed at the embellishment of their communities with statues, fountains, and memorial arches; a new movement—"the city functional," representing a more pragmatic conception of planning—had largely supplanted it even as *The Lansing Plan* was published. Nor did Bartholemew's plan anticipate the remarkable proliferation of the automobile, which would soon make obsolete all city planning that did not take it into account.

Although the common council never officially adopted the Bartholemew plan, Mayor Alfred H. Doughty, City Forester H. Lee Bancroft, and City Engineer Otto E. Eckert, did carry out many of its recommendations. One immediate result was the adoption, in April 1921, of a building code based on that of Gary, Indiana. The downtown area was designated as a "fireproof district"; within that district—bounded by Shiawassee, Capitol, Kalamazoo, and the Grand River—only fireproof structures could be built. A city building commissioner and a city electrician were appointed.

Bartholemew had proposed a zoning ordinance; the *State Journal* agreed that such an ordinance was imperative. The paper reported one case of a speculator who wanted to build 40 houses on a single acre just west of the city; the farmer who owned the land had refused to sell. "To head off such an operation at its very inception," said the *State Journal*, "will be to interfere with business. However, business of some kinds needs to be interfered with." Poor housing conditions, the paper continued, are "among the most harmful and baleful influences that can beset a city"; when bad housing is permitted, "it requires a battle of years to undo the condition." Such had been the experience of New York City, where the reformer Jacob A. Riis had led a battle against the rear tenement. "The rear tenement," warned the *State Journal*, "is gaining a foothold in Lansing," and only a strong zoning ordinance would enable the city to cope with the problem.

In July, the planning commission proposed a zoning ordinance that would divide the city into residential, commercial, industrial, and unrestricted districts. "If the ordinance passes," said the *State Journal*, "every dweller in the city would find himself protected as to living conditions and conditions under which business may be carried on." In addition to restricting the uses of certain areas, the ordinance prohibited rear tenements, "spite" buildings, and structures of irregular heights.

Zoning ordinances were relatively new in 1921, and the proposal touched off a lively debate. Members of the Lansing Real Estate Board, while agreeing with zoning in principle, quarreled with details of the ordinance. A number of areas designated as residential, they maintained, were in fact commercial. "South Washington," argued one realtor, "is destined to be a commercial thoroughfare and nothing else." The realtors also opposed tight restrictions that would keep the central business district within its existing bounds; this, they argued, would raise rents, cause commercial hardship, and retard the growth of the city. Public meetings were held, and the proposed ordinance was defeated. Another zoning law was finally adopted in 1927.

One of Bartholemew's predictions—that Lansing would undergo considerable building in the 1920s—came about, as the city embarked on the most extensive wave of industrial, commercial, residential, and public building in its history. In common with many American cities, Lansing experienced a construction boom in the 1920s, in the course of which many now-familiar downtown buildings and extensive residential tracts were completed.

The boom began in Lansing as prosperity ended the recession of 1920-21. "The best indication of prosperity this city has ever witnessed," said the *State Journal* in June 1921, "is contained in the fact that structures of all sorts—public, semi-public, and private—are being built on a larger scale than ever before." In May, the city heard the astonishing news that William C. Durant, who had left General Motors and formed his own company, would build a $3-million plant in Lansing. Another $2 million had previously been committed to Lansing construction projects, and the new total of $5 million—unprecedented in the history of the city—seemed incredible.

Work on the Durant factory proceeded quickly; a month later, the *State Journal* could report that the new plant, "on a site covered with dandelions and tall grass," had "risen like a dream and already holds a commanding

view of the countryside." City building reports showed record numbers of new houses and residential subdivisions all over the city. And in the summer of 1921, the city of Lansing began a record number of public-works projects, including street repairs, major bridge renovations, and a pavilion at Potter Park.

Nowhere did the building boom of the 1920s have a more dramatic effect than on downtown Lansing, where many new structures altered the skyline. One of the first to appear was the seven-story neoclassical State Office Building, now the Lewis Cass Building, on a site bounded by Kalamazoo, Chestnut, Walnut, and Lenawee. The sandstone and granite structure—described by architect, Edwyn A. Bowd of Lansing, as "a free adaptation of the Roman Ionic order"—exceeded the floor space of the capitol.

In April 1921, builders completed one of Lansing's most architecturally distinguished buildings, the Strand Theater and Arcade on South Washington Avenue. To the *State Journal*, the Strand—familiar to later generations of Lansing theatergoers as the Michigan Theater—marked "an innovation in luxuriousness and practical utility." John Eberson, a well-known theater architect of the period, placed a scintillating electric marquee against an Italian Renaissance facade of mottled terra cotta. He selected the Strand's interior appointments from a variety of architectural styles. The 14-shop arcade featured a Spanish ceiling studded with cathedral glass, which, according to a reporter present on opening day, cast "a gentle, golden radiance ... through the entire passage." The thickly carpeted, 2,000-seat auditorium, done in the style of Louis XV, was capped at its apex by a vast sky-blue oval.

A block away, at the southwest corner of Washington and Michigan, a new Prudden Building began to rise even before the debris of the old structure, which burned in December 1920, had been removed from the site. The handsome 10-story structure, now the Washington Square Building, has a facade of green and white marble on its 20-foot first floor, gray-tinted pressed brick from the third to the eighth floor, and terra cotta on its upper two stories. It was designed by the architect Sam Butterworth.

Even as the Bartholemew report appeared, downtown Lansing was undergoing dramatic changes. As early as July 1921, the *State Journal*, taking note of the architectural excellence of recent downtown construction, thought that Lansing was indeed becoming a "city beautiful," with more improvements than at any time in its history. In October 1921, the cornerstone for the Masonic Temple on South Capitol Avenue, now occupied by the Cooley Law School, was laid with impressive ceremony; a new telephone building appeared nearby. By the summer of 1924—with much downtown construction still in the future—Lansing's skyline had changed so dramatically that a 1912 panoramic photograph, published in the *State Journal*, seemed to have been taken in a different city. "After more than a decade," the *State Journal* declared, "Lansing has assumed new shapes and styles of architecture and added new groups of buildings which tend to obscure the Lansing of 1912." Some old buildings still

RIGHT: **In the summer of 1921 the City of Lansing began a number of public-work projects, which included this pavilion at Potter Park. Courtesy of Michigan State Archives.**

BELOW: **In December, 1920, the Prudden Building was destroyed by fire. A second Prudden Building (now the Washington Square building) was constructed on the site, located on the southwest corner of Michigan and Washington avenues. Courtesy of Lansing Public Library.**

LEFT: **The 100 block of South Washington Avenue, west side. The Prudden Building can be seen at the right. The Washington Square building now occupies this site. Note the sidewalk obstructions and overhead wires; city planner Harland Bartholemew criticized these eyesores in downtown Lansing. Courtesy of Michigan State Archives.**

ABOVE: **Moore's Park swimming pool, 1925. Recreational facilities were expanded in the 1920s as a result of Lansing's economic prosperity. Courtesy of Michigan State Archives.**

Lansing Between the Wars

stood—"the ragged rows of old fashioned stores, many of which are perfect landmarks of the earliest period in the city's history"—but the paper considered them eyesores and hoped they would disappear as increased prosperity enhanced land values. But tastes change, and today the surviving old buildings, in North Lansing as well as downtown, are considered part of the city's unique charm.

When the Regent Theater (formerly the Bijou), at the southwest corner of Michigan and Capitol, was destroyed by fire on December 28, 1923, a premium parcel of downtown real estate became available for development. On September 16, 1924, the *State Journal* published an architect's sketch of a new $1.6-million hotel proposed for the site, providing that $650,000 could be raised by local subscription. The following day R.E. Olds, convinced of the need for a first-class downtown hotel, announced his personal subscription of $100,000 toward the cost, and by mid-December the entire sum had been raised. In fact, Olds had privately agreed to subscribe the entire amount should the fund-raising effort fail.

The Hotel Olds—so named in honor of the man who had done so much to promote it—went up quickly, dramatically altering Lansing's skyline and the environs of the state capitol. It contained more than 300 guest rooms, plus an attractive lobby, spacious ballrooms, and convention halls. The Reniger Company, one of Lansing's major contractors, built the hotel, and Arbaugh's provided most of the furnishings. The use of dark gray figured marble slabs as pilasters on the entrance lobby, the Georgian style of much of the interior, the French-styled ballroom, and the Wisteria Room, patterned after a house in Maryland, all evoked much favorable comment.

By the mid-1920s, the continued industrial prosperity, the construction boom, and a marked increase in civic pride had ended the wave of complaints with which the decade had begun. On August 30, 1924, citizens turned out en masse for a City of Lansing Day celebration that sought, by means of an enormous parade, to acquaint the citizenry—many of whom were new arrivals in the city—with the scope of municipal services. The parade of city officials, employees, and schoolteachers required an hour to pass the reviewing stand where former mayors Reutter, Kyes, John Crotty, and Silas F. Main—all veterans of the political wars of the past—watched with interest.

Mayor Alfred H. Doughty led the parade, bearing aloft the key to the city, which on ordinary days reposed in a niche above his office door. Next came the Reo Motor Band, followed by the city treasurer, city clerk, assessor, weightmaster, marketmaster, the municipal court, and their staffs. Superintendent Jay W. Sexton marched at the head of the Lansing School District corps of teachers and custodians; Chief Alfred H. Seymour led a platoon of police; several fire engines crept slowly forward. The Board of Health paraded floats depicting the work of school nurses, health-center nurses, and physicians; one float contained an exact representation of a schoolroom with nurses on duty. H. Lee Bancroft, the city park commissioner, displayed a caged lion and bear from the Potter Park Zoo. The Board of Water and Light—by then a huge corporation—paraded trucks showing the work of its various divisions. Two city garbage trucks brought up the rear—the first containing a bevy of squealing young piglets, and the second a load of enormous hogs who had dined on the city's garbage and were ready for market.

East Lansing and Michigan Agricultural College, after a brief postwar crisis, also grew remarkably during the 1920s. From 1916 to 1919, enrollment at the college had declined nearly 10 percent, from 1,482 to 1,341. Enrollment in the agricultural program fell by 25 percent while the number of engineering students increased. The agricultural community from which the college traditionally drew most of its students was then in an economic depression.

With economic conditions making farm life less attractive, the college broadened its offerings; in the course of the next decade, it established a division of applied science and liberal arts, refurbished its graduate program, created a music school, and initiated programs in biology, physical education, business administration, and hotel management. These were considerable achievements, all the more remarkable considering that four different presidents—Frank S. Kedzie (1915-1921), David Friday (1921-1923), Kenyon L. Butterfield (1924-1928), and Robert S. Shaw (1928-1941)—served the institution during the decade. In 1925, the name of the college was changed from Michigan Agricultural College to Michigan State College of Agriculture and Applied Science, reflecting its new mission and more diverse academic program. By 1926, enrollment had climbed to 2,500—an increase of 1,000 in five years—and new campus facilities included a chemistry building, library, home-economics building, student union, and a new concrete, 16,000-seat athletic stadium. By 1928, enrollment in liberal arts was double that in agriculture.

The city of East Lansing grew with the college; its population of homeowners in 1926 was estimated at 3,600. According to the Lansing Chamber of Commerce, the city had become "a preferred suburb of Lansing businessmen." It had "not a single factory within its confines—and not one is desired." In 1926, East Lansing adopted a zoning ordinance proposed by C.P. Halligan, professor of landscape architecture, with relatively little debate. Handsome new residential subdivisions appeared all over the city; their street plans, many of which followed land contours, might have been drawn by Bartholemew himself. Improving the road between Lansing and East Lansing required the removal of "Split Rock," or "Half Way Rock," a local freak of nature that stood midway between the two cities in front of the residence of Charles Foster. When the *State Journal* announced the demise of the rock and the tree that split it, hundreds of persons came from miles around "to drop a tear and get a little sliver of stone by way of compensation."

Several new structures changed the character of downtown East Lansing. In 1926, People's Church moved into its new collegiate Gothic, limestone-trimmed, tapestry-brick edifice on Grand River Avenue just east of Abbott Road. The interdenominational church, founded in 1912 served both city residents and college students and was in

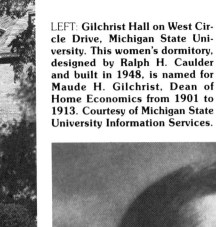

LEFT: **Gilchrist Hall on West Circle Drive, Michigan State University. This women's dormitory, designed by Ralph H. Caulder and built in 1948, is named for Maude H. Gilchrist, Dean of Home Economics from 1901 to 1913. Courtesy of Michigan State University Information Services.**

BELOW: **Alfred H. Doughty, mayor of Lansing from 1923 to 1926, was one of Lansing's most controversial mayors. His opposition to extending the services of the Board of Water and Light beyond city limits caused a major political dispute in the 1920s. Courtesy of Lansing Public Library.**

ABOVE: **Michigan State College President Robert S. Shaw and graduate Daniel Strange in 1939. Shaw served as president of the college from 1928 to 1941. Courtesy of Michigan State University Archives and Historical Collections.**

RIGHT: **Mayor Alfred H. Doughty, aldermen, and officers of the City of Lansing, January 5, 1925. From the Wiskemann Collection.**

95

Lansing Between the Wars

many respects a center of East Lansing life. In 1927, the Abbott Building—a neoclassical, five-story theater, bank, and apartment building—appeared at Grand River Avenue and Abbott Road; the Hesperian House, a Queen Anne-styled student cooperative that had formerly occupied the site, was moved to Ann Street. The new building, which housed the offices of the East Lansing State Bank as well as the Abbott Theater (now the State Theater), drastically changed the appearance of downtown East Lansing. An unsuccessful drive to prohibit the movie theater from operating on Sundays led to one of East Lansing's most bitter political disputes. With the construction of College Manor on Abbott Road just across from the Abbott Building, East Lansing acquired another of its important commercial buildings. This building contained 26 apartments and two retail stores, occupied today by Washburn Travel and "Beggar's Banquet," a favorite East Lansing watering place.

The national issues of Prohibition and the Ku Klux Klan, which deadlocked the Democratic party during the campaign of 1924, had repercussions in the capital region. The Klan, originally founded in the post-Civil War South, revived in Atlanta in 1915 and spread after the First World War to many Northern states, including Michigan. The Klan was anti-Catholic, antiblack, and anti-Semitic, but its principal activity in Michigan during the 1920s seems to have been a crusade against Catholic schools.

On July 5, 1924, the *State Journal* reported that "a large Ingham County delegation" attended a huge Klan gathering at Jackson. Lansing, however, was the scene of the largest Michigan "Klonvocation" of the decade, a gathering of 50,000 persons on Labor Day, 1924, that included a parade of 15,000 white-robed figures on Michigan Avenue. The actual attendance fell far short of the 150,000 persons the Klan hoped to attract, and plans to build a huge "Klavern" or Klan convention hall in Lansing with the proceeds of a "tag day" did not materialize. Two days after the Lansing meeting, an overflow crowd attended an anti-Klan meeting at the Prudden Auditorium. After the fall of 1924, the Klan began to decline, and by 1926 news of its activities largely disappeared from the Lansing press.

The capital region was the scene of one of the worst tragedies of the decade, the Bath School disaster of May 18, 1927. This incident—probably the largest case of mass murder in American history—is the subject of *Mayday*, a recently published detailed history by Grant Parker. One Andrew Kehoe, a Bath Township farmer and former treasurer of the school board, planted about half a ton of dynamite in the cellar of the recently consolidated school, and at 9:45 a.m. the building exploded. As rescue workers frantically removed the dead and injured, state police found an additional 500 pounds of unexploded dynamite. Kehoe drove to the scene in a dynamite-laden Model T, and a second explosion killed him and several bystanders, including Emory E. Hyck, superintendent of the Bath School. A total of 44 persons were killed in the two explosions, and another 58 were injured; Kehoe's wife was found murdered at his farm.

In the fall of 1924, radio broadcasting came to Lansing.

Before station WREO, operated by the Reo Motor Car Company, went on the air, there was no radio station closer than Detroit, and only a relatively expensive set could receive programs. With a station in the city, broadcasts could be received with relatively simple, crystal-headset equipment. Commercial radio was still in its infancy, and WREO was on the air only a few hours each day, offering organ music in the morning, and evening programs only on Tuesdays, Thursdays, and Saturdays. Wires were placed in the Prudden Auditorium and several downtown churches where programs originated. WKAR, operated by Michigan State College, went on the air a short time later.

A Lansing radio performer, whose identity was never revealed, enjoyed a brief flurry of radio stardom as the "LanSinger." Regarded for a time as the best radio tenor and yodeler, he had a repertory that included such selections as "Sleep Baby, Sleep," and "Roll on Silvery Moon." In the summer of 1926, the LanSinger, his identity carefully concealed, went on a national tour of radio stations on behalf of the United Engine Company, a Lansing manufacturer of farm machinery. His performances at radio stations around the country, reported the *State Journal* in its radio supplement, "brought forth a veritable flood of requests and applause from enthusiastic listeners." The United Engine Company, in order to capitalize on the publicity, marketed the "LanSing" line of radio receivers, featuring the "LanSing MonoGlide" tuning condenser.

It appeared during the 1920s that Lansing had arrived at a plateau of permanent prosperity. Never before had the city's economy seemed so sound and its future so bright. Evidence of good times abounded—in full employment, record production, factory expansions, new downtown buildings, miles of new homes, and a surge of civic pride. In 1926, the city of Lansing and the Chamber of Commerce published a handsome brochure, *Lansing: A City of Stable Industries, Satisfied Workers, and Civic Soundness,* which attests to a general faith that the prosperity of the Coolidge years would continue for the forseeable future. The brochure, part of a campaign to attract more diverse industries to the city, pointed to Lansing's remarkable history of economic stability: "In 1921, when the country at large was suffering from an industrial headache following the commercial orgy of 1919 and '20, Lansing's prosperity was never more evident, and its building permits for the year totalled the greatest sum in its history." During the depression of 1920-21, Lansing had "no gigantic failures, no shutdowns, [and] no breadlines." This was no mere puffery—it was based on hard facts and fed a growing belief that since the city's economy had stood firm not only in 1920-21 but also in the recessions of 1907 and 1914, its fundamentally sound economic structure had made it somehow impervious to the occasional downturns of the national economy.

If Lansing withstood storms, it prospered in good weather, and the city shared fully in the industrial prosperity of the Coolidge years. In 1926, Reo introduced its Flying Cloud and entered the luxury-car market; the company reported that May was the best month in its

LEFT: The Wentworth Hotel on West Michigan Avenue at Grand, circa 1920. The Wentworth Hotel deteriorated over the years and was razed in 1966. Courtesy of Michigan State University Archives and Historical Collections.

BELOW: Beaumont Tower on the campus of Michigan State University was built on the site of College Hall, the first structure built for the teaching of scientific agriculture. Courtesy of Michigan State University Archives and Historical Collections.

CENTER: Howard Finch (left) and Earl Parchment (right) were popular broadcasters on WJIM radio station in the 1930s. From the Yellow Brick Road Collection.

ABOVE: Michigan Agricultural College students engaged in a struggle on the old football field. Courtesy of Michigan State University Publications.

history, with more orders than it could handle and many employees on overtime and night shifts. "Lansing is in the best condition I know of," said Charles H. Davis, secretary of the Chamber of Commerce. It was "the only city around" with all industries working full time and practically no unemployment. Bank clearances during 1926—a rough indicator of economic activity—reached a record high of $144 million.

It surprised no one that 1927 was even better than 1926. Net sales of the Reo Motor Company—which amounted that year to about 22 percent of the value of Lansing's manufactured products—reached $67.2 million, having increased 65 percent in a single year. And good news continued in 1928—in October, the *State Journal* reported a 24-percent increase in bank clearances and record employment in local industry, and predicted in a year-end economic wrap up that "1929 will be the greatest year in the city's history." Reo, Oldsmobile, Durant, and Motor Wheel announced plant expansions, and local unemployment was so small it could not be measured.

The balance sheets, however, tell another story. Sometime in 1927, the automobile industry—on which the prosperity of the 1920s depended—had saturated its market, and the demand for new cars fell sharply. In 1928, Reo car sales dropped by one-third, or 10,000 units, below the 1927 peak; early in 1929, the company began losing money. Reo hoped that its Flying Cloud Junior would improve business in 1929, but the downward curve gained momentum and sales plummeted disastrously to 16,100 cars, less than half the 1927 figure. Between March and August, 1929, even before the stock-market crash, employment in Lansing's 18 largest industries dropped 60 percent. Durant Motors went bankrupt shortly after the stock-market crash, and by August 1930, the city's industries employed only one-third the number who had worked in March 1929.

Until the depression reached bottom, the *State Journal* tried to promote confidence by giving prominent coverage and editorial approval to "upbeat" statements by President Herbert Hoover and other national leaders, and somehow finding reassurance even in the face of bad news. When heavy withdrawals forced the American State Savings Bank to close in December 1931, the *State Journal* took comfort in the fact that the city's other banks had withstood a brief panic. The City National Bank, of which Richard H. Scott of Reo was president, almost folded; it survived only because Capital National Bank, headed by R.E. Olds, guaranteed City National's deposits. But there was a price—Reo had to deposit $1 million for a year in Capital National, and guarantee that bank against any loss.

The incident of the bank failure and the precarious rescue of City National sent a shudder of fear through the community. Reverend R.O. Thomas of the First Presbyterian Church spoke for many in a well-publicized sermon in which he declared that "the immediate future of Lansing was in the balance." The stability of Lansing's banks had been purchased at the high cost of placing Reo, then losing heavily, at risk. But to the *State Journal,* the lesson of

the incident was that "the organization of [Lansing's economy is still intact. It is as a fat man grown lean, bu[t] still decidedly among those present."

But the bad news continued, and by the summer o[f] 1932 even the *State Journal,* which had boosted the city for years, gave vent to a spasm of doubt about the funda[-]mental soundness of the city's economy, which had de[-]pended so heavily on the automobile industry. A remark[-]able editorial wondered whether the city's miraculou[s] revival from earlier slumps had been caused not by some singular quality of the city's economy, but by timely infu[-]sions of substantial amounts of capital by R.E. Olds, General Motors, Durant, and others. During the Coolidge boom, the paper suggested, Lansing residents had "over[-]bought, over built, over expanded, and over expected . . . without much foundation." The Depression, it argued, ha[d] been caused by precisely the kind of economic over[-]expansion as had occurred in Lansing—and from the present crisis there would be no spontaneous revival. The *State Journal* and other community leaders embraced the "mature economy" view of the origins of the Depression[;] the paper warned that recovery would come only by "the slow, hard process of debt paying and saving up," which meant severe retrenchment in the private as well as the public sector.

Unemployment might have been even worse had no[t] the construction industry, another mainstay of Lansing's economy, maintained reasonably high activity through 1931. In fact, 1930 was a peak year for residential sub[-]divisions, and downtown construction continued into the early 1930s. In 1931, the 26-story Capital National Bank Tower, now the Michigan National Tower and the talles[t] building in Michigan outside Detroit, appeared at Capito[l] Avenue at Allegan, just south of the Hotel Olds. I[n] November 1932, builders completed the architecturall[y] significant 15-story Indiana-limestone Bank of Lansing a[t] the northwest corner of Michigan and Washington. The building, designed by Lansing architects Lee and Kennet[h] Black and built by the Reniger Company, omitted tellers[] cages in the banking area—a new departure in ban[k] design. Figures carved in the entrance pilasters and in the bank's huge bronze main entrance doors symbolical[ly] represented Lansing's history, and are seen today as out[-]standing examples of outdoor sculpture.

In 1931, the federal government announced a majo[r] new downtown edifice, the Lansing Post Office, now the Federal Building, whose cornerstone was laid with im[-]pressive ceremony on May 17, 1933. The $850,00[0] structure was Lansing's share of President Hoover's majo[r] program of public works. The building, covered with Min[-]nesota dolomite and decorated with marble, was seen a[s] "an excellent example of modern civic architecture." The cornerstone ceremony, however, caused a comedy of er[-]rors. By that time, the Roosevelt administration had take[n] office, and a telegram from Washington insisted that the Republican names on the cornerstone—"Ogden L. Mills[,] Secretary of the Treasury, and Ferry K. Heath, Assistan[t] Secretary"—be changed to those of Democratic officials[.] By the time the telegram arrived, however, the cor[-]nerstone had already been laid and surmounted by severa[l]

TOP: A group of Reo Motor Car Company's apprentices in front of the Reo clubhouse, 1924. The Reo Motor Car Company took great pride in its apprentice classes. Courtesy of Michigan State Archives.

The Bank of Lansing, one of the most notable structures in the downtown area, was designed by Lansing architect Kenneth Black. The building was completed in 1932. Courtesy of The Warren Holmes-Kenneth Black Company.

The interior of the Bank of Lansing. Note the carved relief at the top of the wall representing Benjamin F. Davis, president of the bank and dean of Lansing bankers. Courtesy of The Warren Holmes-Kenneth Black Company.

Lansing Between the Wars

layers of stone. Participating in the ceremony were Governor William Comstock, former Governor Wilber M. Brucker, Mayor Gray, and Grant M. Hudson, the "bone dry" former Republican Congressman who had been largely responsible for the post-office appropriation.

East Lansing's post office, now the site of the Pantree Restaurant, was built under the same program and completed later in 1933. Its construction, however, was rife with controversy. Residents complained that so much wood was used in the building's interior that it would not measure up to East Lansing's fireproof zoning ordinance for ordinary commercial buildings. Others complained that the building's architecture was "more becoming to a garage, factory, or jail than a post office" and that the building's "sore thumb" smokestack detracted from the beauty of the city. Ardent Republicans, of whom there were many in East Lansing, described the cornerstone—which bore the names of Democrats Henry J. Morgenthau and James J. Farley—as a "Democratic Monument," and wondered why the cornerstone was placed not in the traditional northeast corner of the building but in the southeast. Nor was this all. Federal officials had heard that East Lansing residents wanted a cornerstone ceremony, but by the time B.A. Faunce, East Lansing postmaster, got the invitation, the construction company already had the cornerstone in place.

Chamber of Commerce employment figures show that the economy of the capital region fluctuated considerably from 1929 to 1933, reaching bottom in November 1932, when the city's largest industries employed the full-time equivalent of only 6,000 workers. An upward trend began in 1933, and by the end of the year 11,000 workers were employed. Employment during 1934 peaked at 16,000 in March, then fell to less than 8,000 in November. By the spring of 1935, with employment hovering between 14,000 and 16,000, the worst of the unemployment crisis had passed, and the economy of the capital region, while still precarious, had weathered the worst of the Depression.

There seems little doubt that a remarkable improvement in Oldsmobile sales paced Lansing's recovery. Oldsmobile's pre-Depression sales had peaked in 1929, two years later than Reo's; even during the darkest days of the Depression, its sales showed remarkable vitality. Oldsmobile sales picked up dramatically in the spring of 1933; in May, the company reported a 25-percent increase over the first four months of 1932. In November, the company announced that its 1934 model had been so well received that it would spend $2.5 million to expand plant capacity for the production of approximately 1,000 cars a day.

The expansion was more than justified; during the 1934 model year, Oldsmobile sales were exceeded only by the lower-priced three (Ford, Chevrolet, and Plymouth). Record production continued in the spring of 1935. March output surpassed that of any previous month in the company's history, and President C.L. McCuen announced that March 12 "marked an all time peak schedule in our facilities, with the building and shipping of 931 cars." On April 9, McCuen announced that his company

had purchased the old Durant plant, which had lain idle since 1931, as the new site for Fisher Body, which would make bodies exclusively for Oldsmobiles. The ultramodern facility, when joined with Oldsmobile's other Lansing facilities, boosted daily production capacity to 1,500 cars and made Oldsmobile the fourth largest unit in the automobile industry.

McCuen's announcement, made shortly after the company had broken all previous sales and production records, caused a jubilant reaction in the city. "This appears to be the history of the city," said a "booster" quoted by the State Journal. "Just when growth seems to have reached its apex, something bobs up to stimulate a further expansion. This has been the history of Lansing, call it luck or any other name."

As the Olds Motor Works began to prosper, Reo, beset by internal dissension and mounting losses, never recovered its share of the market. In October 1930, Richard H. Scott, who had succeeded R.E. Olds as president and general manager, was forced to resign as general manager, though he retained the office of president. William Robert Wilson, an experienced automotive executive, became general manager; but the losses continued. The introduction of the Reo Royale—regarded as the most beautiful American car—and a new line of Flying Cloud models resulted in disappointing sales. The Royale and the "self-shifter," the first successful automatic transmission, had cost the company $6 million. In March 1932, Wilson resigned as general manager, and Scott resumed the position.

Losses and dissension continued, Scott was forced out again, and for a time Olds returned to active management in the affairs of the company. Finally, in May 1936, after years of losses in its automotive division, Reo withdrew from the passenger-car field and moved its truck-assembly division into its main manufacturing plant. Truck manufacturing, which had remained profitable, had kept the company from going under. "We find that the day has passed," said Reo President Donald Bates, "when trucks and buses can be considered sidelines." The company would continue to manufacture trucks and buses for the remainder of its corporate life.

Not until the 1930s did organized labor become a powerful force in the life of the capital region. Craft unions of skilled workers, mainly in the construction trades, had existed in Lansing since the 1890s, but as late as 1926 the Chamber of Commerce reported that since only one-half of one percent of the city's labor force was organized, and there were no organizations in the automobile, metal, and woodworking industries, "Lansing is totally free from union influence." Lansing had a history of industrial peace, reported the Chamber. "No serious strikes have occurred for a number of years, and industrial failures of any consequence are unknown in the city's history."

The Chamber of Commerce attributed Lansing's "wholesome labor market" to several factors. Employers—most notably, Reo—had organized programs of social and recreational activities for their workers. A large part of Lansing's recreational life

100

BELOW: The administration building of Olds Motor Works, 1931. Amazingly, Oldsmobile sales showed vitality even during the Depression years. Courtesy of the Oldsmobile Division, General Motors.

RIGHT: Reo Motor Car Company truck engines ready for installation, circa 1940. Courtesy of Michigan State University Archives and Historical Collection.

LEFT: One of the earliest aerial views of Lansing, 1932. From Abrams Aerial Survey.

Lansing Between the Wars

revolved around the Reo Clubhouse. The Industrial Branch of the YMCA "played no small part in promoting harmonious relations between employer and employee." But there were also hard economic facts. More than half of Lansing's workers, said the Chamber, "enjoy a work year of more than 260 days of employment"—a considerable achievement at a time when employment in many basic industries, including automobiles, was often seasonal and erratic. Although higher average wages were paid in other parts of the country, the "consistency of employment" and "ideal conditions under which workers live in Lansing" tended to diminish interest in labor unions.

The Depression changed everything. In October 1932, the employees of the Lansing Transportation Company, which operated the city's streetcar service, went out on strike. Some strikers operated "jitney cabs," picking up passengers ahead of the streetcars. In the spring of 1933, the company, already in the hands of receivers, suspended operations, and for the first time in 30 years the city was without public transportation. For a time the Muskegon Bus Company operated its buses on Lansing streets, and soon the streetcar tracks and loading docks disappeared.

Labor unrest in Lansing reached a peak in the spring and summer of 1937, during a wave of sit-down strikes in many automotive cities. On March 10, 90 percent of the Reo workers, angered at the firing of 15 men and a cut in wages, "sat down" 10 minutes before closing and refused to leave the factory until their demands—which included recognition of the United Auto Workers, CIO, as their sole bargaining agent—were met. This strike, which lasted a month, was the first major labor incident involving a Lansing automobile manufacturer. Mayor Max A. Templeton offered to mediate the dispute, but not until Governor Frank Murphy intervened was the strike settled. On April 7, the company agreed to recognize the union; the settlement paralleled that accepted by Chrysler 12 hours earlier.

The attempt of the UAW to organize the workers of the Capitol City Wrecking Company led to the "Labor Holiday" of 1937, one of the most remembered incidents of the 1930s in Lansing. Lester Washburn, president of Local 182 of the UAW-CIO, led the drive to organize the 25 workers at the lumbering and wrecking company. Six employees who joined the union were dismissed on the grounds that there was no work; a week later, the company hired six new employees. Washburn's attempts to negotiate with the company were rebuffed, and on May 21, 100 Local 182 pickets appeared at the plant and discouraged employees from going to work. The company, forced to suspend operations, sought an injunction to prevent picketing, and the struggle widened as workers in building-materials companies began a slowdown to force a settlement of the strike. On June 1, after complicated legal proceedings, Judge Leland W. Carr issued the injunction, but picketing continued in the face of his order. Sheriff Allan MacDonald issued an ultimatum, but as the hour struck, declined to interfere with the pickets in order to avoid violence.

Sheriff MacDonald, perhaps impetuously, decided on a course of action that had remarkable repercussions. On Monday, June 7, at 2:00 a.m., MacDonald and his deputies descended on the homes of Washburn and several other strike leaders, but found Washburn absent. They arrested eight persons, including Mrs. Washburn, and charged that they had used threats and intimidation to interfere with an employee of the company who had attempted to go to work.

Years later, Washburn recalled that he learned of the arrests when he returned from Detroit at 2:30 a.m.; he contacted other labor leaders, and all agreed that Lansing automobile workers would be asked to take a one-day holiday. A ringing statement was issued to the press, denouncing the "superlatively brave action" of Sheriff MacDonald in "dragging a harmless and innocent woman out of her bed in the middle of the night" and leaving several young children alone. To celebrate the sheriff's "brave act," the local UAW proclaimed a labor holiday, "so the world will never forget Sheriff MacDonald and his courageous deed."

It seemed ironic that Lansing, with its history of industrial peace, should become the scene of a general strike, a relatively rare phenomenon in American labor history. By 9:00 a.m., crowds of workers flooded downtown, stopped traffic, and demanded that all stores and offices be closed. Traffic came to a standstill. Many drivers abandoned their cars, and a parade of about 2,000 persons marching four abreast, led by two flag bearers and including many women in housedresses, descended on City Hall and demanded the release of the prisoners. Mayor Templeton said that he could not release the prisoners, and the crowd then moved toward the capitol to see the governor.

The "general strike" had limited objectives—the release of the prisoners and negotiations to end the Capitol City Wrecking Company strike. By early afternoon, the crowd downtown was apparently becoming restless, and much credit must be given to Governor Murphy, who returned to Lansing from Detroit as soon as he heard of the strike, for preventing an escalation of the incident. Murphy called a meeting of all persons involved in the dispute and assured the crowd from the capitol balcony that "there will be no injustices practiced on you while the governor can prevent it. It is not necessary for you to do any extreme or dangerous thing. You know you will get your rights." Five of the prisoners were released at 5:00 p.m., and the remainder were discharged the following morning after posting $200 bonds.

The Lansing Labor Holiday spilled into neighboring East Lansing and touched off a series of incidents that have become known as the Battle of Grand River Avenue. Some union members drove to East Lansing to close stores, including the cafeterias on Grand River Avenue at which many students took their meals. Store owners generally complied, but a crowd of about 500 students gathered and the union men met resistance at the shoe store of one James Brakeman, located on Grand River Avenue between Abbott Road and MAC Avenue. The students began to clear the streets of cars that had blocked traffic, and they tipped one car over. When additional cars of union men, dressed in light blue capes, appeared, some students removed the passengers and threw them into the

LEFT: An early-day photograph of Lansing's Labor Holiday, 1937. In this scene workers have begun to block traffic on Michigan Avenue. Courtesy of Ralph Lewis.

BELOW: Max A. Templeton, mayor of Lansing from 1933 to 1941, led the city during the depths of the Depression. His conservative "pay as you go" financial program was controversial, but it won Lansing its exceptionally high credit rating. Courtesy of Lansing Public Library.

ABOVE: Headline news of the Lansing Labor Holiday in 1937. Courtesy of Ralph Lewis.

RIGHT: Strikers gathered at the front of Michigan's capitol on Labor Holiday, 1937. Courtesy of Ralph Lewis.

Lansing Between the Wars

Red Cedar River. Tension was high; no one, however, was seriously hurt. When the crowd of students began to push the union men back toward Lansing, East Lansing Police Chief Castle Pratt attempted to come between the contending factions, and about five minutes of fistfights ensued. When a group of students charged their flank, the outnumbered union men called for a cessation of hostilities.

Much of the fighting occurred in close quarters. A spectator described the scene as "the Battle of Bunker Hill and a mardi gras all rolled into one." The bright blue capes of the union organizers became prized souvenirs. The *State Journal* reported that "candid camera fiends" found the campus battle "a prolific source of rare shots." It seems that everyone who owned a camera recorded the scene; the local camera shop ran out of film. Governor Murphy, who lived in Cowles House on campus, first learned of the trouble when a group of students asked his permission to take several cavalry horses, kept by the college ROTC program, to ride down the UAW men. The governor thought the idea "too Cossack like." For a time, Murphy and a state police aide watched the fight from a hill near the college hospital, but they did not intervene as the fight seemed to be winding down.

The Lansing Labor Holiday came just at the time when the local economy was being revived from an unexpected source—the construction industry. Lansing-area construction contracts had totaled slightly more than $1 million in 1935; that figure doubled in 1936, and quadrupled in 1937. Early in 1937, the *State Journal* reported that more construction was going on in Lansing than in any other city in outstate Michigan; only Detroit had more building activity. The real-estate market picked up, with lot sales in 1937 reaching the levels of 1927 and 1928.

It became apparent early in 1936 that the capital region was undergoing another construction boom. The most significant new downtown structure of the new building wave was the J.W. Knapp department store on the Washington Avenue site of the old Downey Hotel. The new five-story Art Deco structure, of glass brick and tan-enameled stone with windows only at entrance doors and the fifth floor, contrasted starkly with the Victorian-era mansard-roofed store buildings nearby. To the *State Journal*, the new store symbolized not merely a daring innovation in downtown store architecture but "a symbol of the new era in America. The old is giving way to the new and modern construction is replacing the old style everywhere."

The new store, with its brave new architecture, symbolized a willingness to break with the past and face the future with confidence; but building the new store caused the destruction of an old and venerated Lansing landmark. The night before the Downey was razed, the members of the Lansing Newspaper Guild, many of whose members had fond memories of the old hotel, met in its Red Room for a final "threnody," or dirge. Lou Rowley, Roy Vandercook, and other old newsmen recalled incidents when the Downey was "on the capitol beat." But *State Journal* publisher Paul Martin closed the evening with the toast: "Today."

Michigan State College also weathered the Depression

and expanded during the 1930s. The legislature trimmed appropriations for 1932-33; during the banking crisis of 1933, with college funds frozen in closed banks, President Shaw brought in cash by armored car to pay salaries. Shaw managed to reduce expenses without compromising the mission of the college; in 1933-34, expenses generally were cut 11 percent, but salaries were reduced only 7 percent.

At the same time, in order to lessen the impact of bad times on the students, fees were reduced from $35 to $30, and loan funds were increased. The National Youth Administration, a New Deal agency, made it possible for thousands of students to attend college by a work-study arrangement under which students might receive about $15 dollars a month, enough for books and expenses. "The students on the East Lansing campus," reported the *State Journal* during the banking holiday, "are somehow getting along, and there is no evidence that any are going hungry." Rooming house proprietors generally extended credit, but payment for board was demanded every week.

During the early 1930s, the college was involved in a financial scandal. Ingham County Circuit Judge Leland W. Carr, acting as a one-man grand jury, and Assistant Attorney General Joseph A. Baldwin conducted separate investigations into a series of charges: that campus salaries were deposited in local banks of which college personnel were officers; that the college had paid exorbitant fees for landscape gardening; that members of the music-school faculty had used campus buildings for private lessons.

While the charges made sensational newspaper copy, Carr and Baldwin found no substance to them. The college routinely deposited employees' paychecks in banks of their own choice, some of them far from the area. Baldwin wrote that "ninety-nine percent of the people interviewed by me voluntarily expressed themselves as having absolute confidence in the ability and integrity of President Shaw." Carr agreed; in his view, the charges originated in "critical remarks, magnified and distorted by repetition." Other charges were made, but these, too, were found to be without substance.

The incident led to the greatest shake-up in the history of the college. The board fired three staff members who had circulated the charges: Dean of Agriculture Joseph F. Cox; Professor James B. Hasselman, head of journalism and sports announcer; and Frank S. Kedzie, former president and dean of applied science. For the first time since the 1860s, there would be no Kedzie on campus. To place the college operations beyond reproach, Shaw also made several administrative changes, including a modification of the office of college secretary, whose power had begun to rival that of the president. The incumbent secretary retired in 1935; John A. Hannah, his successor, was placed in charge of the college property, but subject to the board through the president.

Hannah's appearance on the scene was an important event in the history not merely of the college but of the capital region. He succeeded Shaw as president in 1941 and contributed powerfully toward building the college, which became Michigan State University in 1955, to its present eminence. His importance in the area is at least equal to that of R.E. Olds.

Despite the Depression, Shaw and Hannah began a campus building program. The net worth of the college buildings, grounds, and equipment increased from $6 million in 1928, the first year of Shaw's administration, to $15 million in 1941, when Hannah became president. The building program was so extensive, wrote Madison Kuhn, that a student graduated in 1928 who returned in 1941 "might have thought that the Depression had not touched his alma mater."

The campus building wave began in 1928 with the completion of Beaumont Tower on the site of Old College Hall. A Detroit lawyer, James W. Beaumont of the class of 1882, and his wife donated the money for the campanile tower "to commemorate the spot" that had given him "the greatest pleasures" of his student days. The tower now contains a carillon bell and clock. Despite the financial crisis, the college building program proceeded throughout the 1930s, thanks to private funds early in the decade and grants from federal relief and recovery programs after 1935.

Since the college lacked the authority to borrow directly, the Detroit and Security Trust Company sold 6-percent certificates and built and leased to the college the Mary Mayo dormitory for women in 1931; student rentals retired the debt. The Mary Mayo dormitory, near the Beal entrance to the campus, is an outstanding collegiate Gothic structure with interesting buttresses and arches. Other dormitories—named for Sarah Langdon Williams, Theophilus C. Abbott, Stevens T. Mason, and Mrs. Louise C. Campbell—were built after the authority of the college to borrow on its own was established. Public Works Administration funds assisted in the construction of such major campus structures as the Auditorium and Theater, Jenison Fieldhouse, the Music Building, and the Olin Memorial Health Center.

The building wave revived interest in city planning. A generation had passed since the last city plan; in December 1936, Mayor Max A. Templeton appointed a group of distinguished citizens—H. Lee Bancroft, Otto Eckert, and Kenneth Black—to form a new planning commission. Bancroft and Eckert, both long-term city officials, had served on the planning commission of 1921; Black was a Lansing architect. The commission recommended that the city once again engage the firm of Harland Bartholemew to prepare a master plan; significantly, the state of Michigan cooperated by retaining the same firm to prepare a plan for state buildings.

The assumptions of the new plan differed sharply from that of 1921; the "city beautiful" approach was much less evident, having been replaced by "city functional" planning, a straightforward engineering solution to such problems as traffic flow and the probable direction of population growth. Compared with that of 1921, the 1938 re-

John A. Hannah as an extension agent, shortly after he graduated from Michigan Agricultural College in 1923. Hannah became college secretary in 1935 and president in 1941. Courtesy of Michigan State University Archives and Historical Collections.

port showed more sophistication in its analyses of land use and demography, and perhaps most significantly, an awareness of the need for regional planning. By 1938, the automobile had transformed Lansing's relationship with the surrounding area; the city's economic reach—as shown in commuting distances and a greatly expanded market region—meant that the future of the city and a growing area of its hinterland were intertwined.

Bartholemew complimented Lansing on the progress made under his original plan, which, though never officially adopted, appeared to have influenced city officials and real-estate developers. The earlier Bartholemew report had stimulated, among other things, an improved street plan with about seven miles of new thoroughfares, 300 acres of new parks, including Groesbeck and Red Cedar golf courses, additions to Potter Park, Scott Field, two new school sites "of adequate size," and nearly 11,000 street trees. And Bartholemew was pleased that "a decided improvement has been made in the design of new subdivisions."

The city had also adopted a zoning ordinance—fundamental to orderly growth—in 1927. "Much undesirable development," said Bartholemew, "has been excluded from residential districts by the enforcement of the zoning ordinance." The fact that the city had undergone considerable commercial and industrial growth showed that "zoning does not retard desirable growth but merely guides it along proper lines." Bartholemew noted that "some undesirable modifications and variations had been made" in the zoning ordinance, but stressed that the city would have had "a much greater amount of scattered and undesirable development if there had been no zoning ordinance."

Sophisticated analysis of probable population growth was a hallmark of Bartholemew's new approach to city planning. Industrial employees—among whom Bartholemew included construction workers—accounted for nearly half of the employed persons in Lansing. Bartholemew, influenced by the "mature economy" ideas of the Depression era, doubted that Lansing would ever again experience significant growth from this source. "This type of industry," he wrote, "is probably approaching its capacity for employment and it is doubtful that its future growth will ever be comparable to that of the recent past." Unless one or more large Lansing plants closed, however, "the present ratio of industrial employment will continue and a large percentage of wage earners will be employed by industry."

Bartholemew found that slightly more than half of the Lansing labor force was engaged in nonindustrial pursuits. "This diversification of employment," he wrote, "minimizes dangers present in a town concentrating on one single type of industry." By the mid-1930s, the functions of state government had expanded to the point that 2,700 state employees—more than the Reo labor force of 1936—lived in Lansing, and there was no longer any question that the presence of the capital stabilized the local economy. As state government grew, so did the number of visitors and sightseers, a factor of growing importance to the city's retail trade. And Michigan State

College—whose enrollment had doubled in a decade—was becoming an important factor in the area. In 1937, college students and faculty spent an estimated $5 million directly or indirectly in Lansing; Bartholemew believed that "the anticipated gradual increase in such expenditure will continue to be an important influence."

Lansing's population remained relatively stable during the 1930s, increasing by only 356 persons, or one half of one percent, between 1930 and 1940. This small population increase is sometimes cited as an effect of the Depression. But if Lansing's population remained relatively stable, that of the surrounding area did not; the "five-township area," which included the cities of Lansing and East Lansing, grew 12.6 percent during the decade, substantially more than the average for cities in Michigan (4.6 percent), the state generally (8.5 percent), and the country at large (7.2 percent). During the 1920s, the five-township area had grown by 51.4 percent, compared with 36.8 percent in Lansing. The fact that Lansing land values had increased and vacant land had largely disappeared within city limits largely explains the greater population growth of contiguous areas.

Bartholemew was not sanguine, however, about continued population growth in the capital region. In addition to the "mature economy" as a factor limiting population growth, the birth rate had declined during the 1930s. The population of the capital region, Bartholemew predicted, would gradually increase to a peak of about 146,000 by 1960, then level off and remain stationary. He could not, of course, have predicted the economic growth of the 1940s or the "baby boom" of the 1950s, which would cause the population of the five-township area to reach 158,293 by 1950 and 198,142 by 1960.

Much of Bartholemew's 1938 report dealt with such technical matters as traffic flow and zoning. His recommendations in these areas were eventually adopted and had an important effect on the development of the city. The 1938 report also included a plan for city and state buildings in downtown Lansing. This plan, eventually adopted in its broad outlines, continues to have an important effect on the central core of the capital region.

For the state of Michigan, Bartholemew proposed a "general plan for State Capitol Development"—a complex of buildings behind the western portico of the capitol. Bartholemew considered the capitol adequate, but suggested a new capitol site several blocks to the west should the state decide that a new edifice was needed. He recommended building three office structures and a state auditorium close to the capitol, and a governor's mansion on a site on South Capitol Avenue. The three office buildings would barely meet existing needs, as the state was then renting space all over downtown Lansing. The auditorium would house the state library and museum and become a cultural center as well as a locale for public functions.

For the city, Bartholemew proposed a city hall, jail, and "civic center" or large auditorium for conventions and public meetings. These structures, too, were eventually built, but the coming of the Second World War disrupted life in the capital region and their completion was delayed for a generation.

LEFT: This often photographed freak of nature was removed in 1925 for the purpose of widening the road. It was sometimes called "half way rock," as it stood midway between Lansing and East Lansing. Courtesy of Michigan State Archives.

BELOW: The J.W. Knapp store, South Washington Avenue, Lansing. Built in 1937, it was a dazzling addition to the downtown district. In 1980 the store's parent firm went bankrupt, causing the J.W. Knapp store to close its doors. Photograph by author.

Chapter 11

THE SECOND WORLD WAR AND AFTER

The 1930s began in Depression and ended in war, and both these traumas profoundly affected the life of the capital region. President Franklin D. Roosevelt's New Deal program had begun to wind down in 1936, and after the court-packing fight and sit-down strikes of 1937, national attention shifted increasingly from the waning Depression at home to the ominous events abroad. The Second World War began in September 1939, and the election of 1940 largely revolved around issues of defense and foreign policy. The voters, strongly influenced by the fall of France, Dunkirk, and the bombing of London, elected Roosevelt for a third term and endorsed his policies of defense spending, peacetime draft, and all-out aid to the Allies.

An immediate effect of the prewar defense program in the capital region was a great reduction in unemployment, as government contracts sparked an expansion of local industry. That Lansing had become a major center of war production even before Pearl Harbor may be seen in a *State Journal* estimate of December 5, 1941, that 20 to 25 percent of the city's labor force was engaged in war work, a higher proportion than in any other Michigan city except Detroit. Atlas Drop Forge had begun manufacturing tank and aircraft castings. The Nash-Kelvinator Company, occupying two vacant Reo buildings on South Washington Avenue, began manufacturing three-bladed propellers and aircraft-engine parts; the company announced plans to hire 8,000 additional employees by the end of 1942.

The Pearl Harbor attack on December 7, 1941, shocked Lansing residents as it did other Americans. Rumors flew thick and fast on the fateful day, and the *State Journal* was forced to delay its "War Extra" for eight hours. At noon on the following day, a *State Journal* reporter heard the broadcast of Roosevelt's war message in a crowded downtown Lansing Chinese restaurant. "Throughout the talk by the President," he wrote, "there was a prayer-like stillness among the people, and when the band struck up *The Star Spangled Banner,* there was a rumble of chairs as the crowd came to attention."

With the coming of War, Lansing's "defense industries" became war plants, and before long the city became a vital center for the production of armaments. On February 5, 1942, the last Oldsmobile—a Series 98 four-door sedan—rolled off the assembly line, as the company shut down to retool for war production. The shutdown was the first since 1897 at that time of the model year. During the war, Oldsmobile manufactured tank cannon, various types of antiaircraft guns, and artillery shells in prodigious numbers.

The city quickly assumed a war footing. By Christmas 1941, all industries were working round-the-clock, 24-hour schedules; production continued even on Christmas and other holidays for the duration of the war. Lansing Mayor Sam Street Hughes organized a civil-defense program. At 2:00 a.m. on February 8, 1942, Austin Deford, the city-hall custodian, advanced the municipal clock one hour to conform with "war time," and there it remained until the close of hostilities. A government "brownout" order dimmed outdoor lights on all retail stores, theaters, and the capitol dome.

Before the war ended, 24 Lansing war plants held government contracts, and scores of smaller firms produced component parts on a subcontract basis. Reo manufactured trucks and heavy equipment. By 1943, the Nash-Kelvinator plant had become the world's largest producer of airplane propellers, employing 8,500 workers in its $80-million facility. Its three- and four-bladed, controlled-pitch, hydromatic propellers were used on B-17 and B-24 bombers, on several types of carrier-based aircraft, and even on the British Lancaster, York, and Mosquito bombers. Fisher Body—which manufactured ailerons, rudders, and elevators for the B-29—had one of the largest war contracts in the area. Federal, Lindell, and Atlas Drop Forge made castings of every conceivable variety; Abrams Instrument, Dail Steel Products, Olofsson Tool and Die, and the Novo Engine Company also held major war contracts. With wartime labor shortages, thousands of women worked in these and other Lansing industries.

The war placed strains on Lansing's already tight housing market; federal officials eased restrictions to permit the building of several thousand housing units, mainly in the Everett School district and areas north and east of Lansing. But housing continued to be in short supply, and during the war thousands of workers, forced to reside from 10 to 60 miles from the city, had to commute great distances. Early in 1942, the *State Journal* estimated that housing shortages had compelled 35 percent of Lansing's industrial workers to live outside the city limits.

The war years were an important interlude in the transformation of Michigan State College into Michigan State University. The war sharply reduced the number of male students; by the spring of 1945, the student body contained 2,705 women and only 946 men, most of them under draft age, handicapped, or in a few cases returned veterans. Traditional college activities—intercollegiate athletics, the yearbook, the annual water carnival, and even the campus Christmas tree—were suspended for the duration. "Many of the trimmings are gone," wrote the

One of the first postwar Oldsmobiles, 1945. Courtesy of the Oldsmobile Division, General Motors.

109

editor of the campus newspaper, "but it is still Michigan State."

Between the spring of 1943 and the end of the war, some 10,000 army and air-corps personnel received training on campus. In March 1943, the 310th College Training (Aircrew) Detachment arrived for five months of intensive general education before beginning flight training. Five similar contingents, each with 300 men, began training and were replaced by others at the end of five months until the program ended in June 1944. The Army Specialist Training Program enrolled hundreds in an engineering program. The soldiers marched to class in groups of 25 on a campus from which automobiles had largely disappeared. "As they marched," remembered Professor Madison Kuhn, "they sang of the wild blue yonder, and, as well, of the banks of the Red Cedar."

The general-education program—in which the air cadets received instruction in physics, chemistry, mathematics through trigonometry, and the history of the war—was not narrowly technical. "As students," wrote Kuhn, who taught them, "the cadets proved to be a gratifying surprise." Kuhn had expected that the cadets would be "indifferent scholars" in liberal-arts courses; he soon found that they were "highly motivated" and alert "out of proportion" to their demanding schedule, which included military training, vigorous physical education, and dual-flight instruction in addition to academic classes.

Other soldiers were trained as engineers under the Army Specialist Training Program; these men, too, had courses in English, chemistry, mathematics, physics, and history in addition to military training. In July 1943, 300 men began preparing for postwar military government; they received three hours daily of intense language drill and also studied the history, culture, and social and economic organization of various countries. "Student progress," wrote Kuhn, "was phenomenal."

The college underwent no intellectual decline in teaching the military students; the army had shown that even wartime technical training could not omit the arts and sciences. At the same time, thousands of military personnel from all parts of the country had positive experiences on the Michigan State campus, thus enormously enhancing the reputation of the institution nationwide.

For its regular students, the college created a whole series of war-related courses, including mapmaking from aerial photographs, geopolitics, food technology, and contemporary history. Research—much of it secret—focused on food production and preservation. Horticultural specialists searched for the substance that spoiled dehydrated vegetables; other researchers found more effective means of preserving food shipped to combat zones and discovered a way of speeding up the production of the raw material from which penicillin was made.

Little but war news appeared in the local press. The *State Journal* published daily news of Lansing-area service personnel, and casualty lists lengthened. The most stirring event in the war—the Normandy invasion of June 6, 1944—occurred shortly after the city celebrated the 80th birthday of R.E. Olds on June 2; the municipal birthday celebration honored the man more responsible than

anyone for Lansing's automobile industry and its emergence as a wartime armaments center. On June 4, Olds gave the city the gift of Grand River Park. At 10:00 a.m. on June 6, church bells tolled and factory whistles sounded, and in all of Lansing's war industries workers paused for a moment of silent prayer. "The invasion," reported the *State Journal*, "dissolved the air of expectancy, and replaced it with one of concentrated effort."

As victory became imminent, Lansing turned to planning for the postwar era, when the city's excellent financial position would at last make possible the execution of Bartholemew's plan for downtown buildings. By 1944, the city had eliminated its debt, and on June 4, Mayor Ralph W. Crego inaugurated postwar planning by appointing a committee of aldermen to study the city's needs and propose a plan of action. The long-discussed new city hall, Crego announced, would cost about $1.5 million; the city had ample funds in reserve, and the Board of Water and Light had agreed not only to participate in paying for the structure but also to locate its offices there. The Junior Chamber of Commerce, concerned that the end of the war would bring unemployment to the city, suggested that Lansing annex heavily populated areas in Lansing Township "to provide years of postwar improvement work." The JCs also suggested that the Lansing and East Lansing city limits be joined, and H. Lee Bancroft, an old hand at city planning, suggested that Lansing push its city limits south to Cavanaugh Road.

The state of Michigan began planning its capitol group, and by late June 1944, *State Journal* writer Seth Whitmore reported that the city and state had plans for spending $25 million on various Lansing building projects. "To some," wrote Whitmore, "this may seem like an astonishing amount," but the annual cost of city government, including the schools, was about $2.5 million during the war. In addition, enormous sums had been spent in the city by war industries. "When one looks at the figures of war contracts held by local industry since Pearl Harbor," he said, "the $25,000,000 is but a drop in the bucket." Far more than $25 million—$80 million, in fact—had been spent in converting two vacant buildings into the Nash-Kelvinator propeller plant.

Whitmore spoke for a generation that had undergone the privations of the Depression and wartime shortages and was ready for a new wave of civic improvements. "Some city officials," said Whitmore, "are inclined to think in terms of pre-war finances and WPA wages, but those days, like the horse and buggy days, have gone forever." In planning for the future, he urged, "we must think of every desirable improvement that we can make"—including, in addition to the building projects, annexing the greater part of Lansing Township and extending the city's utility services to all populated areas.

As the war approached its end, the postwar plans began to take shape. In May 1945, shortly after V-E Day, the state acquired the first of 30 parcels of real estate for its capitol group; property owners were given a chance to buy back and move their houses. In August 1945, several days before the dropping of the atomic bomb on Hiroshima, the city began taking preliminary steps toward acquiring 13 parcels of real estate on the block of the Prudden Auditorium for its convention center. A *State Journal* editorial urged that the city move quickly, so that construction might begin as soon as the war ended in order to keep local employment at a high level. Later that month, plans for the new city hall, to be erected on the site of the old city hall, were announced by the architect Kenneth Black.

V-E Day in May did not produce the same wild demonstrations in Lansing as in New York and other cities; wartime restrictions were somewhat eased as the red and white floodlights that had illuminated the capitol dome were turned on and thousands of light bulbs were replaced in theater marquees and store windows. The day after the dropping of the atomic bomb, Board of Water and Light president Otto E. Eckert revealed that a turbine generator intended for the city's Ottawa Street power station had been commandeered by the atomic bomb plant at Oak Ridge, Tennessee.

The Japanese surrender, after several false reports, was officially announced about 7:00 p.m. on August 14, 1945. To the *State Journal*, it was "beautifully symbolic of the coming of peace" that the setting sun broke through overcast clouds as thousands converged on downtown for an extraordinary spontaneous celebration. The intersection of Michigan and Washington became a milling throng of college students, factory workers, and service men and women. Factory whistles, church bells, air-raid sirens, and thousands of automobile horns kept up a terrific din for hours; in front of the capitol, a marine was borne aloft by the crowd, and snake dances involving thousands of persons continued downtown and in residential areas until far into the night.

One effect of the Second World War was a significant increase in Lansing's black population. The city had a small black population from the time of its founding; the census of 1850 showed 13 blacks in a population of 1,229, or about one percent of the total. The black population reached a peak of 351 in 1890, or about 2.6 percent of the population, then declined slightly in 1900 to 323 persons, or 2 percent of the total.

Although the number of black persons in Lansing increased during the early 20th century, the white population increased even more rapidly, and the percentage of blacks remained at less than 2 percent until 1940. During the Second World War, the black population almost doubled, from 1,638 in 1940 to 2,971 in 1950, representing 3.3 percent of the population. During the decade of the 1960s, the black population increased again; by 1969 it reached about 11,000, or 8.5 percent of the city's total population.

The blacks, though largely ignored by the press, were a thriving if small community before the Second World War. On August 1, 1907, Lansing blacks held an Emancipation Day celebration that attracted persons from throughout the state. The Lansing Afro-American Business Men's Association sponsored the affair, which included an industrial parade and culminated in an evening celebration at Waverly Park. In 1912, Booker T. Washington addressed a large interracial gathering at the Masonic temple.

An incident occurred in December 1915, involving the film *Birth of a Nation*. This film, which portrayed the post-Civil War Ku Klux Klan in a favorable light, offended blacks; the city council, over the strong protests of the newspapers, passed the "Decke Ordinance," permitting censorship of films "calculated to arouse hatred of Negroes." Although the film was eventually shown in area theaters, the incident showed that the blacks were occasionally able to wield political power.

Neither in Lansing nor in other Northern industrial cities were blacks afforded anything resembling equal employment opportunities. Their jobs in Lansing's growing automobile industry were usually the most menial and dangerous, and though the local Ku Klux Klan seems to have been mainly anti-Catholic, it remained a source of apprehension for Lansing-area blacks.

Perhaps the most important memoir of Negro life in Lansing from the late 1920s to the outbreak of the Second World War is *The Autobiography of Malcolm X*, who grew up in the area as Malcolm Little. Malcolm's father, the Reverend Earl Little, was a Baptist minister and follower of Marcus Garvey, the Black Nationalist leader. In the black community of Lansing during the 1930s, Malcolm X recalled, "to be a janitor at some downtown store was to be highly respected." The "elite" of the black community were "the waiters at the Lansing Country Club and the shoeshine boys at the state capitol." Most blacks, because of the Depression and discrimination in employment, "were either on Welfare, or W.P.A., or they starved." And discrimination went beyond employment. "No Negroes," he wrote, "were allowed on the streets . . . [in East Lansing] after dark."

An early tragedy in the life of Malcolm X was the murder of his father early in the 1930s. "Negroes in Lansing have always whispered," he wrote, "that he was attacked, probably by members of the 'Black Legion,'" an extremist group of the period, "and then laid over some tracks for a streetcar to run over him." Malcolm X got into trouble at school and was sent to a detention home in Mason, where he attended the public schools and made an excellent record before he left the area for Boston in 1943.

Lansing-area blacks began taking steps to secure their rights. A Negro Civil League, formed sometime early in the century, became the nucleus of the Lansing Branch of the National Association for the Advancement of Colored People. The minutes of the first meeting—recorded by Hesper A. Jackson, secretary—reported that "after three months of watchful waiting . . . our Civil Rights Bill was passed yesterday." The Civil Rights Bill, an important goal of the Negro Civil League, outlawed the more blatant forms of denial of public accommodations on racial grounds.

After the bill became law, the Lansing Branch brought legal action against two Lansing restaurants that had refused to serve blacks—the Little Downey and a Chinese cafe. The proprietor of the Little Downey pleaded guilty, paid his fine, and promised "to offer equal service to the colored people." Chief of Police Alfred Seymour, through

111

an interpreter, explained the Civil Rights Act to the proprietor of the Chinese cafe, and thereafter black customers were courteously served.

During the 1950s, as a result of such traditional practices as restrictive covenants, Lansing's blacks found themselves restricted increasingly to the west side of the city; this residential containment was intensified by the building of the I-496 expressway and the expansion of the Oldsmobile plant and the state governmental complex. As a result, by 1960 there were three elementary schools with more than 90 percent black students, and one with 70 percent, as well as a junior high school with more than 90 percent and a senior high school with 95 percent.

In 1963, the Lansing Branch of the NAACP, through its education committee, made representations to the Board of Education for the elimination of segregation. The Lansing Branch asked that the board "make a formal statement favoring the elimination of school segregation wherever it exists regardless of the cause," that the boundaries of West Junior High School—with an overwhelming black enrollment—be redrawn, and that a citizens' advisory committee on integration be appointed. The Lansing Branch also urged the hiring of at least one Negro teacher in every Lansing school.

The board complied, and on June 4, 1964, unanimously approved a statement of equal educational opportunity and appointed the citizens' committee that the Lansing Branch had requested. In April 1964, the board adopted a publication of the Michigan Department of Public Instruction, *The Treatment of Minority Groups in Textbooks,* as a guiding philosophy for the Lansing public schools.

The citizens' committee did its work, and in 1967 the board issued a statement of principles on achieving racial balance in the Lansing schools and announced a plan for busing to achieve integration of the city's three high schools. A group of white citizens brought suit against the plan; the NAACP filed a brief on behalf of the school board, and the court ordered integration to proceed.

By 1969, many blacks who had been actively critical of the system had achieved positions of influence within it. Hortense Canady, a member of the NAACP education committee, was the first black member of the Lansing Board of Education; she is now assistant director of financial aid at Lansing Community College. Dr. Calvin Anderson became principal of Everett High School, the first black principal of a Lansing senior high; Eva Evans became director of elementary education for the Lansing School District; Lee Richardson became assistant principal for adult education and Margaret Groves, consultant in personnel for the Lansing public schools. John Porter became Michigan's superintendent of public instruction, Sandra Huggins served as assistant personnel director for Michigan State University, and Dr. Hazel Turner became an assistant superintendent in the Ann Arbor public schools. Going even further afield, Yvonne Duncan became an administrator in the public schools of Denver, Colorado, and William Ford became an administrator in the Agency for International Development. Joel Ferguson, now a real-estate developer, was the first black person

elected to the Lansing city council.

Plans for integrating Lansing's schools proceeded amid considerable controversy. The Lansing Branch of the NAACP ultimately filed suit in federal court, and on December 19, 1975, Judge Noel Fox, ruling that Lansing "had created and maintained a segregated, dual school system" in violation of the Constitution, ordered that plans for integration be implemented in September of 1976. The school board appealed, and on June 26, 1978, the Supreme Court of the United States upheld Judge Fox's ruling. John Davis, the young NAACP attorney who first entered the case in 1972, is the grandson of Hesper A. Jackson, the first secretary and later president of the Lansing Branch of the NAACP.

The Second World War also had the effect of significantly increasing the Lansing area's Mexican-American community. "Lansing seems pretty far north for a Mexican community," wrote the folklorist Richard M. Dobson in 1947, "and yet some two hundred Mexican people make their permanent home in Lansing." The Mexicans, who had begun to appear in significant numbers about 1941, had been migratory agricultural workers who came every summer from Texas and Mexico; during the war, they found employment in local industry and construction and made the area their permanent home. Many bought homes, mostly along Case Street and along U.S. 27 on the north side of the city.

Lansing's postwar years began in a season of difficulties; several years elapsed before Oldsmobile sales—which paced the city's economy—surpassed the 1941 sales of a quarter of a million cars. The General Motors strike of November 25, 1945, to April 1, 1946, limited sales to only 102,302 in 1946, despite the enormous pent-up demand for consumer durable goods. A recession in 1948 caused a further drop in sales to 70,146 cars, but sales of 270,286 in 1949 at last surpassed those of 1941. Oldsmobile's "Rocket" engine, attractive design, and reputation for quality enabled its sales to hover between fourth and fifth place in the industry. Between 1941 and 1950, the company sold a million cars, and by May 1953, it had sold another million; in the peak year of 1955, a record 609,594 cars were sold, and the company chalked up yet another million sales.

In the 15 years after the Second World War, the city increased in population and expanded its boundaries. Lansing's population, 78,753 in 1940, grew to 92,129 in 1950 and 108,128 in 1960, representing a 37-percent increase in 20 years. While much of this growth was due to natural increase, annexations in 1949, 1950, 1955, 1957, and 1958 extended the city's boundaries to the Clinton and Eaton county lines. The annexation of enclaves between Lansing and East Lansing gave the cities a common boundary, and the city of Lansing now covered more than 20 square miles, an area 10 times greater than the original two square miles of the Town of Michigan.

In April 1947, the city experienced its most disastrous flood. The high-water mark was an inch short of the 1904 disaster, but a 100-square-block area on the city's east side remained under water for a week, and damage was estimated at $2 million. The rapid melting of an unusually

RIGHT: **This special three cent stamp commemorated the centennials of Michigan State College and Pennsylvania State University. Courtesy of Michigan State University Publications.**

BELOW: **Sam Street Hughes, mayor of Lansing from 1941 to 1943, attempted to consolidate local government agencies. Hughes also served as circuit judge. Courtesy of Lansing Public Library.**

FIRST OF THE LAND-GRANT COLLEGES

1855 1955

MICHIGAN STATE COLLEGE

PENNSYLVANIA STATE UNIVERSITY

3¢ UNITED STATES POSTAGE 3¢

ABOVE: **Hesper Jackson was the first secretary of the Lansing branch of the National Association for the Advancement of Colored People. He later became the president of the organization. Courtesy of Saundra Lawrence Redmond.**

CENTER: **Ralph W. Crego, mayor of Lansing from 1943 to 1961, served the longest term of mayor in Lansing. Under his leadership, the city completed its modern city hall and police building and the civic center. Courtesy of Lansing Public Library.**

LEFT: **The *State Journal* rolling off the press, February 28, 1935. Photograph by C.C. Granger. From the Yellow Brick Road Collection.**

113

The Second World War and After

heavy snow, combined with a three-day rain, had caused the deluge; the fact that hundreds of farms upstream had been tilled after the 1904 flood added to the runoff in the city.

In March 1947, the city and state observed the centennial of Lansing's selection as state capital; the event sparked an interest in local history and inspired the publication in 1950 of *State Journal* writer Birt Darling's *City in the Forest: The Story of Lansing,* for years the standard history of the city. Darling's book reflects the unbridled optimism of the immediate postwar years—pride in what Lansing had become and confidence in its future. Paul D. Bagwell, Michigan State professor, two-time gubernatorial candidate, and president of the United States Junior Chamber of Commerce, wrote the introduction to Darling's book. "Many people hold to the mistaken notion," wrote Bagwell, "that a city is what it is because of its natural resources, its transportation facilities, and other similar factors." Lansing's history, he wrote, "disproves this concept," for Lansing had almost no advantages "and yet developed into a city where thirty major industries employ approximately 25,000 workers, a city with a debt free public school system ... no bonded indebtedness, no red light districts, and no vice of any consequence. A city that serves as the seat of state government and the home of Michigan State College, twelfth largest institution of higher learning in the nation."

Darling's book enhanced a civic pride born of postwar prosperity, and within a few years of its publication, the city, under Mayor Ralph W. Crego, completed its long-planned city hall and civic center. The ultramodern city hall and police building, designed by Kenneth Black, appeared where the old city hall and post office had stood; the new civic center occupied the site of the old Prudden Auditorium. The plans for these buildings had been announced during the war; legal problems, opposition to tearing down the old city hall, and the city's policy of paying cash for improvements delayed construction of both projects. In 1957, Lansing Community College began operating in the unused portion of the Central High School building; this institution, which enrolled 424 students in its opening year, was operated by the Lansing Board of Education. The opening of the Frandor Shopping Center on an old golf course just west of Clippert Street on land brought in by annexations foreshadowed the proliferation of outlying shopping malls during the late 1960s and early 1970s.

On April 28, 1955, the *State Journal* celebrated its own centennial with a huge special issue of feature articles on every conceivable aspect of the area's history, written by Darling and other staff members. The special issue, still an important historical source, included a facsimile reprint of the first issue of the *Republican,* the paper from which the *State Journal* had descended. Also in 1955, the assets of the Lansing Historical Society were taken over by the Historical Society of Greater Lansing, which sought to promote interest in the study of the area's growth. The Historical Society remains active today; it publishes a newsletter, holds monthly meetings, and cooperates with the city of Lansing in organizing Family Christmas and the

Art Fete, a juried art-show held annually at the Turner-Dodge mansion.

The celebration of another centennial—that of the founding of Michigan Agricultural College—resulted in the publication of Madison Kuhn's scholarly *Michigan State: The First Hundred Years.* President Hannah, unlike his predecessor Snyder, insisted on celebrating the founding of the college in 1855 rather than its actual opening in 1857. The most extensive historical celebration—that of May 1959—celebrated the centennial of Lansing's incorporation. The observance included an enormous parade, historical pageants, and even a replica of the log house of John Burchard, which was placed on the plaza of the new ultramodern city hall. Burchard was the first settler within Lansing's original city limits.

For Michigan State College, the postwar period marked a shift in its purposes, a marked physical growth, and an enormous enhancement of its reputation. Much of the credit for this transformation must go to John Hannah, who had begun as college secretary in 1935 and became president in 1941. Hannah began postwar planning as soon as the war started. "As I assumed the presidency of what was then M.S.C.," he wrote, "I believed that our first priority was to figure out what the institution wanted to be at the end of the war and beyond." During the war, inspired in part by the military general-education program, Hannah encouraged the faculty to develop a comparable program for the regular students. Committees were appointed, and after much debate, the Basic College—later the University College—began a two-year program for all students regardless of major. "It was remarkable," wrote Hannah, "that our diverse faculty voted without a single no vote to create ... [the] new Basic College for every freshman and sophomore, under the supervision of a separate faculty."

The program was in operation as the postwar student rush began. Three hundred veterans registered in 1944, but the floodgates opened in 1945. In the fall of 1946, 8,600 veterans enrolled; a year later, the figure was 9,000. Total enrollment rose from 15,000 in 1947 to 16,000 in 1949. Before the war, Michigan State had been 23rd in the nation in enrollment of full-time students; in 1949, it reached ninth place.

The college, desperately short of housing for the flood of students, resorted to heroic measures. About a third of the students were married. The college leased a Lansing trailer camp for 50 student families, placed another 500 students in double bunk beds in the Jenison gymnasium, and began constructing new residence halls. Hannah arranged to place 450 wheel-less trailers on the site of an old poultry plant near the Harrison Road headquarters of the Michigan State Police, and 100 quonset huts were erected along Harrison Road. For faculty families, 50 smaller quonset huts were built; later, 11 brick apartment buildings, each named for an alumnus killed during the war, appeared south of Shaw Lane along Harrison.

The peak enrollment of veterans was reached in 1949, and overall enrollment fell off slightly in 1950 and 1951, but in 1952, the institution's student body began an increase that leveled off only during the 1970s. In 1955-56,

114

LEFT: This 1957 photograph of the nearly completed city hall and police building shows the old city hall annex on the site which is now occupied by the plaza of Lansing's modern city hall. The city hall annex was removed in 1958. Courtesy of The Warren Holmes-Kenneth Black Company.

BELOW: Oldsmobile's manufacturing facilities in Lansing, 1950. Courtesy of the Oldsmobile Division, General Motors.

the centennial year, enrollment reached 22,967; a year later, fall-term registration reached 26,540.

Under Hannah's leadership, the institution began an almost frenetic building program. Residence halls, classroom buildings, and other facilities appeared at an incredible rate; a total of 352 separate buildings or major renovations of existing buildings were completed between 1945 and the end of Hannah's presidency in 1969. Many of the buildings were financed in the "self-liquidating" manner Hannah had pioneered, and others with state appropriations. Innovative "living-learning" complexes, which combined dormitory facilities with classroom space, appeared during the early 1960s.

More changed than merely physical facilities. Hannah made an earnest effort to recruit superior faculty. "If we were really going to make substantial progress in improving the faculty," Hannah wrote, "we would have to recruit the brightest young people as soon as they finished their doctorates in the better graduate schools." Many of the institution's most distinguished senior faculty members were recruited in this manner, and Hannah took great pride in the fact that many staff members moved on to other campuses to serve as deans, administrators, and presidents. "At one time," he wrote, "there were twenty or more presidents or principal executive officers of strong universities who had served earlier on the campus in East Lansing."

The admission of Michigan State to the Big Ten, or Western Conference, on May 20, 1949, was a milestone in the history of the institution. "Successful teams alone," said Hannah, "did not necessarily mean that Michigan State would be admitted to the Big Ten. It had to qualify as a worthy member of the conference." The Big Ten members "were all high quality institutions, and it was beginning to be acknowledged that Michigan State was an innovative institution, one that did not necessarily follow precedents." In 1950-51, Michigan State began Big Ten competition in all sports except football; gridiron competition began in 1953.

By the 1950s, the name Michigan State College no longer described a school that had become in all but name a major university. With the approval of the state legislature—and despite the opposition of the University of Michigan at Ann Arbor—the change of name to Michigan State University became official during the school's bicentennial year of 1955.

The many factors that won Big Ten membership for Michigan State, observed Hannah, "were equally important in assisting us in being accepted into the American Association of Universities," which occurred in 1964. The Big Ten and AAU memberships, in turn, "opened the doors of respectability," resulting in the installation of chapters of Phi Beta Kappa and other honorary societies.

Hannah served as president of Michigan State from July 1941 to April 1969, a 28-year period that saw a transformation of the institution that no one could have anticipated. The student enrollment of 6,356 in 1941 grew to 39,949 in 1969, having doubled since 1953. During the final decade of Hannah's presidency, 56 new buildings or major additions appeared, including nine clusters of coeducational academic residence halls, a science complex featuring a cyclotron, veterinary-medicine and food-science buildings, the Abrams Planetarium, the Biology Research Center, the Eppley Center for the College of Business, the Kresge Art Center, and a natural-resources building. Hannah led in the establishment of Michigan State's international program, including centers for Asian, African, and Latin American studies, as well as international institutes for education in communications, agriculture and nutrition, and business management. The value of the university's buildings, grounds, and equipment was $15 million in 1941; in 1969, it was $329 million.

Yet Hannah's activities were by no means confined to the campus. Early in his presidency, he became a nationally recognized spokesman for higher education; at last count, he had received 26 honorary degrees and served as president of several national higher-education associations. In addition, he found time to serve as Assistant Secretary of Defense (February 1953 to July 1954) and to chair the United States section of the Permanent Joint Board of Defense, a Canadian-American defense-coordinating agency; in 1956, he toured the Far East on behalf of the Senate Foreign Relations Committee. From 1957 to 1969—during the height of the civil-rights movement—he served under four Presidents as chairman of the United States Commission on Civil Rights. He even served as a delegate to the Michigan constitutional convention of 1961-62. On April 1, 1969, Hannah resigned as president of the university to become head of the Agency for International Development.

Hannah's announcement stunned the university; choosing a successor was to be no simple undertaking. The Vietnam War, the draft, civil rights, and the very legitimacy of university authority had become issues, and university presidents could no longer be chosen merely by a vote of the trustees. After much campus debate as to whether the faculty or the trustees should make the decision, and on the role of students, alumni, and the black community, the faculty finally proposed the creation of an All-University Search and Selection Committee, to be composed of eight faculty members including one black, 10 undergraduates including one black, one alumni representative, and one administrator with the rank of dean or above.

As the date of Hannah's resignation approached, the committee had not even been appointed, and an interim president had to be chosen. The candidates included former governor G. Mennen ("Soapy") Williams and Howard R. Neville, the university provost, who had the formidable support of Hannah. The choice fell on an unlikely candidate—Walter Adams, a professor of economics with no prior administrative experience and a reputation as a critic of the university establishment. "A cigar smoking economics professor," reported the Associated Press, "who contends that administration 'simply isn't my bag' will take on the job of acting president of Michigan State University on April 1." The Michigan State student daily, the State News, hailed the appointment as not only "a vote of confidence in the ability of the rank and file faculty to competently administer the univer-

FAR LEFT: Hugh ("Duffy") Daugherty was a member of Michigan State's football coaching staff for 26 years. Daugherty's teams won 190 games, lost 69 and tied 5, with 1965 and 1966 teams winning Big Ten and national championships. Courtesy of Michigan State University Sports Information.

LEFT: Coach Amo Bessone played a major role in popularizing the sport of hockey at Michigan State University. Courtesy of Michigan State University Sports Information.

CENTER LEFT: One of the finest all-around football players in Michigan State University's history is Earl Morrall. Morrall was a No. 1 draft choice in the National Football League for the San Francisco 49ers. He later played for the Pittsburgh Steelers, Detroit Lions, New York Giants, Baltimore Colts and Miami Dolphins. While with the Colts, he played in the Super Bowl Games of 1969 and 1971. Courtesy of Michigan State University Sports Information.

CENTER: George Webster was a key member of the Michigan State University Big Ten championship football teams of 1965 and 1966. Webster earned All-Big Ten and All-American honors each year, later garnering awards when playing with the AFL. He was voted the All-Time Greatest Player in MSU history in 1969. Courtesy of Michigan State University Sports Information.

FAR LEFT: Steve Garvey, first baseman for the Los Angeles Dodgers, played both football and baseball at Michigan State. Garvey was the National League's Most Valuable Player in 1974 and the Most Valuable Player in the major All-Star games of 1974 and 1978. Courtesy of Michigan State University Sports Information.

LEFT: Earvin Johnson grew up in Lansing. While a student at Everett High School, he led the basketball team to the state high school championship. Two years later he led the MSU Spartans to the NCAA championship, and the following year he led the Los Angeles Lakers to the NBA championship. Johnson paced MSU to the Big Ten championship in 1978 and 1979, and the NCAA championship in 1979. Currently, Johnson plays for the Los Angeles Lakers. Courtesy of Michigan State University Sports Information.

117

sity" but "a triumph for the university."

Adams' brief tenure began at the height of student radicalism. SDS—Students for a Democratic Society—was a small but vocal campus minority, and within a week Adams set the style of his administration by personally intervening in a dispute at the University Placement Office, where a group of about a hundred SDS-led students were trying to prevent the Oakland, California, Police Department from recruiting MSU students. Adams found that the students had occupied a narrow corridor, blocking access to an interview room. Adams talked to the students, the interviews were held, and the situation was defused without calling in the police.

The overriding issue of the 1960s was the Vietnam War. In the fall of 1969, the student government passed a resolution declaring October 15 a "Vietnam Moratorium" and requested that the university suspend classes and make its facilities available "for community discussion and action toward ending the senseless war in Vietnam." Adams discussed the proposal with student leaders; it was agreed that faculty and students might go about their normal activities if they wished, while those who so desired might take part in the moratorium. It was also agreed to hold a mass meeting in the auditorium, and following that a march to the state capitol. Adams agreed not merely to address the gathering but personally to lead the march to the state capitol. The students assured Adams that they would obtain a parade permit and designate marshals to keep order.

The moratorium went off as scheduled; students and faculty attended class or did not according to their conscience. "Teach-ins" were held on campus, and an overflow crowd heard speeches by Adams, Senator Philip A. Hart, and Congressman (now Senator) Donald Riegle at the auditorium. The march to the capitol, Adams later wrote, "came off without incident."

The selection process for a permanent president ground on, with numerous leaks to the press; again supporters mounted a vigorous campaign for former Governor Williams. Many faculty members opposed Williams and supported Adams, and despite his repeated claims that he did not want the job, a campaign began to make Adams the permanent president. Station WJIM—which had never before endorsed a candidate—editorialized, "Mark Twain once said, when you're looking for a man to put into public office, you can't go wrong picking a fellow who genuinely doesn't want the job." The *State Journal* also supported Adams, and a student petition on his behalf gathered 17,000 signatures. But Adams gave no encouragement to these efforts. By serving as the 13th president of the university, he noted, he "had saved his successor from occupying such a jinxed position." He further noted that the 13th president of the United States had been Millard Fillmore, and expressed the hope that he would be as well known to future generations.

In due course, the trustees announced the selection of Dr. Clifton R. Wharton, Jr., the first black man to head a major university. Wharton's qualifications were impressive; he was a graduate of the Boston Latin School and Harvard College and a major figure in agricultural economics. As Wharton took office on January 1, 1970, student protest had by no means subsided; the Kent State incident of May 1970, in which four students were killed during an antiwar demonstration, had repercussions at Michigan State, including a brief strike in which some students boycotted classes. In May 1972, the announcement of the mining of Haiphong harbor led to a "blockade" of Grand River Avenue, in which student demonstrators blocked traffic. The blockade lasted for several days until it was ended by the state police.

The political scene in East Lansing was transformed not only by the antiwar movement but by the ratification of the 18-year-old vote and a decision by the Michigan Supreme Court allowing students to vote in college communities if they wished. "The most predictable result," Lawrence Kestenbaum has written, "was that anti-war activism was continued in the voting booth." East Lansing, with its student vote, gave George McGovern a heavy majority in both the primary and the general election of 1972.

The students were less likely to vote on local issues, but their support enabled liberal candidates George Colburn and George Griffiths to win election to the city council. Student votes also figured in the defeat of Gordon Thomas, East Lansing mayor since 1961, by Wilbur Brookover, who served as mayor for two terms.

Student radicalism subsided in East Lansing and on campus after 1973. Under Wharton's leadership—he resigned at the end of 1977—the university's enrollment increased slightly, from about 40,000 to 44,000; the university established colleges of human and osteopathic medicine; and the Center for Urban Affairs became the degree-granting College of Urban Affairs. Building projects—including the Munn Ice Arena, the Stephen A. Nisbet Building, the Troy Management Center, and the Clinical Center—continued. The budget grew from $168 million when Wharton took office to $263 million when he resigned to become chancellor of the State University of New York, the difference resulting from inflation.

Wharton, like Hannah, was succeeded by a reluctant interim president. Edgar Harden, described by the *State Journal* as "a 70-going-on-55 businessman," had already retired as president of Northern Michigan University and was president of Story Olds, a local automobile dealership. The *State Journal* contrasted Wharton—"a low key, even cerebral administrator"—with Harden, whose administrative style had earned him the nickname "the Hannah of NMU." Harden, who hoped that his tenure would be brief, sought to improve the university's relationship with the legislature by personal contact, to continue the capital-fund drive begun by Wharton, and to enhance the reputation of the university. His successor, Cecil B. Mackey, former president of Texas Tech, took office on August 6, 1979.

In the city of Lansing, completion of the new city hall had revived concern about downtown—widely seen as deteriorating—and led to a new city plan, *The Comprehensive Master Plan for Lansing and Its Environs, 1960 to 1980.* This time the city employed the planning firm of Ladislas Segoe and Associates of Cincinnati, Ohio. The

118

FAR LEFT: **John A. Hannah began his career at Michigan State College as secretary in 1935, and became president in 1941. Hannah played a major role in expediting postwar changes at the college, changes which marked physical growth and enhanced the school's reputation. Courtesy of Doug Elbinger.**

LEFT: **Michigan State University President Clifton Wharton with his wife, Dolores Wharton. Wharton served as Michigan State's president from 1970 to 1979. Courtesy of Michigan State University Information Services.**

BELOW: **Walter Adams succeeded John Hannah as president of Michigan State University in 1969, a time when student radicalism was at its height. Courtesy of Doug Elbinger.**

ABOVE: **The residence of Darius B. Moon, well-known Lansing architect, built in 1889 on South Logan Street and moved in 1978 to 216 Heron Street, where it now stands. Photograph by author.**

RIGHT: **An aerial view of Michigan State University's "living-learning" complexes, 1968. Michigan State University has the largest population of on-campus student residents in the nation. These dormitories combine living and classroom space. Courtesy of Michigan State University Publications.**

119

The Second World War and After

powers of the City Planning Department, directed by Victor G. Leyrer, were enhanced; the City Planning Board included Dr. Max Stoakes as chair and Walter W. Neller, the highly respected realtor, as vice-chair.

The plan of 1960-1980, unlike that of 1938, was optimistic about the future of the regional economy. Annexations since 1949 had increased the area of the city. At the same time, new home-building techniques and greatly increased use of the automobile had brought rapid growth to the entire five-township area, including Lansing, De Witt, Meridian, Delhi, and Delta townships, as well as the cities of Lansing and East Lansing and the village (now city) of De Witt.

In view of the changing land-use patterns, the comprehensive plan of 1960—a far more complex document than either of its predecessors—considered a wide geographic area, about 87 square miles, including the cities of Lansing and East Lansing and contiguous parts of Ingham, Clinton, and Eaton counties. This area, noted the report, "is sufficiently large to meet the requirements of the urban area in the foreseeable future, with a reasonable margin of supply over probable demand." Since the city of Lansing had control only of its own area, a Tri-County Regional Planning Commission, established in July 1956, was charged with coordinating the planning activities of the entire metropolitan region and assisting in the solution of local problems. Lansing's recent mayors, Willard I. Bowerman (1961-65), Max Murningham (1965-69), and the present mayor Gerald W. Graves have energetically furthered regional planning.

By the mid-1960s, planning in Lansing was becoming a continuing activity. A capital-improvements program was announced by commission chairman Russell H. Fink in January of 1966. Increased population—up by 22,600 since 1960 for a total of 130,400—had placed severe strains on city services. The most serious problem was a projected housing shortage caused by the demolition of buildings in "urban renewal" areas and along the Main Street-St. Joseph corridor, the route of the proposed I-496 or Olds Freeway, which resulted in the eventual relocation of about 960 families and the demolition of such venerated structures as the R.E. Olds mansion.

In 1968, the Department of Housing and Urban Development approved Lansing's plan for participation in the Model Cities program, which sought to improve not only the physical environment of a large swath of Lansing's west side, but the social environment as well. The Lansing program, directed by Jacquelyn Warr, included dental and health clinics, housing assistance, and the Youth Development Program, designed to encourage school dropouts to complete high-school equivalency programs and to acquire salable skills. The Model Cities program was also responsible for organizing garbage collection in Lansing—until then, the largest American city without a public garbage disposal system.

By the mid-1970s, the Greater Lansing area had been transformed beyond the most sanguine expectations of the early postwar years. When Birt Darling published his *City in the Forest* in 1950, the forest—"a man-made forest of street trees"—was very much in evidence; aerial photographs of Lansing in 1950 show the buildings to the west of the state capitol largely obscured by trees. Today all this has changed. Behind the century-old state capitol—still an imposing structure—is the vast, four-square-block "capitol complex," consisting of the Stevens T. Mason, Treasury, Law, and Highway Department buildings. The old commercial structures along North Washington Avenue—eyesores even in the 1930s—were removed during the 1960s. Much of Washington Avenue, now the Washington Square Mall, has been closed to traffic while Lansing Community College occupies a wide stretch of downtown from Shiawassee to Saginaw. The college, which opened in the fall of 1957 with eight faculty members and 425 students, enrolled 18,826 students in the fall of 1979; its broadened curriculum now includes 375 different programs in five divisions, with 205 full-time and 750 part-time faculty members.

In addition to the state complex, Lansing Community College, and recent commercial construction, the city has at last begun to develop a riverfront park out of several parcels of riverfront real estate—one of them a gift from C. Rowland Stebbins, son of Arthur Courtland Stebbins and grandson of Courtland Bliss Stebbins, representing one of Lansing's oldest and most distinguished families.

But problems remain. Lagging automobile sales have depressed the local economy, and Lansing and Meridian malls have drawn retail trade away from downtown. The J.W. Knapp Company, for years one of downtown's "anchor" stores, was forced to close, and another large retailer has announced a move to the Meridian Mall. Two mainstays of the area's economy—Michigan State University and the state government—are in the process of trimming budgets and personnel and examining priorities. The "remarkably stable economy" described by Birt Darling in 1950—based on automobiles, state government, and education—now seems to hinge on the revival of the automobile industry.

There are grounds for optimism. Oldsmobile sales have remained brisk; that company is now engaged in a $40-million plant-expansion program to improve its efficiency and competitive position. The Motor Wheel Corporation, faced with an obsolete plant that has diminished its productivity, is engaged in a similar program of massive investment. The company expects not only to retain its present work force of 1,500 but to employ an additional 300 workers. The city has weathered economic downturns in the past, and it seems likely that a revival will come as the automobile industry improves its competitive position.

The downtown area, too, in spite of its problems, is engaged in a process of renewal and revival. The Washington Square Mall has added enormously to the attractiveness of the area, and the city of Lansing, in cooperation with downtown merchants, has begun a program of beautification and maintenance. New commercial structures—including the 12-story office building and hotel complex planned for Washington and Michigan avenues and the rebuilding of the Michigan Theater to include restaurants, stores, and office space—are important signs of this revival.

ABOVE: **The Michigan capitol complex, photographed from the capitol building. The sculpture "This Equals That" may be seen in the center of the mall. Photograph by author.**

LEFT: **The interior of the Lansing Water Conditioning Plant. Completed in 1939, the building shows the influence of art deco architectural style. Photograph by author.**

Chapter 12

FORTY-FIRST
ANNUAL
MICHIGAN

E PLURIBUS UNUM

SI QUÆRIS PENINSULAM AMŒNAM CIRCUMSPICE

STATE FAIR.
LANSING.
September 9th, 10th, 11th, 12th & 13th,
1889.

THE SURVIVING PAST

History is everywhere to be discovered. In the greater Lansing area, historic buildings, landmarks, and artifacts tell an important story; the story of a transformation. Lansing has been virtually carved from a wilderness, and though the face of the city has changed many times over, the spirit of its foundation remains. The Historical Society of Greater Lansing has played an important role in keeping this spirit alive. It is hoped that the pictures on these next few pages will serve to remind the reader of the importance of preservation.

OPPOSITE PAGE: **A poster for the 41st Annual State Fair, 1889. The State Fair, a major event in late 19th century Lansing, was held on the State Fair Grounds, a 52 acre site now occupied by Oldsmobile. From the Wiskemann Collection.**

ABOVE: **A Victorian style stained glass window by Richard E. Hanley. Hanley has restored many stained glass windows in the Lansing area. Photographs by author.**

RIGHT: **The Lansing Brewing Company ceased operations after the first "local option" or prohibition law was adopted by Ingham County early in the 20th century. Courtesy of Michigan State Museum.**

A magnificent dome highlights the interior of the Michigan capitol. Photograph by author.

LEFT: **Michael Heizer's sculpture "This Equals That" stands in the Michigan capitol complex. The sculpture was dedicated on September 25, 1980. Photograph by author.**

ABOVE: **A Ziegler cigar box, circa 1916. Otto Ziegler, one of Lansing's most influential citizens, manufactured cigars and ran a cigar store on North Washington Avenue. Courtesy of Robert J. Bouck.**

RIGHT: **This residence at 1025 North Washington Avenue, now the Colonial Apartments, was built for George Washington Peck. Peck, who had been Speaker of the House in 1847 when the capital was located in Lansing, was Lansing's first postmaster, a member of Congress, mayor of Lansing in 1867, and publisher of the Lansing *State Journal*. Photograph by author.**

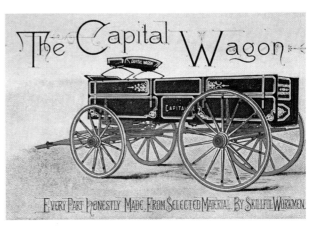

OPPOSITE TOP: **An 1895 painting of Cowles House by William Holdsworth, a professor of drawing. The painting was given by Professor and Mrs. William James Beal to their daughter, Jessie Beal, as a wedding present. Cowles House, since remodeled, is the only survivor of the Faculty Row campus faculty homes. Courtesy of Michigan State University Museum.**

OPPOSITE LEFT: **This chalk sketch depicts the homestead of Wesley and Inez Rusch Clark, who lived there during the late 19th century. The Clark homestead was located on Curtice Road near Onondaga in Aurelius Township, Ingham County. Courtesy of Ellis and Noel Clark.**

ABOVE: **This famous painting by William Harndeon Foster shows a 1910 Oldsmobile "setting the pace" and staying ahead of the railroad train in the background. The illustration was taken from an advertisement published in the *Saturday Evening Post*. Courtesy of Robert J. Bouck.**

TOP RIGHT: **"City Hall" cigars were manufactured by the Queen Bee Cigar Company in Lansing, circa 1890. Courtesy of Michigan State Museum.**

CENTER: **A "New Jack" cigar box, manufactured by Queen Bee Cigar Company, Lansing. Courtesy of Robert J. Bouck.**

BOTTOM: **The Capital Wagon Company, founded in Lansing in the mid-1870s, unfortunately became a casualty of the depression of the 1890s. Courtesy of Lansing Public Library.**

The Surviving Past

RIGHT: **A postcard advertisement for City National Bank, Lansing. This bank was located at the northwest corner of Michigan and Washington avenues, where the Bank of Lansing now stands. From the Yellow Brick Road Collection.**

BOTTOM LEFT: **Linton Hall, built in 1881 on the campus of Michigan Agricultural College, has for years been known simply as the Library and Museum. For many years the building served as the administration building and housed the offices of John A. Hannah and several of his predecessors. Photograph by author.**

BOTTOM RIGHT: **This 1897 horseless carriage, one of the few built by the Olds Motor Vehicle Company in 1897, is one of the valued holdings of the Smithsonian Institution in Washington, D.C. It was returned to Lansing briefly as part of the celebration of the 75th anniversary of Oldsmobile in 1972. Courtesy of the Oldsmobile Division, General Motors.**

ABOVE: **This painting, by an artist identified only as "Wheeler," depicts the residence of John S. Forster on Meridian Road, just south of St. Katherine's Chapel. The house was built in 1883 and torn down to make space for St. Katherine's Episcopal Church. Courtesy of Michigan State Museum.**

RIGHT: **The curved-dash Oldsmobile was manufactured in quantity from 1900 to about 1904; a few were produced between the years 1904 and 1907. The version shown here, with spoke wheels, was manufactured in 1904. Courtesy of the Oldsmobile Division, General Motors.**

TOP: **This common grave in the Summit Cemetery in Ingham County tells a story of 19th century life and death. Mattie Reed, two years and seven months old, died on February 10, 1876; her sisters Stella, aged nine months, and Nellie, aged eleven years, are buried with her. Photograph by author.**

ABOVE: **A bust of Zachariah Chandler, U.S. Senator and Republican leader, who played an important role in the development of the capital region. Photograph by author.**

TOP: **An experimental greenhouse at Michigan State University, where research and experimentation in horticulture is an important activity. Photograph by author.**

ABOVE: **The graves of the Branch children in Foote Cemetery, Ingham county. All died from dysentery within days of each other. Photograph by author.**

ABOVE: **The North Lansing dam, east of the corner of Grand River Avenue and North Washington Avenue. Burchard's cabin, the first house built in Lansing, was built on the west side of the river. Photograph by author.**

LEFT: **The Auto Owners Insurance building is a stunning example of modern architecture in Lansing. Courtesy of The Warren Holmes-Kenneth Black Company.**

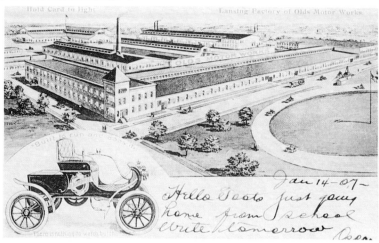

OPPOSITE FAR LEFT: **The Reo Motor Car Company's high expectations for sales of this beautiful car unfortunately did not materialize. Courtesy of Ian McLeod.**

OPPOSITE LEFT: **A 1907 Oldsmobile advertising card. From the Yellow Brick Road Collection.**

OPPOSITE BOTTOM: **A 1908 Oldsmobile touring car. Courtesy of the Oldsmobile Division, General Motors.**

BELOW LEFT: **The Okemos Barn Theater in Okemos, Michigan. Photograph by author.**

BELOW RIGHT: **Two charming late 19th century buildings on Allegan Street, Lansing. Photograph by author.**

BOTTOM: **Turner Park in North Lansing is named for James Turner, one of Lansing's early settlers. Photograph by author.**

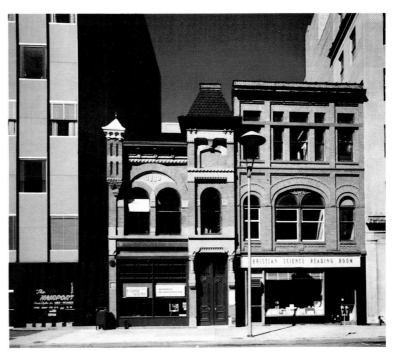

ABOVE LEFT: **Artifacts of Governors Lewis Cass and Stevens T. Mason in the gallery of Michigan State Museum. Courtesy of Michigan State Museum.**

ABOVE RIGHT: **The "child's room" in the Turner-Dodge Mansion in North Lansing, as furnished during a decorator showcase in 1979. The residence, built in the early 1850s, had been occupied by James Turner and Marion Monroe Turner, early Lansing settlers. Frank Dodge, Turner's son-in-law, and his wife Abigail Turner Dodge, later occupied the residence. It is now owned by the City of Lansing. Photograph by author.**

RIGHT: **The Kresge Art Gallery, Michigan State University. The works shown include paintings by Andy Warhol, Morris Lewis, and William Bailey, and sculptures by Alexander Caulder, Theodore Roszak, and George Rickey. Photograph by author.**

OPPOSITE PAGE: **The dome of the Michigan capitol. Photograph by author.**

Chapter 13

The first settlers in Ingham County—the vanguard of a population rush into lower Michigan in the 1830s—found themselves in an almost impenetrable wilderness. They cleared land, planted crops, and built houses. None of them thought they were doing anything remarkable, since others before them had hacked homes out of a wilderness, and countless others would do so again in the vast American forests. There seemed no particular reason why, in that part of Lansing Township where the Red Cedar River flows into the Grand, a town of any size—much less a great city—would ever flourish. But when in 1847 the legislature of Michigan moved its capital from Detroit to the Township of Lansing, remarkable things did indeed begin to happen.

Some thought the move a joke. "No legislature of a civilized state," it was recalled later, "ever convened with cruder surroundings." The first legislature to meet in the hastily built frame capitol found an oasis of stumps in the midst of a vast, magnificent forest. There were few inhabitants and even fewer amenities. But by the mid-19th century the joke had worn thin as the area grew in importance, not merely as a state capital, but as a regional commercial and manufacturing center. The advent of the early railroads encouraged commercial farming in the place of subsistence agriculture; the founding of an agricultural college on a mosquito-infested swamp five miles from the present state capital had enormous implications for the future. Lansing was incorporated as a city in 1859 and its population tripled by 1890. Its increasingly diverse industries manufactured wheelbarrows, carriages

and wagons, and agricultural implements. Its physical face began to change with the completion in 1879 of the present state capitol and the building of many factories, fine residences, hotels, opera houses, and mercantile establishments. A weekly newspaper and rich cultural life attested to the growing importance of the area.

Then came the automobile, beginning in 1885 with a three-wheeled, steam-driven horseless carriage and evolving by 1905 into a gasoline-powered runabout, the first such vehicle to be manufactured in quantity. The manufacture of autos and trucks made Lansing for a brief time before the First World War the leading center of the American automobile industry. That successful industry sparked the growth of other manufacturing and service industries, causing the population of the area to more than double by 1945. By then Lansing so dominated its hinterland that the U.S. Bureau of the Census designated all of Ingham County as the Lansing Metropolitan Area.

Today the "City in the Forest" has changed beyond the wildest dreams of its early settlers. The original forest that blanketed the region is gone. The City of Lansing, now the largest community in a radius of 80 miles, is capital of the eighth most populous American state. The century-old state capitol building dominates the scene of government activity that primarily takes place in an enormous complex of modern state office buildings occupying the spot where a sea of tree stumps greeted early legislators. Government shares the distinction of being a chief employer in the area with one of the nation's leading

automobile manufacturers, whose network of support industries has drawn even more people for more jobs, spawning other industries to provide the goods and services required by every community. The area is a major education center as well—the agricultural college has become a distinguished university that attracts students from all the American states as well as from many foreign countries.

It is probably as difficult to foresee what Lansing will look like a century from now as it was for the original settlers to predict today's thriving combination of industry and business, government and education. But perhaps our best clues to the future are contained in some of the stories of Lansing's fascinating commercial past, as the following pages will illustrate.

Abrams Aerial Survey Corporation

Ted Abrams was taking pictures with a handheld camera from airplanes less than 15 years after the Wright Brothers' historic flight at Kitty Hawk. Soon, he was developing a method of scaling his photos so that measurements could be calculated from them. In the decades that followed, the company that Abrams founded and incorporated in 1923 became a pioneer in the field of aerial photography, introducing numerous technical innovations that established the science of aerial photogrammetry around the world.

Nowadays, the importance of aerial photography for engineering, geology, agriculture, topography, urban planning, construction, and many other areas is well recognized, but it was not until the 1930s that the engineering community realized its potential for reducing expensive, time-consuming field work. As head of one of the first aerial survey operations, Ted Abrams accomplished many firsts in photogrammetry. He achieved the first full aerial inventory study of Isle Royal for the U.S. Park Service; his photographs of the strip of land from Honor to Benzonia, Michigan, was the first aerial survey done for highway layout; and he designed the only airplane used specifically for aerial photography, a plane that is now restored and preserved for display in the Smithsonian Institution.

In the late '30s, Abrams' aerial photos aided the Department of Agriculture in its "pay-not-to-grow" depression-fighting policy. The business also worked with the U.S. Geological Survey in completing maps of the state of Michigan. Then, with the outbreak of World War II, aerial photography really came of age. Both the Pacific and European campaigns were based on extensive mapping projects drawn from aerial surveys. During the war, Abrams Aerial Survey Corporation was instrumental in educating the Marine Corps in photogrammetric interpretation.

Today, the applications of aerial photography are enormous. No engineering project is undertaken without first acquiring complete topographical information of the earth surface, and 75 percent of this information is obtained by aerial survey data. Analytical and digital photogrammetry have brought the power of the computer to photogrammetric processing and storage. As recently as 1970, the firm delivered aerial survey material in conventional map-sheet form; now, sophisticated computer technology can produce punch tapes, magnetic tapes, tabulated numbers—any form compatible with the client's data systems.

From Ted Abrams' sole venture almost 60 years ago, Abrams Aerial has grown into one of the top ten aerial survey firms in the country, employing about 100 scientists, engineers, pilots, mechanics, and administrators. The company serves clients nationwide from its headquarters in Lansing and St. Petersburg, Florida. Ralph Kauffman, who started as a temporary pilot with Abrams in 1948, became president of the corporation in 1962.

Today, Abrams uses sophisticated emulsions, sensors, and scanners to record what cannot be captured on conventional film. First-order plotting systems, introduced by the company, have revolutionized aerial map accuracy standards. The firm offers remote sensing and interpretation services for land and crop classification, energy loss surveys, geological studies, flood damage assessment, pollution monitoring, environmental impact studies, and many other types of projects.

Left
Ted Abrams poses with an aerial survey plane and cameras in this early photograph.

Right
An Abrams explorer flies over Pittsburgh in this photograph taken in 1938.

American Bank and Trust Company

The bustling intersection of Michigan Avenue and Washington Square has been the center of Lansing's commercial activities for more than a century. Back in 1850, J.C. Bailey founded Lansing's first bank and exchange in a small building on the northeast corner of the intersection. Later, in 1872, the Lansing National Bank purchased a 2-story brick building on the southeast corner. Since that time, there has always been a bank on this corner—all direct ancestors of Lansing's oldest "hometown" bank, American Bank and Trust Company.

The bank was born on February 25, 1892, when 82 shareholders incorporated the Lansing State Savings Bank and purchased the corner property from the Lansing National Bank at a public auction. Twenty-six years later, the bank invested a vote of confidence—and a great deal of money—in the future of Lansing by building on that property the most modern and complete banking house in central Michigan.

In 1921, the Lansing State Savings Bank merged with the American Savings Bank, whose building had been destroyed by fire, to form the American State Savings Bank. Gradually, under the leadership of Donald E. Bates, the bank was able to offer a wide range of banking services and by 1944 the word *savings* was dropped from the name to reflect the diversification of services. Another merger in 1958 with the Central Trust Company resulted in the bank's current name.

During the late '40s and early '50s, the bank expanded its physical facilities as well as its services. By the end of 1951, the bank operated five branches in the Lansing area. In 1965, a complete modernization project increased the size of the bank headquarters by 50 percent. Today, American Bank and Trust has 18 full-service branches.

The bank's policies have traditionally emphasized service. A recent innovation was the introduction of "ReadyTeller" in April 1976, the first automated teller machine (ATM) in Lansing. And now American Bank has initiated "Money Saver," a credit union-like service available to local businesses.

Senior officers of the bank are H. Andrews Hays, chairman of the board, and George S. Nugent, president. With over 400 employees and $358 million in total assets, American Bank and Trust Company continues the fine banking traditions that have been its heritage for more than a century.

Top
Lansing State Savings Bank, ancestor of Lansing's oldest "hometown" bank, American Bank and Trust Company, was incorporated in 1892. The bank's original name was still on the facade of the building when this photograph was taken in 1958.

Above
This photograph was taken prior to 1965, when an extensive modernization project increased the size of American Bank and Trust's headquarters by 50 percent. The same building (left) looked remarkably different in 1980.

139

Belen's Flowers

The history of Belen's Flowers, a nationally known, thriving florist business, has been closely tied to the history of Lansing since the early days of the century.

In 1911, Christopher Belen and his young wife Elizabeth moved from Westphalia, Michigan, to the state capital. Elizabeth brought with her an unusual interest in flowers, discovered when she was a student nurse at a Grand Rapids hospital. In those days, flowers sent to patients arrived unarranged. It was the duty of student nurses to take care of such bouquets, and Elizabeth discovered in herself a talent for arrangement. Both her dedication to nursing and her love of flowers were to remain with her throughout her lifetime.

For the next 15 years, Mr. Belen was busy with his trade as a meat cutter. Mrs. Belen, in addition to raising a young family, reentered the nursing profession and became active in social and community affairs.

In 1925 a dream was realized. The Belens opened their first flower shop in their home at 2021 Jerome Street. A glass-enclosed porch showcased their plants and flowers. For the next few years, each day began when Christopher and Elizabeth Belen set out in a Ford truck at 3:00 or 4:00 a.m. for Grand Rapids to pick up plants and flowers. From the beginning, Belen's Flowers was a family affair. This was an especially close-knit family, and everybody was involved. Even during the early '30s, when, for all florists, the demand for flowers was as depressed as the economy, they kept their sights high. "Our parents never permitted us to feel sorry for ourselves," says Lucile.

"We had a lot of fun, too. I don't think we realized that the times were frightening."

In 1935, they opened their new shop at 626 West Kalamazoo Street. The following year, Elizabeth became the first woman in the 57th district to be elected to the Michigan legislature. By this time, Lucile was working for the state of Michigan, but in 1942, when her mother was appointed by the governor as commissioner, Michigan Workmen's Compensation, she resigned to manage Belen's Flowers as a full-time profession.

Frederick also continued to help with the business during his years as a student at Michigan State University. His career led him to Washington and bureaucratic posts, first under President Kennedy and culminating in his appointment as Deputy Postmaster General of the United States under President Lyndon Johnson.

The business continued to flourish. A second shop, managed by Virginia Belen, was opened next to St. Lawrence Hospital. Upon her death in 1963 (Christopher Belen had died in 1960) the two shops were merged, the staff enlarged, and Belen's Flowers opened at its present location at 515 West Ionia. Elizabeth Belen died in 1975.

Today, under the management of Lucile Belen, the flower business that bears so honorable a name continues to flourish. She is the first woman to receive the Retailer of the Year Award from the Michigan Florists Association. Her Belen's School of Floral Design attracts hundreds of young men and women from across the nation. First and foremost, however, she is the manager of Belen's Flowers, and that heritage is

reflected in the dedication she and her talented staff give even the most inexpensive arrangement that leaves her shop. That such dedication also pays is reflected in the fact that Belen's Flowers ranks, in dollar business, among the upper 20 percent of florists in the United States.

Lucile Belen is also the only woman to hold the office of mayor pro tem during three consecutive terms on the Lansing City Council. She is the first woman elected to chair the Ingham County Board of Supervisors. She chairs the Board of Trustees of Ingham Medical Hospital and serves on the Lansing Regional Chamber of Commerce, the Convention Bureau of Greater Lansing, and the Lansing Symphony Association.

Her reason for such wide involvement? For Lucile Belen it is simply stated. "My mother told us that the Lansing community had been very good to us and that we owed something to it." It is a goodly heritage.

Left
Belen's Flowers was first opened in a portion of the residence at 626 West Kalamazoo. Eventually the business occupied the entire three floors, with a staff of six plus family members.

Right
Lucile, Virginia, and Frederick Belen stand in front of their parents' Michigan Floral Company at 2021 Jerome Street, the first flower shop owned by the Belens.

Bunday Furniture

If not for the suggestion of an unemployed friend in 1899, the Bunday Furniture Galleries might never have been born.

Frederick P. Bunday, Sr., was born on October 11, 1860, on a farm in Hillsdale County. In 1879, he moved to St. Johns and took a job as a railway mail clerk on the Grand Trunk Railroad from Detroit to Grand Haven. The railroad was to occupy Bunday's life for 20 years. At 40 years of age, it looked like it would be his life's work. And it might have been, had not an unemployed friend seeking work in the area come up with the idea of starting a business manufacturing hand-tied quilts.

From that suggestion, the Columbian Manufacturing Company was formed in St. Johns. But five years later disaster struck—a fire completely destroyed the plant, and Bunday, with only $100 worth of insurance, was out of business.

Fred found himself working in his uncle Warner Bunday's grocery store and eventually purchased it from him. He tired of the grocery business and sold it. In 1914, at the age of 51, he purchased the property at the corner of North and Center streets in Lansing, sold stock in the Bunday Bedding Company, Inc., and built a new mattress factory.

In a growing city with two railroads for easy shipping, things went smoothly. Due to an illness, his son Fred Jr. was forced into the business in 1933. Bunday's company expanded to a retail operation in the late '30s, specializing in studio couches, daybeds, and baby furniture. World War II and the postwar baby boom led to increased concentration in juvenile furniture. As the retail business grew, other furniture items were added to meet customers' requests. By the mid-1950s, the retail furniture line had expanded and the decision was made to discontinue the manufacture of bedding.

In 1965 the third generation, John Bunday, joined the firm. "We serve our customers with grace and good value," says John. "Biggest does not always mean the best." The company now has 18 employees, most of whom have been with Bunday for many years. With John Bunday serving as president, Ellen-Grey Bunday as vice-president, Norma Bunday as secretary-treasurer, and Fred Jr., who retired from active management in 1978, as chairman of the board, the Bunday Furniture Galleries comprise today the oldest family-owned furniture store in Lansing.

Recent advances include computerized inventory and bookkeeping procedures and a program of residential and professional interior design—proof that perseverance, ingenuity, and family loyalty can overcome even the harshest adversity.

Left
Frederick P. Bunday, Sr., founded Bunday Bedding Company in 1914.

Right
This is how the original building looked after it was constructed in 1914.

Below
Since then, the building has been remodeled, and today Bunday Furniture appears as shown in this photograph.

Capital Area Transportation Authority

During these days of fuel shortages, air pollution, and traffic congestion, public transportation systems perform an important community service by alleviating the extent of these problems. Lansing is particularly fortunate in having perhaps the most efficient and rapidly growing public bus system in the country.

The Capital Area Transportation Authority (CATA) was born in 1972 by an act of the state legislature. During its early years, the Authority's buses were housed in buildings so small that many of the vehicles were stored year-round outdoors on Mill Street. The bus system was still struggling in its infancy when Clare D. Loudenslager assumed the reins in 1973. Within one year, new drivers, buses, and routes were added, and funds were raised for future expansion. In 1976, CATA purchased the Tranter Manufacturing Company building and began a complete remodeling program that was finished and operational by 1978. The Tranter facility now has almost 90,000 square feet for year-round indoor maintenance and storage.

Along with physical expansion came an increase in services. CATA initiated "Spec-Tran" and "CATA Club" services for senior citizens in 1975. A massive passenger information network, including schedule racks, advertising, and telephone information services, provides CATA riders with up-to-the-minute information on routes and scheduling. CATA officials estimate that 76 percent of Lansing residents are now within two blocks of a CATA bus route.

Loudenslager has always emphasized driver safety, dependability, and accountability, and CATA drivers have

won numerous awards for safety and service. A CATA driver won the title of "Number One Driver in North America" at the first national "Bus Roadeo" in 1976. And the Michigan House and Senate passed concurrent resolutions recognizing CATA for safe, reliable bus service. All CATA drivers—both men and women—undergo vigorous training programs for handling emergency situations and for coping with elderly and handicapped passengers.

In 1980, the system purchased 18 new lift-equipped GMC "RTS" buses. Seventy of the 76 buses in the CATA fleet use cost-efficient diesel fuel. Preventive maintenance is also stressed for economy, with three shifts of mechanics working around the clock to assure clean, smooth-running bus service.

In terms of riders, CATA's growth has been extraordinary. From 739,000 passengers in 1972, CATA serviced

more than 3.8 million riders in 1979 and 4.5 million in 1980. CATA drivers traveled 1.9 million miles in 1979.

CATA's appointed 10-member board of directors represents Lansing, East Lansing, and the townships of Delhi, Delta, Lansing, and Meridian. With its operating budget growing steadily, CATA will continue to provide Lansing area residents with safe, comfortable, dependable public transportation in the years to come.

Top
In 1980, CATA purchased 18 new lift-equipped GMC "RTS" buses. Seventy of the 76 buses in the fleet use cost-efficient diesel fuel.

Bottom
CATA's appointed 10-member board of directors operates from corporate headquarters located at 4615 Tranter Avenue in Lansing.

Capitol Park Hotel

It was 1968 and Lansing-raised William Burke, a hotel management student at Michigan State University, needed a job to help pay his way through school. Passing the Capitol Park Hotel one afternoon, he decided to apply for a job as a waiter in the hotel dining room. Why not, he reasoned, he lived nearby and the position would give him the opportunity to explore the hotel business firsthand. Well, Mr. Burke learned quickly, so quickly that he not only worked his way to the top of the hotel's management—he now owns the hotel!

Located at 500 South Capitol Avenue, the main hotel building is a grand, sturdy, completely fireproof structure built in 1917. It was known then as the Porter Hotel, an elegant inn for state politicos who were given the "luxury" of running ice water in every room. In the early 1940s, the hotel was converted to an apartment building and it remained a residential structure until 1948 when the Frank P. Davey Company, a Detroit engineering firm that also built the Roosevelt Hotel, turned it into a hotel once again. Twelve years later, Mr. Davey leased the hotel to the A.W. Gershenson Company, which constructed an adjacent 144-unit motel and renamed the property Capitol Park.

By the time Mr. Burke had graduated from MSU in 1970, Davey once again controlled the hotel's operations under the supervision of William E. Hamilton. Mr. Burke decided to stay on and soon was promoted to food-and-beverage manager and then general manager, a position he held from 1972 to 1977. Recognizing a good investment and by this time knowing every square inch of the structure intimately, Mr. Burke bought the hotel along with Monte Story and Bill Warner in 1978.

Almost immediately, the new owners embarked on a complete $250,000 renovation/remodeling project of the motel structure, installing new carpets, wallpaper, drapes, beds, credenzas, and bathroom fixtures. Meanwhile, the grand old "Porter section," with its 85 apartments and suites, continues its long tradition of catering to legislators, lobbyists, union leaders, and other capitol figures who lease rooms at the hotel year-round. Noted celebrities who have stayed as guests at the Capitol Park include Senators Edward Kennedy and Philip Hart and Vice-President Gerald Ford. "Mrs. Nixon almost took a room on one occasion," Mr. Burke recalls wryly and with little remorse, "but her advance people did not like the color of the carpets."

Future plans call for the sale of the Porter building to a group of developers who will convert the structure once again to residential housing—this time for senior citizens. In 1980 Capitol Park began construction on a new $850,000 restaurant-lounge-banquet complex to be called "Fordney's" after Mr. Burke's mother, Amy Fordney Burke.

The Capitol Park Hotel stresses convenience, location, cleanliness, and comfort. The hotel has been a downtown Lansing tradition for 64 years, and, judging by the consistently high occupancy rate, it will remain a tradition for years to come.

Adjacent to the hotel, "Fordney's" is a new dining complex with a restaurant and lounge on the first floor and elegant banquet rooms on the second.

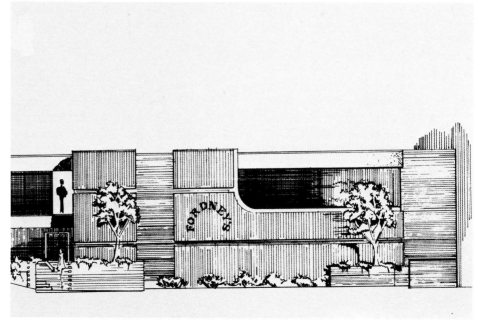

Charles Featherly Construction Company

A major contributor to Lansing's resurgence in growth over the past decade has been a general contractor who started all by himself 15 years ago and built a multimillion-dollar construction company. Charles Featherly arrived in Lansing in 1965 and opened a one-man company from a small office on Cedar Street, just south of the old City Market. Three years later, he was doing well enough to move to a more spacious River Street building, and in 1971 he moved to the firm's present location at 1109 River Street—a 17,000-square-foot facility that is used to store construction materials.

After graduating from Michigan State University with a bachelor of science degree in civil engineering in 1956, Featherly had gained a great deal of experience as an engineer and superintendent with Erickson & Lindstrom, a large Flint construction firm. The experience proved worthwhile, for since coming to Lansing he has been involved in numerous renovation/construction projects that have demanded a wide range of engineering, design, and building skills.

It would require more space than is available here to list all Featherly Construction projects completed over the past 15 years, but a few noteworthy projects have been the Michigan State University observatory; Lansing School District additions; Veterans of Foreign Wars administration building and Community Hospital addition in Eaton Rapids; Lansing police helicopter and pistol range complex; and the Michigan Department of Public Health blood derivative building. For its work on the Quality Electric office building, the company was honored by Braden Metal Building Systems and was its number ten builder in the country.

Featherly Construction's 1980 projects include the MSU football training building; MSU turf grass laboratory building; and the Oldsmobile emissions testing laboratory addition.

Ask Charles Featherly the reasons for the growth of his business—the company did $8.5 million worth of business in 1979 and $12 million in 1980—and he will immediately tell you "quality and reliability." With its current staff, the firm can work directly with the client from the planning stages of the project or on a contract-bid basis after the design stage is completed. "It's a 'we' company," Featherly says, "meaning everyone in the company works together to bring his or her special skills to a coordinated effort."

Besides putting his energies into the physical growth of Lansing, Featherly has also enhanced its spiritual and community growth. He has been president of the Lansing Boys Club, a member of the board of directors of the United Way, and chairman of the small business council of the Lansing Regional Chamber of Commerce.

With his wife Fern, who also serves as secretary of the corporation, Featherly plans to stay in Lansing for a long time. "Lansing," he says knowingly, "is a good town."

Top
An important project undertaken by Charles Featherly in 1980 was the construction of the MSU football training facility.

Bottom
For its work on the Quality Electric office building, Charles Featherly Construction Company was honored by Braden Metal Building Systems.

Dart National Bank

In the early 1900s, private banks handled most banking services in the small towns of the Midwest. Many communities had no chartered banks or associations; the "private bank" was usually the local merchant with the largest safe who could also serve as the "town lender." Rollin Charles "R.C." Dart organized just such an enterprise in 1918 which eventually became the Dart National Bank.

Beginning his career in banking as a teller and assistant cashier with the Farmer's Bank of Mason, R.C. Dart left to form his own insurance, loan, and real estate business in 1906. Twelve years later, he was prepared to convert to a fully operational private banking firm, R.C. Dart and Company, Bankers. During the life of the private bank, one of Rollin's eight children, Doc Campbell Dart, showed a keen interest in the banking business. Together, father and son founded the Dart National Bank of Mason in 1925. Dart National was the third national bank in Ingham County and the first in Mason to hold a charter since 1890. Today Dart is the oldest national bank in Ingham County.

The bank first opened its doors at 100 Ash Street. R.C. served as its first president, and Doc, the first cashier, succeeded to the presidency upon his father's death in 1943. Two brothers and a sister have taken active roles in the bank's success—William F. Dart served on the board for many years and was president from 1962-1964; Gertrude Dart Smith and James A. Dart were both bank directors; and John H. Dart, Harvard law graduate, has given valuable counsel to the bank throughout the years. Doc's son, Rollin B. Dart, has been bank president since 1964 and has

also acted as chief executive and board chairman.

Throughout the bank's history, Dart National's innovations in banking services have guided it through difficult times and have been instrumental in its growth. In the 1920s D.C. recognized the incredible potential of the automobile, and Dart became the first bank in the country to introduce auto financing to its customers. Later, in the '30s, Dart became the first bank to finance buyers of mobile homes.

The stock market crash of 1929 and ensuing Depression toppled many banks, but Dart survived and emerged with sound capital, partly due to its diversified lending policies. Dart was the only national bank in Ingham County to survive the Depression. Since that time, the bank's dedication to providing a wide range of banking services has caused it to seek expansion of its facilities. In 1936, Dart purchased the assets of the First State Savings Bank and moved into its more spacious quarters on the northwest corner of Ash and South Jefferson streets. The bank constructed a modern walk-up, drive-up branch on Park Street in 1960, and in

1969 completed a modern headquarters connected to the drive-up facility. A Holt-South Lansing office became a reality in 1974.

Today, Dart continues to provide *personalized* banking services. The first local bank to offer free checking account services to senior citizens, Dart also provides blind customers with free tape-recorded statements. With assets of $48 million, Dart National Bank will continue to provide the Mason-Holt-Lansing community with the firm financial support and multitude of services that have become Dart tradition.

Top
Doc Campbell "D.C." Dart (left) and Rollin Charles "R.C." Dart stand in the lobby of their privately owned bank, R.C. Dart and Company, Bankers. Two years later, in 1925, the bank was issued a national charter and became Dart National Bank of Mason.

Bottom
Mrs. Temple Christian administers the oath of office to the 1980 board of directors: (left to right) Robert E. Ware, John Davis, Kenneth Hope, John Edgar, Edward Jennings, Valentino DeRosa, and Rollin Dart.

Deepdale Memorial Park

When Harry J. Person bought some farmland next to the Grand River in 1920, he envisioned converting it into a beautiful cemetery for Lansing area residents. He called the land Deepdale Burial Park Association, and at a meeting in the old Capital National Bank building he, his brother James, and two others decided to incorporate the organization. Now, though the name has changed a bit and Harry himself rests peacefully in the land he once purchased, Deepdale Memorial Park has become the magnificent final resting place he imagined 60 years ago.

Person was associated with Deepdale until the 1930s, when Lansing businessman John T. Watkins bought the park and managed it until his death in 1943. The Deepdale stock then went to his daughter, Evelyn Hovey. LaVaughn L. Guill, a St. Louis restaurant owner and cemetery plot salesman, purchased controlling interest from the Hovey family in 1954.

Almost from the first day, Guill set out to transform Deepdale into a regal memorial park. He designed grand religious gardens, landscaped the entire park with stately evergreens, and constructed splendid stone monuments. Over the years, he expanded Deepdale's services; in 1970, Deepdale became the first cemetery in the state to offer lawn crypts—pre-engineered, preset crypts for two people.

Deepdale is the only memorial park in the state—and one of the few in the nation—to offer monument sections, landscaped religious gardens, mausoleum crypts, lawn crypts, cremation niches, and infant plots all on the same grounds. The old mausoleum, built in 1924, was constructed of two-foot thick poured concrete walls, covered outside by six inches of marble and inside by nearly an inch of marble. The new mausoleum, completed in 1975 at a cost of $1 million, is constructed of Sicilian marble and of red granite from Scotland. On its upper level, a chapel is overlooked by two modern stained glass crosses. The cross on the front of the chapel measures 6 feet by 10 feet and is designed so that it is illuminated by the setting sun.

The Deepdale offices, formerly in the Central Trust building, are now located on the park grounds at 4110 Lansing Road. The park has a capacity of 38,000 and sprawls over 65 acres of lush greenery. A six-member grounds crew gives the landscape and the facilities constant, year-round attention.

LaVaughn L. Guill, president and general manager of Deepdale, has been president of the Michigan Cemetery Association (1969-1970) and a board member of the association for many years. LaVaughn's son Jeff assists in managing the park and also serves as its secretary.

Left
This photograph, looking from the mausoleum toward the memorial grounds, was taken in the late 1920s.

Right
One of the many beautifully designed religious gardens at Deepdale Memorial Park is the Garden of Our Savior Jesus Christ.

Below
This recent photograph shows the memorial park from its southern border on the Grand River.

Delta Dental Plan of Michigan

Smiles around the state have been brighter since Delta Dental Plan of Michigan, a nonprofit dental service corporation, began in 1957. In that year, the dentists of the state helped organize the corporation in an attempt to make dental care available to more people in Michigan through the help of dental benefit programs.

Originally called Michigan Dental Service Corporation, the organization was allowed to sell only nonrisk programs. In 1963, enabling legislation was passed to permit sales of programs on a risk basis. Dental Care, Inc., was formed to handle those programs, which emphasized preventive care. The first office, employing only a handful of people, was located in the Stoddard Building in downtown Lansing.

During the '70s, Delta experienced tremendous growth—from 111 groups covering 48,000 subscribers in 1972, enrollment increased to more than 1,000 groups covering 1.5 million people. School business sold through the Michigan Education Special Services Association contributed significantly to Delta's early growth and its present mix of business. By the end of the decade, Delta had become the largest dental benefits carrier in Michigan and had moved its corporate headquarters to a newly constructed building in nearby Okemos.

Responsible in large part for Delta's growth boom were the benefit programs negotiated by the UAW-represented employees of General Motors, Ford, and Chrysler. These programs, which began in 1974, were jointly administered by Delta and Blue Cross/Blue Shield of Michigan. At that time, Delta's present Southfield office was opened. Two years later, in 1976, Delta was selected as sole administrator of the programs covering General Motors' and Chrysler's Michigan UAW-represented employees, retirees, and surviving spouses. Although these are Delta's largest groups, coverage is available to employee groups with as few as 10 people.

From the corporation's inception, the dental profession has shown ongoing support for Delta and its programs. Presently, about 90 percent of the state's dentists have service agreements with Delta. This allows the company to offer unique cost and quality assurances to its customers and subscribers.

Delta looks toward the 1980s with optimism. The acceptance of dental benefit programs is increasingly widespread. The realization that good health includes a healthy smile is certain to have a positive impact on Delta as well as the people of Michigan.

Top
Delta Dental Plan employed fewer than a dozen people before the corporation moved from its headquarters in the Stoddard Building downtown in 1963.

Bottom
Today, Delta Dental Plan's modern, new corporate headquarters is located east of Lansing in Okemos.

Forbes/Cohen Properties-Lansing Mall

The Lansing Mall has been a city landmark since it opened in 1969. Used as a point of reference when giving directions on the west side, the mall was the first of its kind constructed in Lansing, and one of the first built in the state outside the greater Detroit area. An auspicious combination of national and local merchants quickly attracted thousands of shoppers to the "original" 65-store complex.

The exciting atmosphere within the mall was created by two young men born and raised in Michigan who formed a partnership in 1958. Sidney Forbes and Maurice Cohen opened their first shopping center in 1965, just four years before the Lansing Mall was opened. Forbes/Cohen Properties quickly grew to include three other Michigan regional shopping complexes in Grand Rapids, Kalamazoo, and Jackson.

The Lansing Mall's success can be demonstrated by the fact that in 1979, the 65-store complex had nearly doubled in size, housing over 100 specialty shops and three major department stores. By its 10th anniversary, the Lansing Mall looked like an entirely new development containing nearly 700,000 square feet of shopping space with architectural detailing, store variety, and merchandise designed to meet the needs and desires of today's customers.

The new design features an aesthetically pleasing environment of natural woods, cascading fountains, verdant tropical landscaping, and restful seating areas. The 1979 expansion and renovation attracted national attention when it won the International Council of Shopping Centers award for expansion renovation in 1980.

Shoppers at the expansive mall are regularly treated to a series of fashion shows, entertainment, and educational demonstrations at the center court staging area, which creates a focal point for the Lansing community. The mall regularly works with area business and community groups on a variety of interesting activities which take place on the mall throughout the year. Art shows, car and boat shows, community bazaars, and antique shows are but a few of the activities housed on the mall. Additionally, the Lansing Mall boasts a community room which seats over 100 and is booked regularly by area groups.

But the primary attraction of the Lansing Mall continues to be the wonderful variety of merchandise available to shoppers. Without ever leaving the Lansing area, residents can find the latest in fashionable clothing, housewares, furniture, gifts, music, books, and sporting goods. The mall's 105 stores are merchandised with a wide selection of items from across the country and around the world, ensuring that sooner or later, nearly everyone in the Lansing metropolitan area will shop at the Lansing Mall.

Top
Nearly twice the size of the mall which opened in 1969, the 105-store Lansing Mall on West Saginaw is still growing to meet the ever-increasing demands of shoppers from throughout the state.

Bottom
Comfortable seating areas provide respite for the thousands of shoppers who flock each year to the 105 specialty shops and major department stores in the Lansing Mall.

148

Foster, Swift, Collins & Coey P.C.

Lansing's oldest law firm traces its history to 1903, when W.S. Foster commenced the practice of law. The intervening 78 years have seen the emergence of one of the most prestigious firms in the state of Michigan. The organization has grown to 110 men and women, including 48 lawyers, eight paraprofessionals, and numerous other highly trained office employees.

Shortly after World War II, Richard B. Foster, Walter's son, assumed active leadership of the enterprise. The goal was to create a law firm with specialists sufficiently skilled to serve a diversified clientele. The efforts of those who joined the organization at that time were most successful; the firm expanded to provide a broad base and total range of services while remaining personal enough to serve individual needs.

The law firm reorganized as a professional corporation in 1970 and elected its first president and executive committee. A legal administrator was hired to work in cooperation with the executive committee to handle the day-to-day operation of the organization. A computer and word-processing equipment were acquired to expedite the paper flow so vital to a law firm. The past decade has been a period of controlled but rapid growth. From 20 lawyers in 1975, the organization has more than doubled its size.

For internal, administrative, and training purposes, the law firm is organized into four departments. The lawyers within the respective departments meet on a weekly basis to coordinate assignments and to discuss new developments in their respective

fields. Frequent meetings of the entire organization are held to insure a cross-exchange of information.

The law firm has had many homes in its lifetime, all of them located in downtown Lansing within a four-block radius of the courts and state capitol. In 1978, the company's shareholders formed a separate partnership—the South Washington Investment Company—for the sole purpose of acquiring and renovating two old downtown buildings to house the firm. Restoration was completed in May 1979, and Foster, Swift, Collins & Coey, P.C., is now lodged at 313 South Washington Avenue. That structure has been named "The Foster Building."

Today, Foster, Swift, Collins & Coey is engaged in a widely diversified general practice. At the same time, however, the enterprise has developed specialized expertise in a number of areas, including administrative law; insurance; medical and legal malpractice; labor; workers

Top
Corporate offices in the Foster Building provide a pleasant professional environment.

Bottom
Restoration of two old downtown buildings was completed in 1979 and Foster, Swift, Collins & Coey, P.C., is now lodged at 313 South Washington Avenue.

compensation; environmental law; and business, tax, and estate planning. Specific cases are supervised by those attorneys most qualified to complete the task. Frequently, several attorneys from the organization's various internal departments work on different aspects of a particularly complex case. In short, when a client hires an individual lawyer within the firm, he hires the firm itself.

Although its size and form are constantly changing, the firm has not changed its goal during the 78 years of its existence: to provide the highest quality and most complete legal counsel for its clients.

Frandorson Properties

One of the strong-spirited Irish immigrant families of the late 1800s, the first Corrs settled in Lansing almost a century ago. From Ireland they brought a penchant for hard work, the will to succeed, and a broad range of building skills, and they carried on these family traditions in their new hometown. When Francis Joseph Corr, the second generation to live in America, joined with his son Francis John to form Francis J. Corr & Son, general contractors, in the 1930s, the seed was planted for the birth of Frandorson Properties, today one of central Michigan's most active real estate developers.

Francis J. Corr & Son was responsible for building many Lansing landmarks, including portions of the Lansing Oldsmobile Plant and many of the town's Catholic churches. In the 1940s, the Corrs built the Board of Water & Light Power Plant. And you can still see the imprint "F.J. Corr" on sidewalks all over town.

In 1954, after Francis Joseph retired and the business incorporated as F.J. Corr, Inc., the company built Frandor Shopping Center—one of the first shopping centers in the state of Michigan. Originally constructed on 40 acres, the center attracted some of Detroit's largest retail operations to Lansing—Federal Department Stores, Wrigley's, and Winkelmans. Most of the tenants, however, were—and still are—hometown merchants, who can reinvest the profit-dollar into Lansing.

Frandorson Properties received its name from Francis (John), his wife Dorothy, and their four sons—Francis Jerome (Jerry), Thomas, George, and Howard. The sons now own the company in partnership, with Jerry managing the Michigan interests.

Frandorson Properties divides its time between managing interests in Michigan (Frandor Shopping Center, the Corr Building, Point North Office Building, Professional Center West) and in Apollo Beach, Florida, where the company is developing a 5,000-acre planned community, encompassing 16,000 family units, motels, restaurants, and schools.

The company is diversifying into agribusiness as well as planning to build, own, and operate more apartment and office buildings in the Lansing area. In acquiring one of the major heritages in building Lansing's past, Frandorson Properties will continue to invest heavily in its future.

Built in 1954, the Frandor Shopping Center was one of the first of its kind in the country. It furnishes 40 acres of space for over 90 stores and offices, and is centrally located between Lansing and East Lansing.

Freeman, Smith and Associates, Inc.

After a brief glance at the list of projects designed by Freeman, Smith and Associates, Inc., it is apparent that the city of Lansing owes a great deal to this respected architectural firm. Community centers, schools, government buildings, financial institutions, factories, offices, commercial facilities, and residential dwellings attribute their distinctive lines and unique interiors to the company.

Robert Freeman and Robert Smith trace the formation of their partnership to 1957, and since that time they have remained in the vanguard of the Michigan architectural community. On their way to establishing a position of prominence in the Lansing design market, which accounts for approximately 60 percent of their total practice, Freeman and Smith merged with the esteemed company of Laitala and Fowler in 1972.

American Bank and Trust Company, Bank of Lansing, Capitol Savings and Loan Association, and Union Savings and Loan Association have commissioned the firm for the design of many new and remodeled facilities. The company has also maintained a long and valued relationship with the Lansing and Holt School Districts. Freeman, Smith and Associates received professional recognition for their innovative design of a new dealership facility for Story Oldsmobile, and have subsequently planned numerous automotive-related structures throughout the state. Local recognition was attained with the contemporary design for the Holy Trinity Greek Orthodox Church on East Saginaw Street. Another project to excite comment in architectural circles was

also the subject of a nationwide advertising campaign, the Plaza I building in downtown Lansing. With the addition of Plaza II and Plaza III, this development provided a distinctive urban profile which aided in the development of the downtown business district.

The firm's design for renovation of the Eastern-Pattengill Field House and Athletic Complex proved to be of historical importance to sports enthusiasts across the country. It was here that Earvin "Magic" Johnson and Jay Vincent displayed the athletic talents that thrust them into national prominence.

The progress of Freeman, Smith and Associates is directly attributed to their innovative and problematic approach to the design process. Their interdisciplinary emphasis has evolved to include interior design, planning, demographic and feasibility analysis, financial consulting, and analysis of the

psychological and sociological factors affecting space utilization.

The officers and employees of Freeman, Smith and Associates have assumed a leadership role in the evolution of Lansing. They have been activists in state and local affairs by serving as directors and members of various governmental bodies, professional organizations, and civic clubs. As a result of their civic and professional commitment, they have revived the historical structures of our past while advancing the contemporary designs of the future.

Top
Freeman, Smith and Associates were lauded for their innovative design of a new dealership facility for Story Oldsmobile.

Bottom
Local recognition was attained with the contemporary design for the Holy Trinity Greek Orthodox Church on East Saginaw Street.

The year was 1897. John Philip Sousa was writing "Stars and Stripes Forever." Lansing was celebrating its 50th anniversary. And the Olds Motor Vehicle Company, the first enterprise in the state of Michigan organized solely for the manufacture of automobiles, was being formed in Lansing.

The board of directors of the infant company authorized Ransom Eli Olds, a 33-year-old local inventor, "to build one carriage in as nearly perfect a manner as possible." The young manager had been a Lansingite since 1880, when he moved with his parents from Ohio. Attending school in Lansing, he had spent every spare moment working in his father's machine repair shop on River Street. He had completed his first steam car in 1886 and had road tested it during the predawn hours of a summer morning. As the city slept, the first "Oldsmobile" required a push to return home, but the push would prove to be in the direction of Lansing's future.

Over the next 11 years, Olds experimented with a number of electric cars before starting his company in 1897. His first gasoline-powered auto was completed that year. Olds, with unshaken confidence in the future of the automobile, found that Lansing was too narrow a sphere for his early activities and that Detroit presented greater possibilities in his search for more capital to further develop his ideas. He interested S.L. Smith, a Michigan copper and timber capitalist in his project. Smith had not only the commercial vision, but equally important, the money with which to put the young inventor's plan into action.

Accordingly, in 1899 the Olds Motor

Works was organized in Detroit with a capital of $350,000 and R.E. Olds as general manager. A three-story plant was built on the Detroit riverfront. The Lansing facility was retained as an engine plant. Olds' first gasoline-powered auto was completed in the Detroit plant and was the forerunner of the only Olds product to survive a raging fire in March 1901.

Due to the foresight of members of the Lansing Businessmen's Association, a permanent home was established in that city for the automaker at the former Michigan State Fairgrounds. The Olds Motor Works paid nearly $35,000 less for this 52-acre tract than it had paid for the five acres the company had purchased in Detroit in 1899.

Immediately, Olds went ahead with production on his only remaining car— a Curved Dash Runabout, the first car to be built on a progressive assembly system. The cars were moved along on wooden platforms, supported by rolling casters underneath. Parts bins were placed at strategic points along the production line. This was the forerunner of today's mass production.

Beginning in 1902, Oldsmobiles would be produced both in Lansing and in Detroit for a period of three and a half years. Ransom Olds, in addition to serving as general manager of all the Olds manufacturing activities, had immediate responsibility for the Lansing plant; Fred Smith, in addition to continuing to serve as company secretary-treasurer, took over the supervision of the day-to-day operations at the Detroit plant.

The Curved Dash Olds model was built from 1900 through 1904, with minor variations, with some units still

being produced up until 1907. The first Oldsmobile ushered in the era of the automobile publicity campaign, an idea created by Ransom Olds himself. The campaign began with a cost-comparison with horses and climaxed with a flashy demonstration—a "road test" all the

Top left
The ability to climb hills was as important in an automobile in 1901 as it is today, judging from this early photograph of an Oldsmobile. It is being piloted up a steep grade by R.E. Olds, founder of the company that is now Oldsmobile Division of GMC.

Top right
The 1904 Reo (R.E. Olds is at the wheel) established speed records of up to 30 m.p.h.

Below left
R.E. Olds (left) handles the tiller of this 1892 model Olds Gasoline Steam Carriage.

Below right
Economy, dependability, and publicity soon earned Olds a reputation for engineering and design.

Photos courtesy Lansing Regional Chamber of Commerce

General Motors

way to New York by Roy D. Chapin, an Oldsmobile employee. During this same period, Lansingites watched in amazement as a Curved Dash was driven up the steps of the state capitol. Gus Edwards forever memorialized the Oldsmobile in song when he composed "In My Merry Oldsmobile" in 1905.

Economy, dependability, and publicity soon earned Olds a reputation for engineering and design that was enhanced even further by a number of Oldsmobile speed records and an incredible cross-country race from New York City to Portland, Oregon, a race won by Oldsmobile's "Old Scout" in 1905.

Peak production of 36 cars per day was reached that year and from then on there was no stopping the company. The "firsts" were coming thick and fast: nickel plating in 1907, chrome plating in 1925, hydra-matic drive in 1939, high-compression V-8 engine in 1948, front wheel drive on the Toronado in 1966, and, on 1978 Oldsmobiles, the first domestic diesel engine. Oldsmobile, the oldest continuous automaker in the United States, observed its 75th birthday on August 21, 1972. In 1977, Oldsmobile became only the third automaker in history to build more than one million cars in a model year.

Oldsmobile has three Lansing plants, with a fourth under construction—an engine plant designed to build V-6 diesel engines. By 1982, the V-6 plant is expected to employ 1,600 people, and by 1983, 13 percent of all GM-produced cars are expected to be diesel-powered. Oldsmobile is keeping Lansing in the forefront of the worldwide auto industry and securing the city's industrial future.

Granger Associates, Inc.

Granger Associates Inc., a holding company owned by Alton L. Granger, Ronald K. Granger, and Jerry P. Granger, was incorporated on January 10, 1974, for the purpose of providing an ownership entity for several other companies owned by the same three individuals. The firms involved are Granger Construction Company, Granger Container Service, Granger Excavating Company, Granger Land Development Company, and D & K Truck Company.

Granger Construction Company is now in its third generation of serving the construction needs of the mid-Michigan area. It was incorporated in January 1960 by Keith Granger and his sons, Alton, Ronald, and Jerry. Prior to this incorporation, Keith Granger had been in business with his brother Dorr, for more than 20 years, under the name of Granger Brothers Inc.

Granger Construction has grown to become one of the largest general construction companies in the mid-Michigan area. Early projects consisted largely of school facilities, including Lansing Catholic Central and Waverly High School, and commercial buildings. By the middle '60s Michigan State University had become a major customer with such projects as the Biochemistry Building, Holmes Hall, and Hubbard Hall. During the late '60s large commercial buildings occupied much of Granger's time. The 1970s brought such projects as Haslett High School and the State Police Academy. By the late '70s Oldsmobile Division of General Motors had become a major user of Granger Construction Company's services. The year 1980 found the firm completing the

Communication Arts Building at MSU and a new jail facility for Ingham County.

Granger Container Service began operations in August 1966, with one truck unit, 16 containers, and one employee. Today the firm has 15 trucks (all diesel) servicing over 2,300 containers, with 27 employees. They handle commercial, industrial, construction, and apartment waste by containerization, with on-site compaction equipment available for large-volume accounts. They maintain their own vehicles in their new 16,500-square-foot facility, which includes an approved paint booth to handle their largest vehicles.

Granger Excavating Company purchased the assets of Andersen Excavating Company in April 1972. The firm is involved in residential, commercial, and industrial excavating and grading. This includes anything from excavating and backfilling a single family dwelling to moving several hundred thousand cubic yards of earth. To accomplish this, Granger Excavating Company has some of the largest and most modern equipment in central Michigan.

Granger Land Development Company began February 14, 1973, with the purchase of the 120-acre Daggett Sanitary Landfill located in North Lansing. The following January Granger Land Development Company became the operator of the 90-acre sanitary landfill located in Watertown Township, Clinton County. Both sites have been reevaluated geologically and have an established monitoring program to detect any changes in ground-water quality. At present, Granger Land

Development Company disposes of 90 percent of the solid waste in the area, which amounted to 1.25 million cubic yards in 1979. In March 1980 Granger Land Development Company purchased additional adjacent property for future expansion. With this added acreage, the firm will have the capability of handling the disposal of solid waste for the area for another 20 years.

The solid-waste industry is rapidly changing and Granger Land Development Company has been a leader in upgrading sanitary landfills to be an environmentally safe method of solid-waste disposal. In addition, the company allocates funds each year in a continuing effort to establish an economically feasible local resource recovery program.

D & K Truck Company started business in 1948, selling White trucks in the six counties around Lansing. The dealership, first in the area to offer service on diesel engines, was purchased by Granger in 1971. Their claim to fame in the community is their ability to design trucks that will give their customers the best performance, legal payload, and long service life for their particular needs, and to offer those customers the kind of service that will enable them to keep their trucks productive and profitable.

The year 1981 finds D & K with 19 employees with a combined 208 years of service. This experience, coupled with quality trucks such as White, Autocar, Freightliner, and Mercedes-Benz, gives D & K a prominent share of the truck business in the Lansing area.

Headquarters of Granger Associates Inc. are located at 6267 Aurelius Road in Lansing.

Greater Lansing Board of Realtors

The Greater Lansing Board of Realtors, a 73-year-old association of real estate brokers and salespeople, emanated from a modest, loosely knit group of 14 professionals who incorporated themselves as the Lansing Real Estate Board in 1917. The organization was renamed the Lansing Real Estate and Property Owners Association in 1933. Today, membership in the association, which became the Greater Lansing Board of Realtors to better reflect the metropolitan growth and development of the entire service area, exceeds 1,200 people.

Formed before the birth of state and national real estate associations, the Lansing Real Estate Board fostered cooperation among real estate practitioners and established standards of professional conduct, purposes that remain fundamental to today's organization. Services are also very important. The multiple-listing service introduced by the Board in 1941 represents a valuable tool that improves sales opportunities and encourages good will among area realtors.

Other services available to members include a complete professional library, a monthly magazine, legislative updates, political action committee endorsements of candidates, insurance programs, educational seminars, and several informative real estate-oriented publications. The Board also presents awards to outstanding members.

Members continue to take an active interest in the community, just as they did in 1956 when the Board stepped in to resolve Lansing's downtown parking problems, hiring an objective outside firm at a cost of $10,000 to prepare an

engineering study embraced by city planners.

The Board originally set up offices in a remodeled home at 326 Townsend. The organization moved to a site next door, at 332 Townsend, in the 1940s. The first of several expansions was completed in 1946. Today, the growth of the Greater Lansing Board of Realtors has necessitated relocation to larger quarters in the former Horsebrook Elementary School, a structure refitted for office use at a cost of $400,000. Among other things, the new facilities will accommodate the now-computerized multiple-listing service.

The Greater Lansing Board of Realtors looks forward to continued vitality in tandem with Lansing's continued economic and physical development.

Left
The Board's former office at 332 Townsend Street was a delightful Victorian mansion designed by Darius Moon, an architect famous for gingerbread-laden houses built around the turn of the century. It was first remodeled in the 1940s, and later evolved into the rectangular structure shown above.

Right
This recent photograph shows the remodeled Townsend Street offices as they appeared before the Board of Realtors moved for the second time in 73 years to a new location.

Above
Renovated at a cost of $400,000, the new Board offices in the former Horsebrook Elementary School house the many services offered to the growing list of members in the greater Lansing area.

Grunwell-Cashero of Lansing

Lyle Bornor enjoys showing visitors a sign on his office wall that says, "You can't expect to use yesterday's methods today and still be in business tomorrow." Those who are familiar with his position as president of Grunwell-Cashero of Lansing, Inc., appreciate the irony, because that's exactly what he does.

Bornor was engineer superintendent of maintenance at Michigan State University's physical plant from 1957 to 1968. Old buildings on that campus were always in need of architectural medicare. Continuous rehabilitation and restoration of these historic landmarks have been required to keep the ornate structures from going the way of the craftsmen who had labored on them more than a century before.

That's where Grunwell-Cashero Company, Inc., located in Detroit, came into the picture. The Detroit firm was renovating several buildings at MSU and in the Lansing area when the president, Fidell A. Cashero, contacted Bornor. The two soon reached agreement and founded a new corporation, Grunwell-Cashero of Lansing, Inc., in January 1968.

Bornor employs highly skilled artisans and craftsmen to preserve and restore museum-piece buildings in the Lansing area and throughout Michigan. Due to the diligent efforts of Grunwell-Cashero of Lansing, Inc., many architectural marvels have risen from the ashes of Lansing's past to become useful, attractive facilities for Lansing businessmen, students, and government workers.

In the beginning, Bornor worked from his home and from a building located on Vine Street near the State of

Michigan Library near downtown Lansing. The building was small but not too crowded, as Bornor had recruited only a few members of his growing team of craftsmen. Since that time, the office has been moved to a larger structure on the north side of town, at 525 Filley Street. That building was purchased by the firm in 1972.

Bornor speaks with pride of the constant challenge of his company's work. Preservation, rehabilitation, restoration, and reconstruction of older buildings requires workmen who are highly skilled, who must be trained from within. There are no schools to teach new employees. Brick, limestone, sandstone, terra-cotta, marble, wood, asphalt, and coal tar are but a few of the products that make up the shell of a building. Different methods, materials, and tools are required to preserve and/or restore each.

Among Lansing landmarks that Grunwell-Cashero of Lansing, Inc., has restored are the Forestry and Entomology buildings, two of the oldest facilities on the MSU campus; the Goodspeed Building, on the corner of Abbott and East Grand River in East Lansing; Turner-Dodge House on North Street in Lansing; Old Central School, Lansing; Olds Plaza Hotel, Lansing; and the Michigan State Capitol, Lansing.

Maintenance and rehabilitation of the state capitol and other buildings is an ongoing project. Cleaning, painting, masonry replacement, roofing, tuckpointing, caulking, sealing, etc., must be done periodically to preserve any building or structure. This historic site, the state capitol, has been partially restored by Grunwell-Cashero of Lansing, Inc., workers, who sandblasted

and caulked the circular dome in preparation for painting. They also reroofed the entire building.

The forces of nature and the passage of time will continue to provide Grunwell-Cashero of Lansing, Inc., with new work throughout the Lansing area, preserving yesterday's history as new foundations are laid for tomorrow's growth.

Top
Lansing landmarks like the Turner-Dodge House, built more than a century ago, have been transformed into living museum pieces by Grunwell-Cashero of Lansing, Inc.

Bottom
Thanks to the extensive restoration efforts of Grunwell-Cashero of Lansing, Inc., the Michigan State Capitol dome shines today as it did in 1878, when it was fashioned of tin imported from Wales.

Hasselbring-Clark

The tremendous growth of the photocopying machine business over the past 30 years is by now well-known. Large corporations, government offices, small businesses, schools, and individuals have all found photocopying a quick, accurate, and inexpensive means of reproducing important documents and papers. Hasselbring-Clark, a Lansing firm founded 25 years ago, has grown into one of the largest distributors of reprographic machines in the state of Michigan.

The firm began as the Hasselbring Company in 1956, when Reinhart Hasselbring, Seth Bidwell, and James Robertson purchased the office machine division of the Franklin DeKleine Company. Initially selling typewriters, adding machines, addressing machines, and mimeograph equipment, the company was located at 310 Grand Avenue and served a local Lansing market. In the late 1950s, however, the firm made a prophetic and opportune decision—diversifying into photocopiers manufactured at that time by Kodak.

About the same time, important personnel changes were also occurring within the company. Mr. Hasselbring, the driving force of the business, bought out his two partners, and a delivery man by the name of Ellis Clark was hired. He would later run the company. By 1966, Hasselbring had outgrown its Grand Avenue quarters and moved to larger offices at 809 Center Street.

The '70s brought more success and growth, as the firm began to specialize in reprographic equipment. The typewriter and adding machine departments were sold to L.E. Lightheart, a Hasselbring employee,

and Ellis Clark and Louis Willard bought Hasselbring itself, changing the company name to Hasselbring-Clark in 1976.

Today, the company specializes in the sale, rental, service, and supply of Canon and Sharp photocopiers; in fact, it has been the largest dealer of Canon equipment in Michigan since 1977. From its modern plant, showroom, and office facilities at 3942 North East Street, the firm did more than $1 million worth of business in 1979.

The company's expert staff of 15 sales and service employees have all been extensively—and expensively—trained at various colleges and company schools to learn the intricacies of the Canon and Sharp machines. The combination of technical expertise and high-quality service has paid off handsomely for Hasselbring-Clark—many of its clients, including the state

of Michigan, the city of Lansing, and Michigan State University, have been customers for many years.

Current officers are Louis Willard, president; Ellis Clark, vice-president; Noelle Clark, secretary; and Doris Willard, treasurer. They continue to express the company's basic philosophy of dealing with customers as friends. With a market that has expanded to Jackson to the south and Mt. Pleasant to the north, and plans to open a branch office in Jackson, the future looks very bright for Hasselbring-Clark.

Top
Vice-president Ellis Clark and secretary Noelle Clark (at right) pose with members of the company's sales and telephone crew.

Bottom
Service manager Robert Thomann (far right) instructs Hasselbring-Clark's service technicians in the intricacies of the Canon copier.

Heatherwood Farms

Many industries have undergone great changes in the past half century, perhaps none so visibly as the dairy industry. In 1934, when Henry Crouse purchased the Winan Dairy Company and founded Heatherwood Farms, he had a dozen employees and a dozen horses to deliver milk in glass bottles to Lansing homes. Almost 50 years later, the horses are gone, the returnable glass bottles are gone, and home deliveries have all but disappeared. And the product distribution lines of Crouse's firm have grown to include a wide range of dairy items, fruit juices, soft drinks, and even the manufacture of plastic containers to package its own products.

Perhaps the greatest changes in the dairy industry have occurred in the related areas of distribution and packaging; Heatherwood Farms has not only been subject to these innovations but has pioneered them. In the late '50s and early '60s, retail stores and supermarkets replaced home deliveries as the primary dairy distribution outlets, and there was a corresponding shift from glass bottles to paper cartons and plastic containers. Heatherwood Farms was the first dairy in Michigan to introduce in-plant, blow-molding equipment to produce its own plastic containers. The firm now services large retail supermarket chains and institutions throughout the state of Michigan and as far east as Pittsburgh, as far west as Chicago.

Heatherwood began to diversify its product line in the 1960s, when it introduced fruit juices under the Orchard Grove label. The juices arrive in pure concentrate form from Florida and are pasteurized and processed in the firm's own plant at 2701 East Michigan

Avenue. Today, Peninsular Products Company, the parent company of both the Heatherwood and Orchard Grove labels, is the largest chilled orange juice packer in the state.

The family-owned firm has played a vital role in the Lansing community. Henry Crouse was president of the YMCA, chairman of the Community Chest, and a board member of the Jaycees. His son Edward Crouse, who now runs the company, serves as chairman of the Sparrow Hospital board of trustees and on the board of directors of the American Bank and Trust. An avid flyer, Edward has also had an active role in the development of the Capital Regional Airport Authority.

Employing more than 100 people, the company sold $15 million worth of products in Michigan in 1979. The firm services retail outlets, is a specialist in institutional food service, and sells to large corporate dairies, which put their own labels on Heatherwood Farms's vast variety of fruit juices.

Although dairy production and distribution technology have changed,

other aspects of the business have not. Heatherwood Farms milk still comes from local Michigan farms and a few of the plant's large fleet of trucks still make home deliveries. And "personalized service," always a trademark of the firm, is still the key to its success. "We are still small enough," says chief operating officer Wayne Wagoner, "to tailor our distribution to all our customers' needs."

Left
Well into the 1950s, the familiar "clip-clop" of Barney the horse signaled to every child the coming of the milkman and the Heatherwood Farms wagon.

Right
The company has been located at the corner of East Michigan Avenue and LaSalle since the late 1930s.

Below
The heart of the dairy delivery operation is captured in this mid-1950s photograph, which shows the transition from horses and wagons to the new trucks that would soon replace them. The barn in the background housed the horses.

158

Industrial Metal Products Corporation

In the tool and die business, corporate survival depends upon quality workmanship, product durability, and the solid reputation those attributes engender. Edward Judge, Sr., recognized this reality when he and Leonard Deason founded Industrial Metal Products Corporation (IMPCO) in 1937.

Beginning with six screw machines and a small staff of tool and die specialists operating out of a converted dairy, the fledgling firm manufactured brass parts for Oldsmobiles, the sale of which, that first year, earned less than the sale of its residual scrap metal. IMPCO's fine craftsmanship soon gained the respect of Lansing's industrial community, however, and the company started signing work contracts with such entities as the area's growing automaker, Diamond Reo, and Motor Wheel (then Prudden Wheel).

World War II hastened IMPCO's growth and development as military needs created a strong market for tools, fixtures, gauges, and small parts essential to the war effort. By 1945, the company had nearly doubled its original 2,500 feet. Two years later, the corporation was able to introduce the first of a series of high-quality specialty products, a machine that straightened shafts for various industrial uses.

IMPCO initiated a second line of specialty machines by 1951. Defense contracts accounted for 80 percent of the corporation's production at that time. Business volume continued to increase to the point where, in 1955, a new manufacturing facility was required; IMPCO's first plant had already been expanded and remodeled to capacity. The new facility on

Sheridan Street could accommodate machines so large that entire walls sometimes had to be removed in order to ship the completed assemblies.

A micro-finishing machine was invented by an auto worker who discovered that smoothly ground bearings need no breaking-in period, and IMPCO brought out a full line of them shortly thereafter. Today, the automatic micro-finishers built by IMPCO are used worldwide and have effectively eliminated breaking-in periods for modern automobiles.

In the 1960s, IMPCO's auto industry-related production expanded significantly, especially after the introduction of the non-destructive testing machine. The unit, designed to test critical manufacturing parts without destroying them in the process, permitted 100 percent quality control at a lower cost than was possible under audit testing, the previously accepted

Top
By the end of the Great Depression, Industrial Metal Products Corporation had already expanded from the tiny converted dairy building in which the firm was established.

Bottom
Observant Lansing history buffs will spot the original IMPCO office, now engulfed by the continually expanding production plant at 3417 West St. Joseph Street.

inspection method that required the destruction of random parts to test for flaws. Consumer activists applauded IMPCO's new machine. It soon became an industry standard, raising the firm's annual automobile-oriented production to 60 percent by the end of the 1970s.

Today, Edward Judge's sons manage IMPCO, along with other officers, and 250 people work in the corporation's 60,000-square-foot facility. Plans to open new markets in the heavy equipment and farm implement industries are under way.

Lansing Regional Chamber of Commerce

In 1901, a few dozen local businessmen formed a group known as the Lansing Businessmen's Association, for the express purpose of recruiting a young auto manufacturer to Lansing. The Lansing Businessmen's Association, later to become the Lansing Regional Chamber of Commerce, purchased a large parcel of land left vacant by the move of the Michigan State Fairgrounds from Lansing to Detroit. They offered it free of charge, no strings attached, if Ransom E. Olds would move his growing automobile company back to Lansing from Detroit. It looked like a fair trade—the state fairgrounds for a piece of the infant auto industry. No stranger to Lansing, having opened his first Olds Motor Works in the city before moving to Detroit, Olds agreed to build his next factory on the fairgrounds site after fire destroyed his Detroit plant.

On its way to becoming a 1,350-member organization by 1980, the Chamber changed its name from the Lansing Businessmen's Association to the Lansing Chamber of Commerce in 1914, then to the Chamber of Commerce of Greater Lansing in 1956, and to the present name in 1974. Meanwhile, many key members of the Lansing business community assumed positions of leadership in the Chamber in order to promote cooperation among area businesses.

Early presidents of the group included R.E. Olds, inventor of the Oldsmobile, and W.K. Prudden, founder of Motor Wheel Corporation. Prudden donated the chamber's first offices, which were utilized until the Chamber moved into the Lansing Civic Center in 1955.

Today, the Chamber can claim credit for a variety of Lansing developments as it continues to represent area business in government action and economic growth planning. The Chamber is the final word when it comes to small business assistance, providing information, seminars, and advice to new and existing enterprises.

Leading the effort to revitalize Lansing's downtown district, the Lansing Regional Chamber of Commerce looks forward to the coming decades. The Chamber will continue to stress intergovernmental cooperation for increased growth and development, which, like its original success, will benefit all who live and work in the Lansing region.

Top
The automobile was a novelty in 1901, when the newly formed Lansing Business-men's Association purchased a piece of property and offered it free of charge if Ransom E. Olds would move his growing automobile company back to Lansing from Detroit.

Right
Ransom Eli Olds, inventor of the Oldsmobile, was an early president of what is today known as the Lansing Regional Chamber of Commerce.

Leonard Melse Associates

When Holland-born Leonard Melse immigrated to America in 1950, he had only $100 in his pocket. After paying freight on his belongings and buying a bus ticket to Grand Rapids, most of his money was gone. Unable to find a job as an interior designer, the profession for which he had been educated at the Hague Academy of Design, he took a series of odd jobs to make ends meet. He soon found a position with Stow-Davis Furniture Company and was able to begin his interior design career. Eight years later, with many interior designs to his credit, Melse was hired as chief designer by Weger Interiors of Lansing. In 1964, he founded Leonard Melse Associates, and today his firm is one of the most respected commercial and residential interior designers in the country.

Over the past 16 years, Melse has completed design jobs for corporations, colleges, banks, churches, historic building restorations, restaurants, and hotels. Just a few of the company's local clients include Lansing Oldsmobile (executive office design); Consumers Power Company, Jackson (offices, conference rooms, and lobby); Plymouth Congregational Church, Lansing; the Turner/Dodge Mansion, Lansing (historic restoration); and Amway Corporation, Ada (office building design). Melse also designed the interior for the *Enterprise III,* a 130-foot, custom-built yacht constructed in the Netherlands for Amway Corporation.

Melse's interior design service is personal and detailed. Extensive drawings are made to ensure that the client will know how the interior will appear when completed. The drawings include floor plans with furniture locations and elevations of various wall and window treatments; all materials and furnishings are selected and color-coordinated so that everything meets the client's desires. Melse's design philosophy emphasizes that an interior's beauty and functional efficiency depend more on coordination of elements than on money spent.

Melse has managed to keep his staff small so that all clients receive the personal attention they deserve. Douglas Richey, Melse's chief interior designer, has been with the firm since its founding and is also an instructor at Lansing Community College. John M. Melse, Leonard's son, graduated from the Kendall School of Design in 1979 and joined the firm that same year. Leonard Melse has been a member of the American Society of Interior Designers (ASID) since 1962. He is also a member of the Michigan Chamber of Commerce, the Lansing Regional Chamber of Commerce, the National Federation of Independent Businesses, and the National Association of Home Builders.

In addition to his internationally known interior design work, Melse has also instituted a plan of field study with Michigan State University, Lansing Community College, and the Community Design Center, whereby college students work in the studio with Melse designers to gain on-the-job experience. The firm provides the program at no charge to the school or to the students.

Located at 225 South Washington Avenue, the Leonard Melse studio also contains a retail showroom displaying fine quality furniture, decorative accessories, and the work of several local artists. In the future, Leonard Melse Associates will continue to meet the interior design needs of businesses and individuals throughout Lansing and the state of Michigan.

Top
Applying his eye for color and talent for detail, Leonard Melse, ASID, works on an interior design project in his studio at 225 South Washington Square in downtown Lansing.

Bottom
Due to the talents of Leonard Melse Associates, this former meat market built in 1875 is now the headquarters of Melse's interior design studio and an attractive contribution to downtown Lansing.

161

Liebermann's

Although many small Lansing businesses died during the Great Depression, some managed to survive and a few even had their origins during those grim years. One of the latter was Liebermann's, a luggage, gift, and specialty store that today flourishes in three different Lansing-area locations.

The year was 1931 and three Saginaw men, Hugo Boettcher, Julius Liebermann, and Liebermann's son-in-law Heil Rockwell, decided to brave the storm and open a Lansing branch of Saginaw's Liebermann Trunk Company. So they purchased James Edmonds & Son Leathergoods store at 107 South Washington Avenue. Though Julius's Saginaw store already had a reputation for quality and excellent service, the times were difficult and the new store struggled in its infancy. At one point, Boettcher, who moved to Lansing to manage the store, was forced to cash in his life insurance to keep the business going.

As the 1930s wore on, however, things started looking up. Liebermann's developed a reputation for always paying its bills on time; in fact, during the Depression it was not uncommon to see salesmen making special trips in hopes of making a sale, knowing their company would be paid on a timely basis. Hugo's son Art entered the business, and his daughter Betty, who proved to be the driving force in the store's growth later on, introduced crystal and chinaware, the start of Liebermann's well-known gift department. In 1946, Betty's husband Don Price came aboard to run the advertising and luggage departments.

During the next two decades, the store expanded in many directions.

Correctly foreseeing that East Lansing and Michigan State University would grow dramatically, Liebermann's opened an East Lansing store at 209 East Grand River Avenue in 1959. Answering a need for more space, the gift department became the gift store in 1966 at 113 South Washington Avenue. Famed architect George Nelson was hired to design the interior. Nelson's elegant "free-form" motif expressed the store's insistence on quality merchandise. In 1961 Art Boettcher retired to pursue other interests, and Betty and Don Price became owners. Art's son Bill joined the company in 1966.

A major reason for Liebermann's success has been the store's "family" feeling; over the years, many loyal store employees have felt a part of this family, including the bookkeeper, Lottie Vermillion, and buyer, Nellie Bennett, each of whom recently retired after more than 35 years of service. Moreover, employees have regular training sessions with Betty Price on all aspects of the store's merchandise and participate in a profit-sharing plan that is extraordinary for a company of Liebermann's size.

Today, Liebermann's has an unsurpassed reputation for high-quality, well-designed merchandise. The Liebermann "special gift wrap" has become a sign of distinction for discerning gift givers. The store's broad selection of luggage and handbags is considered the best in Michigan. Since the early 1960s Betty and Don have taken buying trips to all corners of the earth to find the best china, antiques, crystal, pewter, and folk artifacts. Don Price quotes Stanley Marcus's axiom that "it is not a question of whether we *can* sell it, but whether we *should* sell it."

Top
Don and Betty Price, who have owned Liebermann's since 1961, stand in the new Rosenthal Studio, part of the 113 South Washington gift store.

Bottom
The early years of Liebermann's clearly established the store's reputation for crisp and elegant display.

Lindell Forge

Forging, a process as old as manufacturing itself, involves the shaping of hot metal under tremendous pressure. As new metal-using industries have arisen and grown in the 20th century, so has the need for high-quality forgings. One of the top names in forgings for more than 70 years has been Lansing's Lindell Drop Forge Company.

The company was founded by Charles E. Lindell, a Swedish apprentice blacksmith who made his way to the Great Lakes region in 1903 as a merchant seaman. Two years later, he settled in Chicago as a tool and die maker, and shortly thereafter he moved to Detroit where he worked in the first drop forge company to operate in that city. After leaving Detroit to work in Jackson, Lindell relocated to Lansing where he took a position as a diesinker for the Emergency Forge Company, which later became the Lansing Drop Forge Company.

In 1910, he established his own business, the Lindell Die and Tool Company, in a small building at 832 West Main Street. The firm remained at that location for 13 years. In 1923, the business was incorporated as the Lindell Drop Forge Company and moved to its present location at 2830 South Logan Street.

Over the years, Lindell has served a wide range of industries, including trucks, passenger cars, railroads, material handling, and earth-moving equipment. Present customers such as TRW, General Motors, and Rockwell International have been with the company since the plant first opened in the 1920s. Although the firm has had many purchase offers from large corporations, it remains independent—the last independent forging shop in the state.

Basically, the forging process is the same as it was a half century ago, but new materials, equipment, and techniques have elevated quality forging to a science. At its 28-acre plant, Lindell engineers all its own die and tooling designs; the firm is a top producer of multiple forging dies. Over the past 20 years, the plant has become completely modernized with the addition of energy-efficient air drop hammers and press machinery.

The company continues to be a family-owned corporation. Arthur Lindell, son of the founder, is currently president and chairman of the board. The remainder of the board is composed of third-generation Lindells—Ronald, Robert D., Walter C., and Douglas— along with Tony Rizzardi and Thomas Beach. For many years, the family has been a "silent" contributor to the Lansing community, donating time and money with little regard for recognition. Charles W. Lindell, for example, was responsible for building the emergency wing to Sparrow Hospital; the Lindell family donated the bells for the St. Thomas Aquinas Church in East Lansing; and Robert C. Lindell was the primary sponsor of the Golden Gloves boxing tournament when it first began. W.E. Lindell, past president and chairman, was one of the founding members of the Drop Forge Association and served on its board of directors from 1955 through 1957. Today known as the Forging Industry Association, it is comprised of 270 forging plants located in the United States and Canada.

In the future, the company will continue its expansive modernization program, concentrating on energy-saving, induction heat forging processes and safety and environmental precautions. From its central Midwest location, excellent for quick and economical shipping to any other location in the country, Lindell Drop Forge will follow the philosophy that has sustained it for more than 70 years—to grow with the city of Lansing.

At its 28-acre plant in Lansing, Lindell Drop Forge Company engineers all of its own die and tooling designs.

163

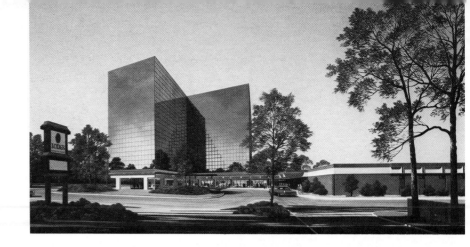

Long Development

Lansing has experienced tremendous physical growth in the past 30 years, and one of the major contributors to this growth has been real estate developer Gordon Long. Raised in Leroy, a small farming community south of Cadillac, Michigan, Long came to Lansing in 1949 and studied accounting and business law at Lansing Business University. After serving in the navy and obtaining his real estate broker's license in Illinois, Long returned to Lansing—this time to stay.

While he attended Michigan State University, he held his first job, with H.J. Novakoski Realty. There he gained valuable sales experience, and, perhaps more important, met William Warner, a co-worker with similar interests and ambitions. It was not long before the two friends were involved in their own real estate projects as general contractors, buying, building, and selling single-family homes in Lansing. In 1955, they formed Warner & Long Realty, a partnership that would last for 12 prosperous years and result in the development and construction of subdivisions, home sites, and apartment complexes, such as Lamoreaux and Mar Scott Meadows.

By 1968, both partners realized it was time to go their separate ways. Long was fascinated with the entire development process from concept to finished product—the search for a good property, the analysis to determine its best possible use, the design and construction of the buildings, and the marketing to potential buyers or tenants. The "complete developer" idea has been carried through to the present day; Long's 500-employee corporation, headquartered in a new million-dollar

facility at 6910 South Cedar Street, has a multi-divisional structure that offers a broad spectrum of development services—building, leasing, full-service brokerage, and maintenance.

The company has been involved in Lansing projects too numerous to mention, but a few of its major achievements include Cedar Park Center, a $9-million shopping center; the $6-million Haslett Village Square Shopping Center; the luxurious 618-unit Oak Park Village Apartments and Athletic Club; Long Commerce Park, a professional office park; the Holiday Plaza office complex; and Long's of Lansing, the well-known banquet, convention, and restaurant center. In the future, Long will develop the Westland Complex in Delta Township, a planned unit industrial park, and will continue developing Country Meadows, a 400-acre planned unit development. The addition of a multimillion-dollar Sheraton Hotel to Long's Convention Center in the near future will make it one of the largest full service convention locations in the state.

Long attributes his success to hard work (he traditionally arrives at the office before 7:30 a.m. and 15-hour workdays were not uncommon in the early years of the company's history) and an astute understanding of people, a skill that he gained from working in a grocery store as a youngster. "I learned how to serve and deal with people," he declares, "and this helped me immeasurably as a salesman. Furthermore, from this experience I knew that someday I would go into business for myself."

Gordon Long has certainly fulfilled that dream and hopes to fulfill the dreams of others as he continues to place his investment stake in the future of the Lansing community.

Top
The addition of a multimillion-dollar Sheraton Hotel to Long's Convention Center in the near future will make it one of the largest full-service convention locations in the state.

Bottom
Long's 500-employee corporation is headquartered in a new million-dollar facility at 6910 South Cedar Street.

Maner, Costerisan & Ellis, P.C.

Michigan first began licensing certified public accountants in 1906, and John J. Jerome was the 14th person in the state to become a licensed CPA. Jerome opened a proprietorship that year in the 200 block of South Capitol Avenue. Over the past 75 years, the proprietorship has grown into Maner, Costerisan & Ellis, a professional corporation with nine owners that is out-state Michigan's leading accounting firm.

Max D. Harris, the 240th Michigan accountant to be certified, joined in partnership with Jerome in 1918. When the new Michigan National Tower building opened in 1933, they moved in immediately, and the firm has had its offices there ever since. After Jerome died in 1951, Harris formed a new partnership, Harris, Reames & Ambrose, which evolved into the present firm.

Once cramped into 400 square feet of space in the Tower building, the firm now occupies 11,000 square feet—three entire floors—of Lansing's only skyscraper. It has grown from a staff of eight in 1951 to more than 50 employees in 1981. And the firm's range of expertise has expanded also, offering accounting services in auditing, tax planning, management consulting, and small business accounting.

With experience in many types of audits, including finance, manufacturing, commercial, retail, governmental, and nonprofit organizations, MC & E accountants belong to specialized industry associations, as well as associations of the accounting profession: the American Institute of Certified Public Accountants and the Financial Accounting Standards Board. The firm is a member of both the Private Companies and SEC Practice Sections of the American Institute of CPAs.

The firm's tax department specialists have backgrounds in the IRS and in representing taxpayers. Through continuing education and a complete library that is updated weekly, they keep current with changes in tax law, regulations, and procedures. They are experts in the areas of individual estate planning, business tax planning, preparation of returns, and governmental audits of tax returns.

MC & E's management advisory clients are served by full-time professional consultants. Typical assignments include accounting system design and installation, cost accounting systems, feasibility studies, budgets, organizational studies, personnel staffing, cost-reduction programs, financing, data-processing studies, and acquisition programs.

The small-business department provides a monthly service to prepare financial statements and various required financial reports to businesses not large enough to warrant the cost of a full accounting department. Services include computerized ledgers, financial statements, employee earnings records, payroll tax reports, and bank reconciliations.

The firm utilizes the most modern computer technology and accounting practices. The Lansing office offers the advantages of state capitol contacts and proximity to many governmental agencies. The stated philosophy of the firm is "to contribute to the community in which we live and the profession to which we belong," and further, "to grow, but never to lose the identity and personal relationship with clients which is the foundation of our practice." With goals like these, Lansing area businesses and organizations know that Maner, Costerisan & Ellis adds up to more than numbers.

Max D. Harris (1894-1980) was one of the founders of the firm known today as Maner, Costerisan & Ellis, P.C.

Maxco, Inc.

One of the nation's leading industrial conglomerates was born right here in Lansing. Maxco, Inc., began operations in 1969, when Max A. Coon and Lloyd C. Barnhart gathered together 10 investors who were willing to entrust their funds to a business dedicated to growth and diversification. Under the banner of Barnhart Industries, Inc., three companies comprised the initial venture (Barnhart Construction Company, Triplex Engineering Company, and Triquet Paper Company) and two others (Ollie's, Inc., and Image Arts, Inc.) were acquired during the first fiscal year. Sales of the five-member conglomerate for that first year totaled just over $5 million. Just 12 years later, Maxco—the corporate descendant of Barnhart—boasts 14 wholly owned subsidiaries and total net sales of more than $72 million.

The conglomerate began to add to its subsidiaries almost immediately after its founding. Purchased were Michigan companies in the construction, auto supply, and paint supply fields. For Lansing residents, perhaps the most important acquisition was the 1975 purchase of Lansing's Planet Corporation, a manufacturer of handling systems for the steel and coal industries and a designer of automobile assembly lines, particularly relevant enterprises during these times of transition to alternative energy sources and smaller American cars.

Although Planet has five Michigan locations, the Lansing plant, under the direction of Gerald Houseman, is by far the largest with 150 employees. Since its acquisition by Maxco, Planet's sales have more than tripled, from $9 million to $29 million. In 1980, Planet entered

the new field of robotics with the introduction of its ARMAX line of industrial robots.

Today, Maxco is structured into three groups to provide maximum continuity and growth, which have been the conglomerate's twin goals since the beginning. The Industrial Systems Group (Planet, Progressive Machinery Corporation, Medar, Inc., and Fox Electric Corporation) produces fully automatic multi-station machining centers, high-technology equipment control systems, and electrical wiring systems, aside from the previously mentioned Planet products. The Distribution Group (Triquet Paper Company, Ersco Corporation, and Auto Body Supply Company) warehouses and distributes products for road and building construction, printing and industrial paper products, and auto and painting supplies. The third Maxco group of companies is engaged in a broad spectrum of activities, from retail clothing to computer processing.

Of the 14 Maxco subsidiaries, 8 are within 20 minutes of the Lansing city limits, providing employment for about 600 area residents. The conglomerate's headquarters are located at 5522 Aurelius Road on the outskirts of the city.

In the years ahead, Maxco, Inc., will not only stress its own productivity but will also move vigorously toward providing the tools and supplies needed to increase industrial activity within many segments of U.S. industry. For Maxco and Lansing, two entities whose destinies are inextricably linked, this accent on growth is a good omen for their economic future.

Top
Built in 1978, the corporate headquarters of Maxco, Inc., are located at 5522 Aurelius Road in Lansing.

Bottom
The Triquet Paper Company was one of Maxco's first acquisitions.

Michigan Millers Mutual Insurance

On June 27, 1881, a committee of Lansing flour millers met in the historic Lansing House to create an insurance company for protection against fires. From that meeting resulted the Michigan Millers Mutual Fire Insurance Company, and today, 100 years later, the descendant of that company celebrates its centennial anniversary as one of Michigan's leading, full-service insurance firms.

The first president of the company, the Honorable D.L. Crossman, was also the first policyholder. The real founder of the firm, however, was Arthur T. Davis, who managed Millers until 1888 as a one-man office and field force. A.D. Baker, a man credited with playing a major role in the pioneering and growth of mutual insurance in this country, began his employment with the firm in 1889. That same year also marked the company's initial entrance into the writing of general business insurance. One year later, the firm erected its first home office building at 120 West Ottawa Street, where it was to remain for 40 years.

By the turn of the century, the scope of the company's operations was widening to other states. Enactment of the Uniform Mutual Law in Michigan and 20 other states permitted the writing of additional lines of insurance. Michigan Millers joined various cooperative efforts, such as the Mill Mutual Fire Prevention Bureau, the Mutual Reinsurance Bureau, and Improved Risk Mutuals, composed of many of the strongest mutual insurance companies in America.

By 1931, the company's 50th anniversary, it had assets of $4.2 million, and its various departments covered clients from coast to coast. The firm's new headquarters at 208 North Capitol Avenue, adjacent to the city hall and across from the capitol grounds, proudly displayed bronze portals, hand-carved balustrades, and a large recreation room and banquet facilities for its employees.

As Michigan Millers celebrates its 100th anniversary in 1981, the company is headquartered on a beautifully landscaped eight-acre site at 2425 East Grand River Avenue. With assets of $100 million and branch and field service offices in 12 states, the firm now covers the full range of insurance needs for commercial and personal lines. Though a multiple-line insurance company, its mill and grain elevator department continues to specialize in the agricultural industry, providing a unique insurance service backed by a century of experience.

Stannard Baker, president from 1944 to 1965 with 59 years of service to the company, is chairman of the board. Charles B. McGill has been president of the firm since 1976. Michigan Millers Mutual Insurance Company is prepared to meet the challenges of the next century, concentrating on goals that will develop greater growth and better service to its mutual customers.

Top
The Honorable D.L. Crossman was both the first president and the first policyholder of Michigan Millers Mutual Fire Insurance Company.

Bottom
Arthur T. Davis constituted the entire office and field force of Michigan Millers from its founding in 1881 until 1888.

Mill Supplies Corporation

When Otto Kirchen hired chemical engineer Carl B. Pfeifer to run his machine shop in 1922, the groundwork was laid for the establishment of Mill Supplies Corporation, a business which has remained in the Pfeifer family for three generations. It didn't start out that way, however. Before adopting the company's future name in 1924, Carl Pfeifer was simply an employee for the ailing Kirchen and the firm was known in the Lansing area as Kirchen Machine Supply Company.

But Pfeifer was bright and ambitious, and after filling one of the shop's first orders, to Motor Wheel Corporation in Lansing, he decided that it would be much more sensible to make and stock the tools needed by local industry in advance, thereby having the parts on hand when they were needed by customers.

Pfeifer's decision to provide a well-stocked shop proved to be an auspicious one; for when customers realized that they could get what they needed from Pfeifer and Kirchen without the usual delays, orders started to roll in. By March 1924 the busy company needed more space and moved from 117 South Grand Avenue to larger quarters at 316 East Michigan Avenue. The firm was renamed Mill Supplies Corporation at that time. With financial assistance from an investor, Rumsey Haynes, Pfeifer purchased Kirchen's interest, and the two-man company quickly grew to include salesmen, buyers, and office employees.

Within a few years, due to the acquisition of lucrative contracts with Oldsmobile, Diamond Reo, and Motor Wheel Corporation—three of Lansing's early industrial giants—Pfeifer

purchased the floor below him. At that time, he hired his 10-year-old son, Jack Pfeifer, on a part-time basis. Paid eight cents an hour, it was Jack's job to retrieve the tiny ball bearings that continually fell into large cracks in the floor.

While Jack was picking up ball bearings, the hardware store for industry continued to grow rapidly, until by 1939 the company had outgrown its building once again. A new facility, just down the street, was purchased after World War II ended in 1945. Jack returned to school at that time, attending his father's alma mater, the University of Michigan, to obtain a degree in aeronautical engineering.

In 1979, with more than two-thirds of its business conducted in the Lansing area, Mill Supplies Corporation recorded nearly $4 million in total sales, an astounding increase from less than $9,000 in 1926, when Pfeifer became

Top
Carl Pfeifer, founder of Mill Supplies Corporation, was active in many civic activities prior to his retirement and is credited with bringing the Crippled Children's Foundation to Lansing.

Above
In 1949, four years after moving into its new headquarters, Mill Supplies Corporation experienced a strong surge of growth. The company reached $1 million in sales two years later, in 1951.

sole owner of the enterprise. Today, Jack is president and chairman of the board of Mill Supplies Corporation, but despite his busy schedule, he finds the time to serve in several service clubs and to direct the local Boy's Club.

Waiting in the wings to assume a position of leadership is Jack's son, David, who at 25 is already working as an inside salesman, learning the ropes to ensure that Mill Supplies Corporation continues to be a Pfeifer family affair.

Motor Wheel Corporation

From the nation's leading producer of wood-spoked wheels in the 1920s, Motor Wheel Corporation has evolved into the world's largest manufacturer of styled wheels. In addition, the company is one of the nation's leading suppliers of brake parts for automobiles and trucks, and the country's number one producer of rims and wheels for earth-moving equipment.

When Motor Wheel was first conceived in Lansing in 1920 by founders Harry F. Harper, D.L. Porter, and B.S. Gier, 90 percent of all vehicles on the road used wood-spoked wheels. Though the company soon became the nation's largest producer of wooden wheels, its leaders foresaw the time when steel would rule the market; by 1924, Motor Wheel had become the world's top manufacturer of both wooden *and* steel wheels. The remainder of the '20s and the '30s was a period of diversification for the company, as it expanded its product line into Duo-Therm oil-fired water heaters, furnaces, and space heaters. Motor Wheel achieved a major milestone in 1931 with its introduction of Centrifuse brake drums for passenger cars.

Between 1933 and 1938, the company devoted a vast amount of research and money to the development of wheels for agricultural equipment, including steel wheels with pneumatic tires for farm tractors and implements. Motor Wheel also pioneered the installation of steel wheels with pneumatic tires on earth-moving equipment, mining and logging machinery, concrete mixers, power shovels, and road rollers. As the house trailer increased in popularity, the firm sold thousands of wheels to trailer

builders. Finalizing a decade of change, Motor Wheel started production of railroad equipment.

In the 1940s, Motor Wheel became an important business force in the American war effort. The company produced cartridge cases, rocket bodies and motors, aluminum propeller domes, and various armament components, and became the country's leading producer of military tank wheels. After the war, the firm pursued an expansion program, purchasing the Nash-Kelvinator Propeller Plant in Lansing for production of Duo-Therm products, adding gas space heaters and water heaters to its Duo-Therm line, and pioneering the production of power adjustable wheels for farm tractors.

Motor Wheel accelerated expansion in the '50s, building a wheel manufacturing plant in Delaware to serve car assembly plants on the East Coast. The firm also kept pace with the accelerated automobile era when it developed the Electrofuse welding process for use with tubeless-tire wheels—a process now used by virtually all automobile wheel manufacturers.

Innovation was the hallmark of the company in the '60s. In 1962, Motor Wheel introduced the Centrue/Light wheel, the lightest and truest-running steel truck wheel on the market at that time, and one year later the firm announced the Unistyle passenger car custom wheel, the first new concept in wheel design since the steel disc wheel replaced the spoke wheel. Motor Wheel became a subsidiary of The Goodyear Tire & Rubber Company in 1964.

Through the years, the company has been a leader in community and

environmental improvements. Many of Motor Wheel's 1,600 Lansing employees hold positions in the United Way, Chamber of Commerce, Boy's Club, Junior Achievement, YMCA, Little League, and many other worthwhile civic groups. And the company has spent over $20 million in the past few years on air purification systems, noise abatement, and waste recovery systems.

In Motor Wheel's 60-year industrial journey, the firm has created innovative technological processes and new products, and has accomplished diversification and expansion, resulting in leadership in the industry and a higher standard of living for Lansing.

Left
A Motor Wheel toolroom employee grinds a die-forming ring for a steel wheel in this 1924 photograph.

Center
In the 1920s, assembling wooden wheels involved ramming the spoke down into the rim.

Right
When Motor Wheel Corporation was established in 1920, more than 90 percent of all vehicles produced in the United States used wheels with wood spokes. It wasn't long until the company became the largest manufacturer of wooden wheels in the country.

169

Mourer-Foster, Inc.

Insurance companies have been known to cover unusual risks in addition to the commonplace policies on automobiles, personal property, business, and so on. Certain entertainers, for example, have insured their legs, noses, and other parts of their anatomies crucial to their livelihoods. An unusual coverage was added by Mourer Insurance Company to its line of automobile and personal policies shortly after December 7, 1941—bomb insurance. For just four dollars, Mourer's customers could insure their homes against a Japanese bombing attack that many thought imminent after the assault on Pearl Harbor.

Since then, Mourer-Foster, Inc., has dropped bomb insurance from its line of coverages, but the company has continued to issue personal, automobile, and home policies. And the agency has evolved into the leading specialist in insurance policies for road construction contractors—throughout Michigan and the entire United States.

Founded by O.W. Mourer in 1926, the agency was originally located in offices on North Capitol Avenue, where cars now speed by on I-496 near downtown Lansing. In 1954, George Foster, Jr., then a partner in the Wilkerson Agency in Detroit, joined Mourer's firm at those offices. At that time, Michigan was building a network of highways later to be recognized as the finest in the nation, and Foster had the expertise necessary to insure the state's burgeoning road construction industry. Soon after he began providing bonds and insuring contractor's casualty and workers compensation, commercial building and road construction accounted for over 50 percent of all the agency's business.

In the 26 years that Foster has managed the company, it has grown to more than 10 times its original size and has expanded its geographical market area to include road construction from Denver, Colorado, to Orlando, Florida.

Ironically, in the early '60s the firm was forced to move because of highway construction; new offices were constructed at 815 North Washington. Within just a few years, however, the agency needed more office space and a twin building was erected next door. By 1977, Foster had found a new office site at 615 Capitol Avenue, north of the capitol. The former home of the inventor of an engine purchased by R.E. Olds, it was built in 1911 sparing no expense. Foster stepped in to save the magnificent mansion at a renovation cost of more than $100,000.

Today, Foster shares the elegant building with businesses that lease space on the lower floors. Foster's own executive officers are lodged on the upper floors; his wife Jacqueline, secretary and treasurer; his son George III, vice-president; Albert Neubacher and John Raap, vice-presidents; and Thomas Ryan, executive vice-president. Foster remains president and chairman of the board, positions he also holds with his former firm, the Wilkerson Agency in Detroit.

Once the home of a wealthy inventor, today's Mourer-Foster offices retain the structure's original character, preserving a bit of Lansing history in a modern business setting.

The Office of the Governor of the State of Michigan

Governor William G. Milliken first assumed office in January 1969, stepping up from the lieutenant governor's post in a brief, quickly arranged ceremony after Governor George Romney was named Secretary of Housing and Urban Development. Supreme Court Justice John R. Dethmers, who administered the oath on a borrowed Bible, apologized for not being formally robed for the occasion.

Despite such inauspicious beginnings, Michigan's 44th governor has served in the office longer than any other governor in the history of the state. He has been elected to office by the people of Michigan for three 4-year terms.

A native of Traverse City, Governor Milliken carried on a family tradition by entering public life. Both his father and grandfather were members of the Michigan State Legislature, and before becoming lieutenant governor he had served as a state senator. After his graduation from Yale University, Governor Milliken joined the family business, J.W. Milliken, Incorporated, which operates department stores in northern Michigan. He served in World War II as a waist gunner on a B-24 bomber and was on 50 combat missions in Europe. He was wounded over Vienna, Austria, and was subsequently awarded the Purple Heart, the Air Medal, and the European Ribbon with three battle stars.

As the leader of the state's Republican Party, the governor has been involved in state and presidential campaigns since entering office. But because of the wide range of issues facing a large industrial state, the governor has on many occasions achieved a unique cooperative effort within both political parties and has brought together many diverse groups.

Governor Milliken conducts the business of government from the second-floor corner office in the 102-year-old capitol, situated in the heart of Lansing. The office, arranged with books and plants, has a commanding view of the city, the seat of state government.

Governor Milliken is noted for his deep concern for people's problems, and he always remains in touch with his constituency. In any one week, the governor may give an address to a high school graduating class; visit mental health facilities, universities, prisons, or other state facilities; lead a group of 26,000 residents across the Mackinac Bridge during the annual Labor Day walk; meet with citizens in his office to talk about their specific concerns; hold numerous meetings to examine critical state issues; participate in a parade; or crown a festival queen.

The governor also is a frequent visitor to the nation's Capitol, meeting with state and national leaders. He headed a trade mission to the People's Republic of China, served as chairman of the National Governors' Association, visited the refugee camps in Cambodia, and spearheaded a refugee relief effort in Michigan.

During Milliken's administration, Michigan has achieved a cleaner environment, a fairer tax system, safer highways, more vibrant urban areas, a higher standard of living, better transportation facilities, more efficient public assistance programs, better mental health services, and a healthier population.

Michigan became the first industrial state, under Governor Milliken, to ban throwaway cans and bottles, making a tremendous impact on reducing litter and waste. Michigan also was a leader in protecting its environment under a number of innovative environmental laws. Michigan consumers are protected by the nation's most comprehensive consumer protection act. In addition, the state has a unique public health code, which has served as a model for other states.

Governor Milliken helped create the Budget Stabilization Fund, which guarantees a more stable budget by saving during affluent economic periods for use during uncertain times.

The governor and his wife, Helen, have a deep interest in the arts. During the Milliken years, the arts in the state have flourished as never before. He formed a special commission to bring public art to the people of the state, which resulted in an art-in-public-places bill.

For the past 12 years, the governor has led the state in a quiet, but determined, manner. He has met the problems which face any governor and has proven his leadership by grappling with the essential issues. During both prosperous and difficult times, Governor Milliken has emerged as a man known for his compassion, his willingness to listen, and his sense of justice.

Michigan Governor William G. Milliken has served in the office longer than any other governor in the history of the state.

171

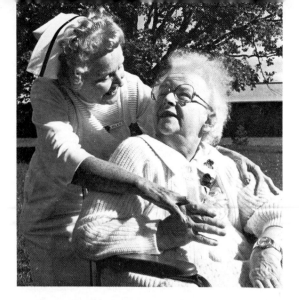

Provincial House, Inc.

In response to the growing need for quality, long-term health care facilities for the elderly, ill, and handicapped, a group of Lansing businessmen began to develop a nursing home in August 1963 that would be the first in a chain of 24 such havens statewide, and one of four that would serve the Lansing area. Monticello House, now known as Provincial House Whitehills, opened as a 115-bed nursing home on Hagadorn Road in East Lansing in May 1965. Community acceptance was strong and immediate.

The resulting demand for similar facilities, coupled with the federal government's willingness to provide reimbursement for their services, spurred their rapid development. Provincial House, Inc., undertook a building program in Michigan that increased its operational facilities at a rate of nearly two each year following the establishment of Monticello House. By 1980, the firm was the largest of its kind in the state, among the 20 largest in the nation, serving over 2,800 residents. It boasted more than 2,600 employees, representing an annual payroll in excess of $16 million.

Provincial House offices, originally located in Monticello House, moved to Medical Center West, a project on Logan Street, as the firm's staff expanded and, in 1971, the corporation took over the former Farm Bureau offices near Lansing's Capitol City Airport. Today, Provincial House's sprawling offices include a centralized laundry facility, a management and consulting operation, and the corporation's Compu-Link subsidiary, a computer network that serves all of Provincial House's nursing homes.

PHI Construction, the corporation's construction arm, has built shopping malls, a hospital, restaurants, schools, a fire station, and a water treatment plant, in addition to the health care facilities.

Provincial House officers are active leaders in the health care field. Patrick J. Callihan, president and chairman of the board since 1969, is a current director of the American Health Care Association and the National Council of Health Care Services. He also served on the Governor's Task Force on Medicaid and Health Care Cost Containment. Vice-presidents Dan Varble, Jeffrey Poorman, Victoria Landolfi, and Lois Lamont often consult with state and federal legislators on matters regarding health care and health care facilities regulation.

Top
Provincial House, Inc., provides long-term care with an emphasis on the quality of life for over 2,800 elderly, ill, and handicapped Michigan residents.

Bottom
Most Provincial House facilities are built according to an "x" plan, with four patient wings meeting at a central nursing station. From this station, nurses on duty have a direct view of each resident's doorway and activity area.

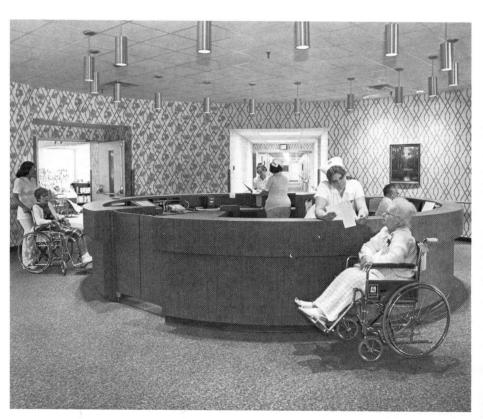

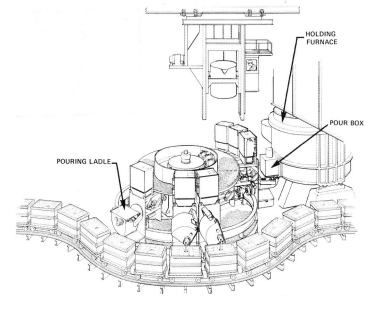

POURING LADLE

HOLDING FURNACE

POUR BOX

Roberts Corporation

Michigan's all-important auto industry relies on foundries to produce cars. Roberts Corporation designs bulk material handling systems, as well as complete foundries, and has performed much of this work for the auto industry.

Roberts was founded in 1964 by Robert E. French, Robert E. Place, and Joseph M. Post, who pooled their resources and opened an office in Southpointe Plaza on Cedar Street. The first employee was Armond R. Sprague, who performed a variety of tasks, including bookkeeping, purchasing, and even handyman tasks. Engineers James Foster, James Gill, and Robert Herner joined the staff later that same year.

Initially, Roberts Corporation was a manufacturers' representative with the capability of custom-designing material handling systems. The company founders originally planned to subcontract any manufacturing requirements. However, by 1965 there had been such a broad acceptance of Roberts products and services that it was necessary to become directly involved in the manufacturing phase. An intensive search for available space was begun in the Lansing area. James Foster discovered a welding shop in Grand Ledge that was about to close, and in 1966 Roberts purchased this facility. The Grand Ledge manufacturing plant has since been expanded nine times in order to keep pace with Roberts's growth. Rapid growth also occurred in the engineering and office staff, and in 1971 the corporate offices were moved to a picturesque location in southwest Lansing. The company's continued pattern of growth led to an expansion of the office facility in 1980.

Roberts merged with a leading machine tool concern, the Cross Company of Fraser, Michigan, in 1973. When the Cross Company merged with Kearney and Trecker Corporation in 1979, Roberts became a Cross and Trecker company. Cross and Trecker is the second largest machine tool company in the United States, with corporate offices in Bloomfield Hills, Michigan.

Today, Roberts Corporation employs 250 people at three locations—the corporate offices in Lansing, and manufacturing facilities in Grand Ledge, Michigan, and Birmingham, Alabama. Roberts has gained recognition as a leader in the design, manufacture, and installation of turnkey systems. ("Turnkey" is a term indicating that a contractor, such as Roberts, builds a complete foundry, hands the customer the key to the front door, and the customer unlocks the door, ready to begin operations.)

Roberts's innovative Roto-Pour® revolutionized automatic iron-pouring, and has been hailed as the biggest breakthrough in the metal castings industry since the ancient Egyptians first began making castings nearly 4,000 years ago. The Roto-Pour® was named Michigan Product of the Year in 1976.

Robert French, president of Roberts Corporation, pinpoints innovation as the key to Roberts' past and future success. Of the original seven staff members, five are still with Roberts in various management and staff positions. Armond Sprague passed away, and Robert Place has retired.

Top
The diagram above illustrates a typical system layout for Roberts Roto-Pour® automatic iron-pouring equipment.

Bottom
This artist's drawing shows one of the largest sand systems in the country, too large to be photographed in a single shot.

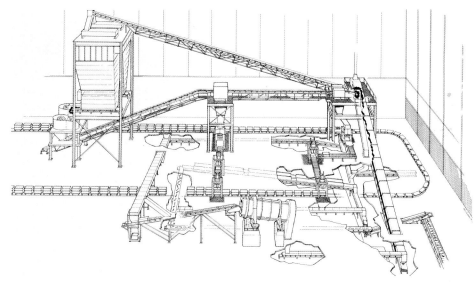

Schaberg Lumber

Schaberg Lumber Company and its sister company, Heart Truss & Engineering, have deep roots in Lansing. In 1923 Arthur Schaberg and William Dietrich came to Lansing from the Saginaw area. They were later joined by their brothers and formed Schaberg-Dietrich hardware stores.

Donald Schaberg was the son of Arthur Schaberg. In 1945, after serving in the U.S. Navy, Don's first job was delivering lumber throughout Michigan. By 1951, he had decided it was time to "go it on his own." From his Beal Street yard, he and two employees began selling lumber purchased from mills in the West to retail lumberyards in Michigan. It was not long before the business required more space and

moved to its present location at 1830 North Grand River.

Schaberg Lumber Company was incorporated in 1953, and Don's brother, Gerald, joined the firm that same year. The company continued to grow. In 1963 Donald, Gerald, and Donald Butcher formed Heart Truss & Engineering, a firm that custom-engineers wood roof and floor trusses.

Today, the combined firms have more than fifty employees. Heart Truss & Engineering markets laminated beams along with its truss systems throughout the lower portion of Michigan. Schaberg Lumber Company purchases lumber from the United States and Canada, and distributes to roof truss fabricators, retail lumber

dealers, and mobile home and industrial manufacturers in a 35-state area. "The Schaberg family," says Don, "has been fortunate to have dedicated partners and excellent employees. They are the reason for continued growth."

Top
The early years of Schaberg Lumber Company found Arthur, Jerry, and Don Schaberg, along with L.J. Earl, on the steps of their North Grand River office.

Bottom
The corporate headquarters of Schaberg Lumber Company encompass 55,000 square feet of plant space and 5,000 square feet of office space.

Shop-Rite Super Food Markets

Lansing's Shop-Rite Markets evolved from three local food stores that banded together in 1949 to compete with the new, large supermarket chains. Today, there are 13 Lansing Shop-Rites, all independently owned and operated by Lansing residents, and the stores account for more than 25 percent of all food sold in the Lansing metropolitan area.

Densteadt's first opened for business in 1922 at 3630 South Cedar. Owned by Mrs. Blen Denstaedt and her son Ken Olson, the store location predated electricity and even pavement on the street. A.G. Popoff's store at 2416 North East Street had been operating for 30 years before the 1949 merger. This location was later sold to Bob Townsend, who kept it until his retirement when he sold it to Jim Moody in September 1974; at that time the store became, and still is, Jim's Shop-Rite. And Louis Willard's grocery at 1910 West Saginaw Street was the first of three stores owned by the Willard family. This original trio of storeowners formed the Shop-Rite trade name that has prospered for more than 30 years.

In 1954, four other stores (then called "Save-A-Ways") joined with the original three:

Walter and Stan Levandowski's L & L Shop-Rite at Jolly and Logan streets had been in business since 1931. Though Walter has passed away, his son Stan and Stan's sons still run the business. The family recently purchased another location in Walled Lake and in 1979 bought Denstaedt's, retaining the Denstaedt name.

Originally located at 2410 West St. Joseph, Goodrich's Shop-Rite moved to 940 Trowbridge Road (formerly "Prince's") in 1967. Goodrich's, also a family-owned store, was run by Al Goodrich, his sons Bruce and Wayne, and a son-in-law, Bob Scheffel. Presently, Bruce and Bob own and manage Goodrich's and are bringing a third generation of the family into the store with them.

Southside Shop-Rite was originally a partnership of Tom Papiernik and Ed Zak. Tom later bought out Ed and took his son, Tom Jr., into the business. In 1972, Tom Sr. moved from South Cedar to Mount Hope, and called the new store "Tom's Shop-Rite"; in 1976, father and son opened "Tom's Shop-Rite No. 2" at 312 Willow Street.

The fourth Save-A-Way store to join Shop-Rite in 1954 was located on East Grand River in East Lansing and was owned by Mike Hauer, who, along with his father and brother, ran the market for many years. After the deaths of Mike's father and brother, Mike sold the business in 1967 to Larry and Helen Fortino, who left the Shop-Rite family in 1980.

Over the next 25 years, several more Lansing stores became members of Shop-Rite:

Mike's Shop-Rite was started in 1921 by Mike Wickenhiser, Sr., with his two sons, Mike Jr. and Robert. They joined in 1956 and moved their North Washington Street store to 2301 East Grand River in 1958. Mike Jr. still manages the store.

With the aid of other Shop-Rite members, Walt Goff started the Haslett store in 1966. In January 1980, Walt moved to a bigger and more convenient location at the corner of Marsh and Haslett roads. Walt's second store,

Carriage Hills Shop-Rite, located in the new Lake Lansing/Hagadorn Road shopping center, opened in 1977.

In 1974, Shop-Rite members founded the West Saginaw Shop-Rite at 4106 West Saginaw Highway, with Bob Blakeman as manager. Blakeman became sole owner in 1980.

Members formed a new corporation, Shop-Rite Properties, Inc., in 1978 and acquired a former Wrigley's location on 5625 West Saginaw Highway in the K-Mart building. The members also leased a store—the Dewitt Shop-Rite—in a shopping center to be built at the corner of Route 27 and Herbison Road.

On November 2, 1980, the newest Shop-Rite was born in Bath, located in that town's new (and only) shopping center. A 2-family operation, the store is co-owned by the Robinsons and the Papierniks, with Bruce Robinson serving as manager.

Today, the Shop-Rite family runs a marketing and operations office on Mount Hope Avenue. Under the guidance of president Ken Olson, "Shop-Rite" will continue to be a trusted name for clean, modern, well-stocked food stores—and for its many convenient locations throughout the Lansing area.

Left
This photograph of the grand opening of Mike's Shop-Rite on North Washington Street was taken in 1921. Mike Wickenhiser, Sr., is at right.

Right
Ken Olson, now president of Shop-Rite Super Food Markets, posed with his sister Ruth and his first delivery truck in the mid-1920s.

Spartan Paper and Office Supply

Spartan Paper and Office Supply Company is as young and dynamic as its founder and executive officers, and at a growth rate of more than 100 percent each year, the business is certain to play an increasingly active part in the future of Lansing.

The company, originally a one-man operation run by Michigan State University graduate David Buxton from his East Lansing home, was founded in April 1975. Providing office supplies and paper goods to the many law firms and associations located in the capital city soon became a full-time job for Buxton, however, and he opened a warehouse in Lansing to stock more goods for his growing group of steady customers.

Within only a few months, he hired a full-time delivery driver, moved to a larger warehouse, and began recruiting salesmen. With the sage advice of Arnold Robinson, who had accrued more than 40 years' experience in the office supply business before joining Spartan Paper and Office Supply Company, Buxton steadily increased his staff and his delivery service. This gave him a unique competitive edge when landing large commercial contracts in the greater Lansing area.

His warehouse space was increased from 480 feet to a sprawling 15,000 feet within five years, and his staff swelled from two to 31 during that same period. Meanwhile, due to the unusual blend of state government, university, and business offices in Lansing, the demand for Spartan's office supplies and products continued to increase.

Specializing in service, Spartan now services the Lansing area, well-stocked with everything from erasers to computers, advising clients on office design systems which improve the work flow and increase the comfort of employees. Four delivery trucks ensure that none of Spartan's clients run out of supplies, and an enormous inventory can accommodate "rush" orders for reams of stationery and thousands of pens within hours.

The potential for advancement within Buxton's company is great. Many of Spartan's officers and top salesmen were hired as delivery drivers and were rewarded for their hard work and incentive. As the firm continues to grow, Buxton and his officers are contemplating a move into markets outside of Michigan, while keeping the capital city as Spartan's home base.

Spartan Paper and Office Supply Company was founded by David Buxton in 1975. Today, the firm continues to specialize in service.

176

Story Incorporated

When Karl D. Story accepted a job in Buffalo, New York, with the Curtis Wright Aircraft Company, he didn't realize that he would develop a keen interest into a multimillion-dollar success story. His growing fascination with the buying and selling of used cars soon created an abiding desire to enter the automotive business.

In 1948, Story became associated with Fincher Motors, an Oldsmobile dealer in his hometown of Rochester, New York. He rapidly rose to the position of sales manager and vice-president of the organization, and two years later, was transferred to Fincher Motors in Miami, Florida, as general manager.

His success with the dealership quickly attracted the attention of General Motors, and in 1954 Story purchased the Lansing Oldsmobile franchise on South Capitol Avenue. The dealership moved in 1960 to its present location at 3165 East Michigan Avenue. During the next few years, Story expanded his franchise and built University Oldsmobile, Inc., at 6420 South Cedar.

With its multiple showrooms and service facilities, the dealership offers recreational vehicles, GMC trucks, Datsuns, and the complete line of Oldsmobiles. Both locations, along with the body shop, employ over 200 people. The corporate record of achievement is a strong one. Story's Oldsmobile dealership is the nation's largest Oldsmobile dealership in terms of retail sales. With three Datsun franchises in Michigan, Story is recognized as the largest volume Datsun dealer east of the Mississippi River.

Today, Story has expanded his dealerships to other locations in Michigan and Florida and has established two insurance companies and a real estate investment firm, which combined, gross more than $100 million per year. Anticipating the changes inherent in the current gasoline shortage, Story Inc. has developed a subsidiary to engage in distributing diesel engines throughout the United States.

Despite his many business responsibilities, Karl Story has been actively involved in the development of Lansing and Michigan. Story serves on the board of directors of Sparrow Hospital and of the American Bank and Trust Company, and is a trustee of the Northwood Institute in Midland, Michigan. He has received numerous Dealer of the Year awards and service awards from Oldsmobile, along with wide auto industry recognition. Mr. Story was awarded the Distinguished Citizen Award by the MSU Board of Trustees.

A significant keystone in the company's commitment to the rehabilitation of downtown Lansing occurred in 1975, when Story purchased the 400 block of South Washington. The Arbaugh Department Store building, which had been a landmark since 1906, was completely remodeled into a professional office building and renamed Plaza I. Also included in this refurbished block are the corporate offices of Story Inc., located at 124 East Kalamazoo, and the Michigan Manufacturers Association. At the southwest portion of the block is the Michigan AFL-CIO headquarters.

Mr. Story is married and has two daughters. Eleanor Jean, the older daughter, is married to Leo Jerome and they have two children, Christopher and Tiffany. Nancy, the younger daughter, is married to Douglas Milbury and they have three children, Mark, Todd and Christyna. Mr. and Mrs. Jerome live in Birmingham, Michigan. The Milburys have recently returned to Lansing from Rochester, New York, to take a more active part in the overall Story Enterprises.

In 1954, Karl D. Story purchased the Oldsmobile dealership that bears his name today.

Tiffany Place

In 1907, a young Greek immigrant named James E. Vlahakis arrived in America with ambitious dreams and high hopes for his new homeland. After working on the railroads in Kansas and Oklahoma, he decided to come east to make his mark in his new country. He settled in Lansing, where in 1914 he founded what was to become the city's oldest restaurant—and one of the most renowned and honored eating places in America—Jim's Tiffany Place.

Originally named "The Lansing Cafe," the restaurant opened at 203 South Washington Avenue. In 1937, the restaurant moved to its present location at 116 East Michigan Avenue, just one block south of the capitol. Expansion to an adjacent building in 1949 allowed the introduction of banquet and cocktail lounge facilities for a present-day total capacity of 255.

Tiffany's Greek-American-Continental menu, ranging from quiches and salads to complete gourmet dinners, has been recognized as one of the finest in America. Over the years, the restaurant has won almost every conceivable award for dining excellence: three-star recognition by *Mobil Travel Guide;* recommendations by *AAA, Weight Watchers, Signature,* and *Gourmet* magazines; and a testimonial by *Restaurant Business* magazine as one of the "most eminent independent restaurants in America." The July 1980 issue of *Lansing* magazine announced Tiffany's greatest accolade when the restaurant was voted—by other Lansing restaurants— as the city's first four-star dining establishment.

Over the years, the restaurant's Tiffany motif has developed to the point where today it owns one of the three largest and finest collections of authentic Tiffany-era lamps in the world. More than 100 lamps have been collected from New York, San Francisco, Cleveland, and Sault Ste. Marie, with about 70 on display at any one time. Another well-known feature of the restaurant is its outdoor greenhouse cafe, perhaps Lansing's most highly identifiable landmark after the state capitol.

The restaurant has always been very active in national and state trade and business organizations, including the National Restaurant Association, the Michigan Restaurant Association, and the Lansing Regional Chamber of Commerce.

The management and staff's dedication to quality is the primary reason for the restaurant's success. The dining rooms and kitchen area are immaculate; in fact, the Ingham County Health Department awarded the restaurant for its "outstanding effort in sanitation"—the only full-service restaurant in 1980 to receive the award out of 822 food licensees.

Almost every prominent Michigan statesman, politician, and governor has made the short walk from the capitol to dine at Tiffany's during its 67-year history—but the capitol tour guides and janitors have been just as welcome.

In December 1980 the Vlahakis family announced the sale of the restaurant to one they felt possessed the highest level of expertise—Craig E. DeHaven. DeHaven, a Lansing native, returned to Lansing after holding several top-management positions with Hyatt, Ramada Inn, Inc., and Holiday Inn, Inc. Vlahakis was quoted as saying that he wanted to find an operator to maintain the sophistication of the restaurant and also not to sell the famous independent restaurant to a chain. As quoted by the *State Journal* newspaper, ". . . DeHaven has the easy manner, speech, and humor of someone well-trained in working with the public. He can be gracious without being ingratiating, witty but not clownish."

Tiffany Place, located at 116 East Michigan Avenue, is one of the most renowned eating places in the United States.

Waldo Travel

Mortimer A. Waldo, founder of central Michigan's first travel agency, was a Lansing native who attended old Central High School before moving to Charlotte. After graduating from Adrian College, Waldo studied international law at Yale University under former President William Howard Taft and historian and explorer Hiram Bingham. In 1916, he was assigned to war-relief work for the international Red Cross and YMCA in Omsk (Siberia), Russia.

Following the March 1917 revolution, he was recalled to Petrograd to participate in United Services activities. In Petrograd he paid official visits to Kerensky during his term as head of the Social Democratic regime and to Madame Lenin, then director of the continuing education program. In 1918 Waldo was appointed vice-consul and transferred to Helsinki, Finland.

As American involvement in the war increased, Waldo felt he should return home; he secured leave and arrived in New York on Armistice Day. Though his intention was to continue in the Foreign Service, Mr. C.E. Bement offered him a position in the export department of the Novo Engine Company. Waldo traveled in the Caribbean, South America, and the Orient, representing both Novo and Reo Motors.

From his travels and residence abroad, Waldo had seen the growing interest in world travel. He had crossed hundreds of miles of the Siberian plains by rail and sledge, sailed in tramp steamers, and flown on some of the earliest commercial airplanes. He believed that travel would increase and that—as a Waldo Christmas poster has proclaimed for many years—"Wise men still travel, for travel leads to understanding and understanding to peace."

"The Travel Bureau" was opened in 1931 on the balcony of the old J.W. Knapp building, and later moved as Waldo Travel Agency to the Hollister Building, then the Liebermann Trunk Company Building, before establishing the present office in the Bauch (now Capitol Hall) Building, 115 West Allegan, in 1957. A branch office was established in the Union Building at Michigan State University in 1948, and expanded as College Travel Office to its present location at 130 West Grand River Avenue, East Lansing, in 1953. Corporate offices for central accounting, the president's office, and the Group Services Department were consolidated at the East Lansing address in 1963.

Mr. Waldo was active in travel agency trade association affairs and was elected president of the Michigan, Ohio, Indiana, and Kentucky agents group in 1957 and 1958. In 1955, on an association visit to the headquarters of the American Society of Travel Agents in New York, Waldo met James A. Miller, another Michigan native who had attended Michigan State University.

Miller's extensive background in travel work began in Alaska, then with American and American Overseas Airlines, and five years of travel agency management on Long Island in New York after assisting the establishment of U.S.-flag airline service to Sweden and Norway and work as system reservations manager of Colonial Airlines in New York. All this resulted in an agreement to manage College Travel Office as a partner in the Waldo firm. As Mr. Waldo's health declined, Miller assumed management of both agency offices and purchased the business upon Mr. Waldo's death in 1963.

Since that time, Miller has become prominent in the travel industry, following in Waldo's footsteps as president of the travel agents trade group for Michigan, Ohio, Indiana, and Kentucky in 1965, then as national director for this area, various national officer posts, and finally as national president of the American Society of Travel Agents, Inc. (16,000 worldwide members) in 1976, serving for two years. As immediate past chairman, he continues as a member of ASTA's board, executive and finance committees, and is presently USA director to the 87-nation body, the Universal Federation of Travel Agency Associations.

Over the years, each travel agency office has grown steadily, and now employs a total of 36 full-time travel industry professionals serving over 100 central Michigan travelers each day. Each office is a fully automated, full-service agency, booking air, rail, cruise, tour, hotel and resort facilities, complete with full worldwide travel information materials, and extensive traveler assistance publications. The Group Services Department of the agencies now processes over 50 special programs per year in addition to the regular daily customer service functions.

The two offices have created an impeccable customer and industry reputation in processing travel planning for over 250,000 customers and proudly continue a tradition of excellence in their field. Lansingites can observe with pleasure the professional maintenance and improvement efforts of central Michigan's oldest travel agencies as they prepare to serve travel customers in the years ahead.

Left
Mortimer A. Waldo founded central Michigan's first travel agency, "The Travel Bureau," in 1931.

Right
James A. Miller purchased Waldo Travel Agency upon Mr. Waldo's death in 1963.

Whitehills
Development Company

When Albert and George White pooled their respective resources and took an option to buy the 100-acre George A. Brown farm at the corner of Abbott and Saginaw Road in 1946, many in the Lansing area knowledgeable about real estate considered the land too far from the city to be of any practical use as a residential or commercial building site.

But after purchasing the property in January of the following year, the two brothers soon broke ground and began construction on what was to be the first of many homes in a unique pattern of winding streets later known as Whitehills Estates.

Albert White, a 1940 graduate of Michigan State University, was joined by his brother George in the late '40s after George received his degree in civil engineering from MSU. George's technical training and experience were important in providing the expertise in planning and developing the subdivision, thereby helping to make Al's dream come true—a dream which began as a child when he purchased his first piece of property with earnings from a paper route.

After construction of Albert's first home began, the two worked out of a portable field office that was moved from building site to building site. George worked on a drafting table in the basement of his home laying out the streets, sewers, lot lines, and storm drains, while Al supervised progress at the construction sites.

Meanwhile, Al's plans were drawing home buyers interested in quiet neighborhoods with spacious homes on large lots. The combination of innovation and strict adherence to high-quality workmanship soon began to show results. By the time the brothers formally incorporated under three different companies, with Al as

president and George as vice-president, word had begun to spread about Whitehills Estates and Albert A. White, Builder.

As the years passed, Al continued to build only two or three homes a year despite pressures to accelerate his schedule. The low volume was due to the stringent review of all plans, thereby maintaining the quality and aesthetic value of the neighborhoods, and because Al insisted on personally inspecting the progress of every home under construction by his subcontractors. Today, the average cost of a home built by Al White is roughly 10 times the cost of the first one he built in 1950.

The Whites have donated land to local government for parks and a school and are responsible for the building sites of the Michigan Education Association, Michigan Medical Association, the East Lansing Post Office, the new East

Lansing Fire Station, and the Carriage Hills Shopping Center, among many others. But Albert White is still best known for his homes—homes so well loved that many families have owned several, insisting on a second or third White-built home when they've grown out of their first.

Above left
George G. White has served as a trustee and vice-chairman of the East Lansing-Meridian Township Water and Sewer Authority. Actively involved in YMCA work, he is past president of the Parkwood Y's Men's Club.

Above right
Albert A. White, an active member of the Meridian Township Building Authority and the Urban Land Institute, is honorary life director of the National Association of Home Builders.

Below
Typical of the many homes built by Al White in the past 30 years, this house on Pebblebrook in Whitehills Estates is located on a quiet street in a neighborhood of steadily appreciating property values.

180

ACKNOWLEDGMENTS

Many persons assisted the author in creating this book. George and Geneva Wiskemann—both scholars in their own right—gave generously of their time and encouragement. Their vast knowledge of the sources of the history of the area, and their commitment to high standards of research and writing of local history, as well as their unfailing good humor, were continuously inspiring. Jane McClary of the Local History Room of the Lansing Public Library cheerfully searched through musty files, gave up free time, and directed the author to significant materials which might have been overlooked. Beth Shapiro of the Michigan State University Library helped unravel the mysteries of urban planning. Lee Barnett shared his expert knowledge of Michigan cartography as well as the vast holdings of the Michigan State Archives; his colleague John Curry found obscure but significant photographs. Richard Hathaway and the staff of the Michigan Unit of the Michigan State Library—Carol Lachance, Mary Jane Trout, Judy Dow, Richard Lucas, Merle Ann Besonen, and Beverly Tremaine—went out of their way to ease access to their important holdings. Ruby Rogers, Rose Victory, and Marc Bennett of the Michigan State Museum furnished artifacts, photographs, and much useful information. Helen Early of the Oldsmobile Division of General Motors, and Patricia Marvin of The Warren Holmes-Kenneth Black Company, loaned photographs and searched out obscure but important facts. Mary R. Patton and Richard E. Harms eased the author's use of the significant manuscript and photographic holdings of the Michigan State University Archives and Historical Collections. Val R. Berryman and Terry Shaffer of the Michigan State University Museum assisted in locating significant paintings and artifacts.

Nor were these all. George K. Kooistra, Michigan State University editor, located photographs and explained many mysteries of book production. Edward J. Zabriski of Michigan State University Information Services placed information and photographs at the author's disposal. The author's photographic collaborator, Robert Turney, assisted in many phases of copy and on-location photography. Douglas Elbinger and Saundra Lawrence Redmond provided photographs, information, and encouragement. Les Kirby, manager of Marks Photo Shop, assisted the author's photography in myriad ways.

The author is grateful for the assistance of many others who participated in the making of this book. Barbara Marinacci of Windsor Publications provided encouragement; the work of project editor Margaret Tropp, copy editor Phyllis Rifkin, picture editor Judith Zauner, and the History Book Department coordinator Katherine Cooper proved vital. The chapter on business histories was written by Nancy Ironside, Peter Bronson, and Hal Straus, and was edited by Karen Story.

I also wish to thank Maryhelen Kestenbaum for her excellent index and Cliff Fox, graduate student at Michigan State, for his invaluable assistance.

The author's colleagues in the Department of History at Michigan State University supported the project from its inception. Professors Richard White and Joseph Konvitz shared their knowledge respectively of the American westward movement and city planning in Europe and America. The author owes a special debt to Professor Donald Lammers, Chairman of the Department of History, for his interest in the project.

Many other people—too many to mention—provided useful information and insights. Professor J. Geoffrey Moore recounted his adventures in growing up in Lansing; Walter Neller and former Mayor Ralph W. Crego gave invaluable insights on the history of Lansing. Lawrence Kestenbaum read the manuscript and saved the author from many pitfalls. And Jan Parisian showed patience and understanding.

All these persons helped to strengthen the book. The author alone assumes responsibility for its shortcomings.

APPENDIX

1807	Treaty of Detroit: Indians cede lands in southeast Michigan, including Ingham County east of Meridian Road.
1819	Treaty of Saginaw: Indians cede most of remaining lands in lower peninsula, including Ingham County west of Meridian Road.
1824-1827	Survey of lands in the Greater Lansing area.
1825	Opening of the Erie Canal.
1829	Ingham and the other "cabinet counties" are "set off" or delineated by the Michigan legislature. Eastern half of Ingham County opened for sale.
1830	Western half of Ingham County opened for sale.
1838	Ingham County organized.
1840	Mason designated as "seat of justice" of Ingham County.
1842	Organization of Lansing Township.
1843	John Burchard—first settler in the original limits of the City of Lansing—builds house and dam in North Lansing.
1847	Michigan legislature locates capital in Lansing Township.
1848	First legislature meets in Lansing Township; name of capital site changed to Lansing.
1850	Michigan Constitutional Convention meets in Lansing. Compromise of 1850, including stringent Fugitive Slave Act.
1852	Publication of *Uncle Tom's Cabin* by Harriet Beecher Stowe.
1853	Opening of Lansing-Howell Plank Road.
1854	Passage of Kansas-Nebraska Act and formation of the Republican Party.
1855	Founding of the *State Republican* (forerunner of the *State Journal*). Founding of Michigan Female College. Founding of Michigan Agricultural College.
1856	Founding of the "House of Correction for Young Offenders," later the Michigan Reform School.
1857	Opening of Michigan Agricultural College.
1858	Death of Chief Okemos.
1859	Founding of the *Ingham County News*. Incorporation of the City of Lansing.
1861	State legislature establishes Lansing School District.
1863	First railroad—the Amboy, Lansing and Traverse Bay Railroad—comes to the City of Lansing.
1865	Establishment of Lansing High School
1867	Michigan Constitutional Convention meets in Lansing.
1868	Founding of the Bement Company.
1871	Michigan legislature authorizes a new capitol. Mark Twain's Lansing appearance.
1873	Cornerstone for new capitol laid.
1875	Dedication of Lansing High School, now "Old Central" on campus of Lansing Community College. Ice buildup in Grand River destroys all of city's bridges.
1879	Dedication of present state capitol.
1880	Telephone service comes to Lansing.
1882	Old capitol—built in 1847—lost in fire.
1885	Formation of Lansing Wheel Company by W.K. Prudden.
1886	Establishment of Board of Water Commissioners.
1887	R.E. Olds' first horseless carriage.
1890	First electric streetcar in Lansing.
1892	R.E. Olds' second horseless carriage. Board of Water Commissioners becomes Board of Water and Electric Light Commissioners.
1897	R.E. Olds' third horseless carriage. Organization of Olds Motor Vehicle Company. City celebrates sesquicentennial of capital location.
1900	Olds begins manufacture of motor vehicles in Detroit.
1901	Fire destroys Olds' Detroit factory; R.E. Olds builds new factory in Lansing. Opening of Central School in East Lansing.
1904	R.E. Olds resigns from Olds Motor Works; forms Reo Motor Car Company. Most disastrous flood in city's history.

1905	Opening of Pine Lake (now Lake Lansing) resort.
1907	Michigan Constitutional Convention meets in Lansing. Michigan Agricultural College celebrates sesquicentennial; Theodore Roosevelt visits. City of East Lansing is incorporated.
1908	Olds Motor Works acquired by General Motors.
1910	Ingham County voters approve prohibition. R.E. Olds forms Reo Motor Truck Company.
1912	Ingham County voters repeal prohibition. William Jennings Bryan speaks at Lansing Chautauqua.
1914	Ingham County voters reinstate prohibition.
1915	Dedication of Potter Park.
1916	Ingham County voters uphold prohibition in record turnout.
1919	Formation of the Lansing Branch of the National Association for the Advancement of Colored People.
1921	First Bartholemew City Planning Report. Durant Motors builds plant (now Fisher Body). Dedication of Strand (later Michigan) Theater and Arcade.
1924	WREO—city's first radio station—goes on air.
1925	Michigan Agricultural College becomes Michigan State College.
1926	Opening of the Hotel Olds.
1927	Bath School Disaster.
1928	Dedication of Beaumont Tower on campus of Michigan State College.
1931	Completion of Capital National Bank Tower, now Michigan National Tower.
1932	Completion of the City National Bank Building, now the Bank of Lansing.
1933	Dedication of the Lansing Post Office. Dedication of East Lansing Post Office. Lansing streetcars cease operation.
1934	Hotel Kerns fire; greatest loss of life (perhaps 100 casualties) in city's history.
1935	John A. Hannah becomes Secretary of Michigan State College.
1936	Reo ceases manufacturing automobiles.
1937	Lansing "Labor Holiday" and "Battle of Grand River Avenue." Completion of J.W. Knapp downtown Lansing store.
1938	Second Bartholemew Report.
1941	John A. Hannah becomes President of Michigan State College.
1947	Lansing's second most disastrous flood. City observes centennial of its selection as state capital.
1949	Admission of Michigan State College to Western Conference, or "Big 10."
1950	Publication of City in the Forest: The Story of Lansing by Birt Darling.
1955	Centennial of Michigan State College, which becomes Michigan State University. Centennial of Lansing State Journal.
1958	Completion of Lansing City Hall, Police Building, and Board of Water and Light Building.
1959	City observes centennial of incorporation.
1964	Michigan State University joins the American Association of Universities.
1969	John A. Hannah resigns as President of Michigan State University; Walter Adams becomes interim president.
1975	Disastrous flood.

Mayors of Lansing

1859	Hiram H. Smith
1860	John A. Kerr
1861-62	William H. Chapman
1863-65	Dr. Ira H. Bartholemew
1866	Dr. William H. Haze
1867	George W. Peck
1868-69	Cyrus Hewitt
1870	Dr. Solomon W. Wright
1871	John Robson
1872-73	John S. Tooker
1874-75	Daniel W. Buck
1876	John S. Tooker
1877	Orlando Mack Barnes
1878	Joseph E. Warner
1879-80	William Van Buren
1881	John Robson
1882-83	Orlando F. Barnes
1884-85	William Donovan
1886	Daniel W. Buck
1887	Jacob F. Schultz
1888	John Crotty
1889	James M. Turner
1890-91	Frank B. Johnson
1892-93	A.O. Bement
1894	A.A. Wilbur
1895	Russell C. Ostrander
1896	James M. Turner
1897-99	Charles J. Davis
1900-03	James F. Hammell
1904-07	Hugh Lyons
1908-11	John S. Bennett
1912-17	J. Gottlieb Reutter
1918-19	Jacob W. Ferle
1920-21	Benjamin F. Kyes
1922	Jacob W. Ferle
1922-23	Silas F. Main
1923-26	Alfred H. Doughty
1927-30	Laird J. Troyer
1931-32	Peter F. Gray
1933-41	Max A. Templeton
1941	Arthur E. Stoppel
1941-42	Sam Street Hughes
1943-61	Ralph W. Crego
1961-65	Willard Bowerman
1965-69	Max Murningham
1969-	Gerald W. Graves

Mayors of East Lansing

1907-1908	Clinton D. Smith
1908-1909	Warren Babcock
1909-1914	Thomas Gunson
1914-1918	Jacob Schepers
1918-1925	Edward H. Ryder
1925-1928	Luther H. Baker
1928-1929	Henry B. Dirks
1929-1931	Benjamin A. Faunce
1931-1933	Bert J. Ford
1933-1937	Lyman L. Frimodig
1937-1947	Carl G. Card
1947-1949	Richard P. Lyman, Jr.
1949-1951	Burr O. Twichell
1951-1953	Cornelius Wagenvoord
1953-1959	Max R. Strother
1959-1961	Harold Pletz
1961-1971	Gordon L. Thomas
1971-1975	Wilbur B. Brookover
1975-1979	George Griffiths
1979-	Larry Owen

Presidents of Michigan State University

1857-1859	Joseph R. Williams
1859-1862	Lewis R. Fisk
1862-1884	Theophilus C. Abbott
1885-1889	Edwin Willits
1889-1893	Oscar Clute
1893-1895	Lewis G. Gorton
1896-1915	Jonathan L. Snyder
1915-1921	Frank S. Kedzie
1921-1923	David Friday
1924-1928	Kenyon L. Butterfield
1928-1941	Robert S. Shaw
1941-1969	John A. Hannah
1969-1970	Walter Adams
1970-1978	Clifton R. Wharton, Jr.
1978-1979	Edgar L. Harden
1979-	Cecil Mackey

INDEX

This book was set in
Sovran and Windsor types,
printed on
70 pound Warrenflo
and bound by
Walsworth Publishing Company.
Cover and text designed by
John Fish.
Editorial layout by
Lisa Sherer.
Partners in Progress
layout by
Linda Robertson.

Boy workers with paint brushes, Lansing Wheelbarrow Company, circa 1900. Courtesy of Michigan State University Archives and Historical Collections.